PROGENY OF GHOSTS

Also by David Manicom

Poetry

Sense of Season (Press Porcépic, 1989)
Theology of Swallows (Oolichan Books, 1991)
The Older Graces (Oolichan Books, 1997)

Fiction

Ice in Dark Water (Véhicule, 1997)

PROGENY OF GHOSTS

Travels in Russia and the Old Empire

by

David Manicom

OOLICHAN BOOKS

LANTZVILLE, BRITISH COLUMBIA, CANADA

1998

Canadian Cataloguing in Publication Data

Manicom, David, 1960
    Progeny of ghosts

ISBN 0-88982-170-4 (bound)—ISBN 0-88982-168-2 (pbk.)
  1. Manicom, David, 1960—Journeys—Former Soviet Republics.
  2. Former Soviet Republics—Description and travel.
I. Title.

DK29.2.M36 1998   947.086   C98-910279-3

We acknowledge the support of the Canada Council for the Arts for our
publishing programme.

THE CANADA COUNCIL | LE CONSEIL DES ARTS
FOR THE ARTS | DU CANADA
SINCE 1957 | DEPUIS 1957

Grateful acknowledgement is made to the BC Ministry of Tourism, Small
Business and Culture for their financial support.

We acknowledge the financial support of the Government of Canada
through the Book Publishing Industry Development Program for our
publishing activities.

Published by
Oolichan Books
P.O. Box 10, Lantzville
British Columbia, Canada
V0R 2H0

Printed in Canada by
Hignell Printing Limited
Winnipeg, Manitoba

For Charlie Foran

ACKNOWLEDGEMENTS

Parts of this book first appeared, in somewhat different form, in *Brick* and *Quarry Magazine*. Grateful acknowledgement is made to Pat McGrath and the *Ottawa Citizen* for the photgraph of David Manicom on the inside back flap of the cover, and to David Manicom for his cover images from Tblisi, Georgia.

The tradition of all dead generations weighs like a nightmare on the brain of the living. And just when they seem engaged in revolutionising themselves and things, in creating something entirely new, precisely in such epochs of revolutionary crisis they anxiously conjure up the spirits of the past.

Karl Marx

Moscow's sleeping like a wooden coffin.
There's no escaping the tyrant century.
After all these years the snow still smells of apples.

Osip Mandelshtam

CONTENTS

PREFACE

*[After Gorbatchev] every year seems like an
entire era.*

David Remnick, *Lenin's Tomb*

During the three years I lived in Moscow and travelled in
the former Soviet Union, I was a diplomat employed by
the departments of External Affairs (now Foreign Affairs)
and Citizenship and Immigration Canada. My work involved interviewing prospective Canadian immigrants and
reporting on migration issues in Russia and many of the
newly independent states of the Soviet world. This gave
my family the opportunity to travel and live through a
fascinating if wrackingly difficult era, and I must first of
all be grateful to my many colleagues at the Canadian
Embassy, both Canadian and Russian: I doubt I will ever
again work among such a talented, passionate, eccentric,
and richly human group of people. My work also gave me
the chance to talk to thousands of citizens of the former
Soviet Union in Moscow as well as on working trips to
Ukraine, Kazakhstan, Georgia, Armenia, Belarus, central
Russia, St. Petersburg and elsewhere.

In spite of that, these colleagues and the embassy do
not, by and large, appear in this book. I have not written

11

as a Canadian representative, because I feel it important that the border between my own observations and my work as a diplomat and visa officer remain as hermetic as possible. Of course the many individuals who talked with me in those official capacities formed a deep well of experience upon which I draw: I got to know Russia and the old Union mainly through their eyes and words. But their conversations with me were primarily part of immigration applications and must remain private. Government trips I took as part of my reporting responsibilities form the backdrops to several sections, but I have written mainly of the unofficial parts of these journeys. The opinions expressed are my own, and in no way represent the views of the Canadian government or the embassy.

Various real individuals do appear in this book. I have often changed their names, or omitted surnames, where it seemed important to safeguard their privacy. The words of those who speak in the following chapters are taken sometimes from journals written hours or days after the event, sometimes from memory a year or two later. As they are thus inaccurate—generalisations, adaptations, summaries, rephrasings—they have not been put between quotation marks. That said, I have reproduced both words and happenings as accurately as I could.

Many people enriched our years in Moscow, but none more than Katya Novskolsova, Bob and Gabbie Hannah, Grigory Chartishvili, the Russian staff of the embassy's immigration section—especially Tatiana, Marina, and Natasha—my Russian teacher Natalia, and many Canadian colleagues, particularly Louis Dumas, Elizabeth Alt, Millie Morton, Margaret Skok, Patrick Armstrong, and

Graeme McIntyre. Ambassadors Bell and Kinsman were always supportive of both my official and unofficial jobs, as were my program managers Dominique Collinge and Gordon Barnett. Two special people kept me (somewhat) sane day in and day out for the entire three years: Peter Bates and Nicole Mailhot.

1

SHIP OF STATE, DREAMS OF EARTH

A giant ship at a terrible height
Is rushing on, spreading its wings.

Osip Mandelshtam, 1918

The first thing I learned in Moscow was that the great Russian poets are always looking over your shoulder, writing about tonight. Pasternak, Mandelshtam, Akhmatova and Tsvetaeva refuse to let Russia be—more ghosts. It was 4:00 a.m., August 30, 1991. We had been in Moscow for four hours. I was standing in the dark living room of our still unfamiliar apartment gazing out of its ninth-floor windows, facing north, the city all around yet distant and unreal, a primal hum beneath the brain. Somewhere behind me we had put the children down to sleep in strange beds. Two kilometres away, the dim jumble of streets and low-voltage alleys and exhausted buildings was interrupted by ethereal illumination from toy-like fairy-tale cream-and-yellow battlements topped by burning golden domes, afloat in the night beside the green-and-maroon harlequin swirl of St. Basil's cathedral.

The Kremlin. It was beautiful. It was not supposed to

be beautiful. Terrible, sure. Even grand; spectacular yet vulgar, no doubt. Foreboding. Drawbridges up. But enchanted? A hovering dream? Music?

Yet it *was* August, 1991. The aesthetic moment passed, interrupted by a thuggish grip on my shoulder. Yeltsin was barely down from his tank. Gorbatchev had just stumbled off a plane from the Crimea, oddly uncertain of himself, wearing the sort of short jacket everybody's father puts on to go to the hardware store, his wife Raisa black-eyed and shivering under a blanket behind him. I scanned the sky over the glories of the Kremlin towers, the first of a hundred such reflexes. All calm. Whenever all hell breaks loose, we'll know for sure, from here. Tonight, no helicopter gunships jousting in the spotlights. One of the capital's ubiquitous ancient trucks— surely every truck in Moscow was brand new, one day, in 1962?—backfired, and I heard a rifle crack. No, all calm. Just a home, a place to live.

I looked out again, Osip Mandelshtam looking out with me from his last gulag hut at the nighttime looming of the Kremlin. The second thing you learn in Russia is that here beauty hurts, because of all the blood. Because the pointless, brutal ugliness is inhaled in your very gasp of delight. The diamond is in the mud, under an ox cart, and probably radioactive. In the poet's haunting image, the stars are like salt on the blade of an axe. The golden domes, I was to learn over the next three years, are usually under dishwater skies. And you can't stop looking anyway.

*

A week before finding myself facing the stage-lit Kremlin,

16

the state for which it had long served as synecdoche began to crumble. At 8:00 a.m. in our Canadian kitchen, I was the first one up, with the movers due in two days to pack our belongings for storage or shipment to Moscow. The radio news interrupted my cereal with the bombshell that Gorbatchev was being held at his dacha, and the eight-man junta which had engineered the coup was busily pumping out Brezhnevian bombast about marching steadfastly backward into the future to save the motherland. I stopped chewing.

But as we all know now, the jig was up; time had folded itself when no one was looking. The coup leaders themselves didn't know where to turn. When they gave press conferences they seemed to be speaking Etruscan; no one could quite translate the words coming out of their mouths. The simplest of facts became subject to the official line. I vividly remember an Italian journalist asking, with insouciant reference to the explanation for Gorbatchev's unavailability, "I am wondering, how are you? Do you feel well, able to work?" Yaneyev entered into extensive consultations with his identically-suited colleagues on either side before replying, "Yes." When a young reporter from *Nezavisimaya Gazeta*, one of the most popular of the *glasnost* newspapers, asked, "Tell me please, do you realize you have carried out a state coup?" the totalitarian pretenders looked more nervous than furious and never even got around to having her arrested or shot. The old attention to detail was gone. As for the Soviet citizenry, they had for decades realized that if you went into the front office of the great proletarian revolution, talked your way past the receptionist—a scowling crone wearing twenty pounds of sweaters—and marched through the

17

doorway to the inner sanctum, you would find yourself back on the street. There was no *there* there.

Nothing is more difficult to deceive than an audience which has seen the puppet's strings. The quality of the extraordinarily temporary leadership didn't help: the putative head Gennady Yaneyev managed to remain in a drunken stupor throughout his week "in power," to the extent that he took a phone call from the Kazakhstan leader Nazarbayev, a crucial player in late-Soviet politics, without understanding to whom he was speaking. As the American journalist David Remnick points out, it is difficult "to describe just how hard it is to acquire a reputation as a drunk in Russia."

So the edifice of the putsch was falling over from the moment it was put up. Philosophers have endlessly debated the idea of a social contract, a set of often inexplicable assumptions silently governing a society's every function. All that is clear is that no one has been able to say exactly what the contract consists of, how it is created, and what makes it change. And I'm no exception. But the Yeltsin years in Russia, which began in earnest as Yaneyev's chin slumped toward his bottle-strewn desk, proved how very real the contract is, and how painful and dangerous a thing is its dissolution. The assumptions of everyday living that had kept the Communist theocracy in place, an apparently untouchable brick monolith, had been quietly dissolving until, with the mortar gone, it was all astonishingly easy to push over.

Not that the coup's immediate collapse—before we even learned to pronounce the names of the junta, as one commentator put it—was inevitable. The abrupt failure was unexpected, even if the day after it was over every journalist was explaining how evident it had been all along. I didn't believe that. A few regiments prepared to shoot to kill would have made a very great difference indeed, as they had so recently in Tiananmen. And even if reformist forces had nevertheless gone on to win the day in another year or ten, how many thousands of lives would have been blighted in that interregnum?

Yet however appalling the society created by the Communist "contract" had been—and it was worse than the most illiberal of cold warriors ever imagined, most appalling of all in its titanic contempt for the simplest of daily human pleasures—the citizens of the old empire, and those lucky enough to live in their midst through the terrible and fascinating years that followed, were soon to learn how exhausting and degrading a journey it would be through a land where all verities were overthrown. A rough parallel to what Soviet and post-Soviet citizens endured week after week would be to wake up in your Canadian suburban home to find frost on the sheets because the power had been off all night, flip on the radio only to hear the CBC announcer reciting solemnly from *Mein Kampf*, go out to get the paper by climbing over three weeks of uncollected garbage that the neighbour's kids are going through looking for something to sell for food, discover the corner store had been firebombed in the night but that an enterprising entrepreneur is selling newspapers in the burned-out shell— mind you the *Globe and Mail* has gone out of business overnight and *Le Devoir* has started carrying grainy black- and-white porno on the front page. The bread is okay, but a loaf costs twenty-five bucks, so you buy a half. On the way back to the house you notice two teachers from your child's school bundled against the cold standing at the bus stop and selling potatoes from the back of their Honda Civic. The bus is up the street, tipped half over, its axle broken. A policeman passing by notices you staring and suggests you can avoid the new two-hundred-dollar fine for loitering by giving him a mere hundred.

It is a hard lesson for fragile Westerners, for whom societal stability is so strong that slight shifts in voting patterns are described as revolutions, ten percent annual inflation is considered "spiralling," and no-smoking sections in restaurants constitute barometers of societal sea-change: unlacing the ties that bind can for us be the comfortable dream of every youth, and isn't apt to find us giving up tenured university jobs to stand ten hours in a damp underpass selling pantyhose or kiwi liqueur, where the real money is.

Two days after my leaden breakfast-table visions of life in Stalinism redux, newspaper headlines cried "New Regime Shows Signs of Strain," and Moscow's formidable babushkas were telling the lads in the tanks to behave themselves. One more day and we could read "*Gorbatchev reprend son poste*" with our morning coffee. The tanks were lumbering back out the chewed-up boulevards.

*

My perch, my viewing platform, hadn't been easily reached. What was still the Soviet Union seemed determined to impress both its epic character (so large that parts of it are closer to Ottawa than to Moscow) and its ongoing insistence that life is intolerably symbolic by making our arrival an odyssey, an admittedly trivial personal taste of the country's destinies of endurance, discomfort, waiting, and *lugging*. One might choose to believe that the events of our travel itinerary between Canada and the flat on Dobrininskaya Street (named after a Bolshevik hero; later renamed Korovy Val, "Cow Embankment," in honour of a more ancient role) were mere coincidence, bad luck, rather than emblematic and replete with meaning. But three years in Russia and its old empire were to purge such reasonableness. No, Russia meant us to suffer so as to understand her a little better, love her and hate her a little more.

The coup had fallen apart so quickly we hadn't needed to change our tickets. We boarded on time in Ottawa, having checked enough heavy bags to keep us and the children—Caitlin four, John one-and-a-half—going until our shipment arrived in a month or two, and also clutching too many carry-ons in case Moscow's notorious airport gangs ravaged the checked luggage. Arms aching. Lugging. The Soviet national sport, we would learn; why not begin training now? Even the most privileged of foreigners would have no immunity, trudging through slush and mud soup from hard-currency shop to metro with a week's groceries in plastic bags cutting through the palm, car left at home with only enough fuel in the tank to make futile trips in search of gas.

Boarding was the last thing that happened on time. We were beginning a slightly new relationship with time. Midafternoon. We sat in the 747, trying to distract the kids. Waited. On the runway the engines fired up, then shut down. The pilot tried again. We waited. We taxied back to the terminal. Technicians could be glimpsed out the window, peering into the maw of an engine the size of a hatchback. Various announcements. Unpredictable delays. A new part required. Fidgeting four-year-old, crying one-year-old. An ominous decision, after the first hour, to serve the hot meal on board, on the ground. Everybody ate. Into the third hour of delay the well-fed children curled up and drifted off. Finally, four hours late, we were airborne in time for the coffee and cognac.

Over the Canadian east coast, trying to get comfortable after an already too long sit, we were nervous from wondering if the jet could pick up enough time to make our connecting flight in Amsterdam, and, in spite of ourselves, daunted by facing the dark beast of the Soviet Union: the cold war geopolitical archetype had clearly been sedimented too deeply in the era to resist—a half-seen, grey, wintry shape. But best grab the chance for a bit of rest, the next day would be a challenge. The Atlantic now below, the jet motionless as time, did a slow roll beneath us: try to sleep. At that moment, the voyage thrown off by the delay, both kids woke up, convinced they'd had a grand afternoon nap and eager to play.

At first light, with the overhead screens showing us slicing the top edge off Ireland, we were better able, amidst exhaustion and nerves, to make calculations about the odds. They weren't reassuring. A flight attendant confirmed it: we would touch down in Amsterdam about twenty minutes before the flight to Moscow was scheduled to take off. Our luggage was checked through, and didn't need to be retrieved. There was a chance, she thought. It was just after 10:00 a.m. in Holland, 4:00 a.m. to our bodies. The children dozed off and on. We closed our eyes and thought about how unable we were to think about Moscow. I remembered the night, a month or so earlier, when, as I was putting her down to sleep, Caitlin had told me matter-of-factly that until now—we had been doing inventories for our shipment—she hadn't believed me when I said we were going to Russia. What could it mean to her, after all? And what did her new belief consist of? What did mine? A recent article in the *Washington Post* had mused that in its rampant unformedness Moscow was the place to be, the Paris-in-the-twenties of the 1990s. That notion would later require clarification: a Paris-in-the-twenties of the nineties with ten million people and not a single decent café . . .

Having agonized and checked watches each ten seconds as the jet lumbered slowly from runway to terminal, we pushed our way off as quickly as we could. It was our first time in Schipol's immensity, but, grateful for its efficient design and clear signage, we soon picked up our connecting flight on the monitors and began the dash toward the designated gate. As luck would have it, the gate was at the opposite extremity of the airport's wingspan— it may not have been two miles but certainly seemed it as we trotted and jogged on and off conveyors and escalators with carry-ons and exhausted children in our arms. Soon the arms ached, then they grew numb, then stabs of real pain made it impossible to carry on without brief, panting stops. The KLM cabin staff had understood the flight was being held for connecting passengers, and this, once our biceps were refuelled with oxygen, spurred us on. With five minutes left to scheduled departure, the gate hoved into view. To our delight—even astonishment—the throng there bespoke a delayed boarding. We had made it.

I flung the tickets on the counter, trying to get air, beyond caring about the fine points of courtesy. "Moscow," I said.

The fellow seemed puzzled. He picked up the documents, read them slowly, threw a confirming glance at his computer screen, and handed them back. He was sorry.

But all these people? The flight hasn't boarded yet? We're here! We're late, but we're here. Of course we'll get on. There's no reason . . .

Yes, the flight was delayed. It would board in a few minutes. But the silken logic of a computer's program had made the doubtless reasonable assumption that we could not possibly make the connection. Calculating rapidly, it had already rerouted our checked baggage to Frankfurt.

Frankfurt?

Yes. We were booked on a 2:00 p.m. flight to Frankfurt—three hours hence—then a 4:00 p.m. Lufthansa linkup to Moscow. Throw in a few more time zones, with three hours in the air, and we were due to arrive at 9:00 p.m. Moscow time, or 1:00 p.m. Ottawa time, a mere twenty-four sleepless hours after we had left our hotel for the airport.

So *let* our luggage go via Lufthansa. We wished it well. We could get on here, and . . .

No. Anti-terrorism rules. You must travel with your bags.

We turned slowly, beginning to inhale fatalism, and lurched back toward the central regions of the terminal, moving more deliberately now, with frequent stops to set down the baby, recharge arms and legs. We camped out near the pay phones. The hours waned slowly around us. From time to time one of us dozed. I haunted the phones at the airline desk fruitlessly dialling the embassy in Moscow to rearrange our airport pick-up. The Soviet Union was no doubt still out there, covering a sixth of the earth's land mass, but it certainly was not tethered to Europe's phone lines. This was already beginning to feel like a caustic script; we were characters the director regarded with barely concealed disdain.

Eventually we found ourselves seated on the flight for the short hop into Germany. And of course as takeoff time approached there was an ominous lack of activity from the flight crew, and then the click of the pilot's intercom. It was midday at Schipol, one of the world's busiest airports. We were fifteenth in queue for a takeoff window. We hoped to be departing in about thirty minutes. Thirty. Calculations began all over again. If we *did* have wheels up in thirty minutes, and if there were no planes stacked up over Frankfurt, and given that we had our boarding passes for the ongoing flight, it was possible we would make it.

We waited. Our four-year-old, Caitlin, noted the advantages of an airplane seat over airport-lounge moulded plastic and turned off like a light switch, cuddled up with her stuffed pink bear. John, eighteen months, cried. I felt too many remaining shreds of dignity to join him, yet. Thirty minutes late we taxied out, forty minutes late we lifted over the red-tiled roofs and lush green grid of Dutch countryside. The time-window was closing fast. Our stomachs knotted. We waited.

There *were* other flights orbiting Frankfurt, waiting for openings. We circled above dark woods, occasionally catching the sun flashing off the glass towers of the financial metropolis lying along the slowly revolving horizon. As the plane at last found the runway racing beneath it, we were waking the children, gathering bags, gauging watches, preparing for a well-nigh impossible dash with far greater pessimism than earlier that morning. Then, a little voice had chirpily suggested, "Oh, we'll make it, disasters don't happen, never quite." Now we knew better.

Déjà vu. We had witnessed ourselves in this role only hours earlier: lamentable panicked travellers hauling and lugging fantastic armloads of children and possessions. We sprinted Frankfurt International as we had sprinted Schipol. Although we have subsequently transited its overcrowded terminal many times, and know its inconveniences intimately, I have no mental map from that first run. Eyes scanned departure screens, logged numbers into the brain, hurried off after the necessary digits. Down the endless succession of gates, arms oxygen dead again. Ten minutes to departure. Five. This way. Lufthansa. *Moscow* on the board near a red eye blinking above an open doorway leading into the downward slope to the tarmac. No passengers in sight; a lone steward at the desk.

We showed our boarding passes not as a plea but by way of information, as our identities. Our psyches were hardening toward acceptance of this running, harried nationality. He folded, split and tore them professionally, handing us stubs, inviting us *onward,* last to board the bus to the plane. He seemed unaware of epic.

As it turned out, there was no rush. Low, flat transports ferried luggage to the shadow of the Airbus for passengers to identify. A bit surprised, we found ours, and crossed one anxiety factor—arriving in Moscow with two kids and no *stuff*—off a mental tote sheet, and boarded. No hurry. Cabin crew sat in their bulkheads and gossiped. The departure hour ticked away. The plane was half-full. In the back rows, Russians—mainly the leather-jacketed import-export crowd that is one of the emblems of the post-Soviet sphere—were busy smoking, playing cards, scratching the black shadows on their faces, rearranging huge cord-bound boxes of stereos and TVs, and giving off a tough vinegar-and-earth odour.

Any thought of a 9:00 p.m. Moscow-time arrival had fled. After a while a co-pilot came on to mention a minor mechanical adjustment. We weren't surprised, but I *was* wondering about the odds of three major flight delays inside twenty-four hours on two of the world's most reliable airlines. We *were* inside twenty-four hours, weren't we? Was today still Monday, or was it Tuesday? Almost surely not Wednesday. Forty-five minutes later everything was shipshape, but we had lost our place in the take-off queue. A pilot commented was it *ever* busy out there this evening. Evening? Kids dozed. I remembered how, on the tarmac bus, Caitlin had clambered on, noted without concern that it was jampacked (too many stereos and microwaves), and tossed her own little backpack onto the floor and sat on it, with all the cool of a sixties world wanderer after eighteen months on the road. I didn't doze. I was, absurdly, wide awake, although my brain felt glazed as an icy window and garnered only indistinct ghosts from its surroundings. Then we were in the air, and quickly over the old Iron Curtain—still a very real fault line, where two plates grated. The arrival time proffered was 11:00 p.m. local. The pilot, however, noted a strong head wind . . .

*

Nearing midnight. Though the plane had been descending for some time, we could see nothing below. As if the
clouds conspired with the oppression of Russian history
to keep things under wraps, when we finally emerged we
were racing above the runway, search lights strobing past,
touching down.

Even a lifetime of absorbing stereotypes had failed to
prepare us for Sheremetyeva airport at night (as it turned
out, one of the best airports in the country). Off the plane,
along a corridor, to the top of a set of stairs—a descent.
Shabbiness, smell, lassitude, wariness, coarseness, impa-
tience, desperation—all submerged in ill-lit gloom. One
couldn't credit the architects with mere incompetence: they
had gone out of their way. A very low ceiling was composed of thousands of dark metal cones about two feet
long, a few containing dim bulbs. Knots of uniformed
youths with bad skin lounged about militarily; you felt as
though all the disoriented, over-hormoned, lost trouble-
makers from brutal households had been taken out of class
and put in charge of the school. Optimism roused by the
relative shortness of the passport-control lines was soon
dashed by the realisation that the inspectors spent five minutes leafing, reading, poking, prodding, stamping even the
passport of our one-year-old. In occasional fits of detach-
ment, Teresa and I grinned at each other maniacally. We
waited. When a sombre Charon peered out of his booth to
match my daughter's face to her photo he smiled slightly, a
seam of light. We were through, across, inside.

Luggage? Sure enough, a wheezing black belt surged

28

arrhythmically out of a cinder-block wall from under old rubber flaps, bearing the string-tied behemoths the size of washer-dryers Russians call parcels. An aggressive mob was jostling for position near the conveyor, elbows high. We had packed our maximum allotment, two bags for each of the four of us. We would need a luggage cart; two would be better. People *were* driving a number of them about, battering shins. I spotted a counter where a clerk with peroxide hair not seen in Canada in decades and lipstick the colour of beets appeared to be dispensing them. Approaching, I tried for the first time to put my Russian lessons to practical use by deciphering the sign in front of her. Fatigue had washed out my brain, and the Cyrillic script at first refused to speak. But eventually I got the gist. *Tolka rubliey.* Roubles only. There was a fee for a cart, a barbarism shared by those few airports in the world apparently trying to *discourage* visitors. For a mere ten roubles, about fifty cents then, the present hurdle could be leapt. This was an interesting situation. They would only accept roubles. That was the rule. But we were on the *outside* of customs control, and in 1991 it was certainly very illegal to take roubles out of the country. And since the rouble was not convertible, you could not buy them outside the Soviet Union. The currency exchange desk was on the other side of customs. But you couldn't go through customs without your luggage. You couldn't move your luggage without a cart. I remembered once trying to explain the phrase "Catch-22" to a Francophone friend who had never read Joseph Heller. Here, finally, was the illustration I had needed.

It was obvious the totalitarian empire was finished. They were having trouble keeping their prohibitions properly lined up. One could a) break the law and bring out roubles so as to have some with you coming back, or b) break the law and offer a U.S. dollar (at which point, myth and security briefings had it, a KGB moll would seduce you in the taxi into town and threaten to expose you for currency marketeering unless you told her all you knew about NATO nuclear codes), or c) steal a cart. With a month's experience I would not have hesitated—give the lady a dollar, for heaven's sake. My brain was still unformed. I hovered, hoping something would somehow happen to resolve my dilemma and return me heroically to my exhausted family back at the floppy conveyor belt. Stress was making my chest muscles hurt. I will never understand how, or why (since these things were valuable commodities), but as I stood, drifting within, an empty luggage cart appeared, sitting alone in a little clearing amidst the swirling crowd, like a Christmas bicycle. It was that kind of country, too.

With our eight suitcases balanced precariously on the rattling vehicle, arms holding combos of carry-on bags and whichever child was currently asleep, legs holding us up, we moved to the back of an enormous, unmoving customs queue. There were a half-dozen channels, but only one was manned. Each person in the line was ferrying enough goods to supply a hardware store for a month. The light was dull, so yellow everyone appeared jaundiced. The floor was gritty. The air was acrid with smoke and unidentifiable fumes. The carts were dented and unpainted and disinclined to roll. The guards' coats didn't fit right. The tobacco in everyone's cigarettes was badly cured. The toilet was broken. The water fountain had no water. It was already difficult, a one-hour veteran of the East Bloc, not to curse the "system." But wasn't that a cop-out, an evasion of responsibility? *People* are the cause of systems, right? But it was difficult to imagine that any group of human beings acting at random could generate such consummate *unpleasantness.* Mere apathy would hardly have done the job. The dispiritedness of poverty, even in the Pakistans of the world, could not have generated such aggravatingly unnecessary, pointless discomfort. For that, ideology was an essential ingredient—otherwise human stupidity would dilute in other elements, and could not achieve this acme of concentration.

This queue seemed an official, final affront, a gratuitous insult to add to the injuries of the past "day." We waited. We took turns strolling the children around the rank confines of the luggage zone. A tiny Duty Free had perfume and booze and portable phones. We went back to the line. The kids cried, though less than we had any right to expect. We waited. Eventually we reached a counter controlled by bored youths who glared balefully at our documents, applied a languorous selection of stamps, waved us on.

We funnelled into a narrow doorway. Beyond, even now, in the small hours, a pressing mob left only the narrowest of channels. People pushed forward and inward on all sides, necks craning, holding signs, shouting *Taxi! Veui khotyetye taxi?* Hands reached out. We pulled the children close with free fingers. I pushed the groaning cart. In the main terminal the ceiling was higher, but the walls browner still and the lighting no better. A quick survey showed a short row of tourist info offices, taxi and car rental bureaus, an Intourist office—all closed tight (if they

31

had ever been open). After buying roubles—and not understanding why the clerk was shouting and abusing me, after all I was *dumping* my U.S. dollars—we pushed our way toward the exit doors. Our thoroughgoing western minds, having accepted the dismal fact that there was indeed no one to meet us here in Moscow in the middle of the night, presumed that outside we would escape the free-lancers of dubious visage now following us around the terminal and find licensed cabs lined up at the curb. It had dawned on us, after all, that we would need two, and as both options available—either putting me, a "rich" foreign male, in one unknown Russian car with one child and half the bags, and my wife, a "rich" foreign female, in a second unknown Russian car with the other child and the other half of the bags; or loading all four of us into one and all our belongings into another—seemed equally bad, the best we could hope was that regular, licensed cabbies might be slightly less inclined toward 1:00 a.m. muggings on abandoned airport service roads.

Outside was more pandemonium. A hundred free-lancers pushed forward, knowing an easy mark when they saw one. No sign of a queue, much less a licence. A blast of gas and diesel fumes swirled in a fog of smoke and yellow glare. Underfoot—mud. A couple of gentlemen with battered faces and leather jackets seemed to want to help push the cart. I got my elbows up like Gordie Howe going into a corner. We panicked a bit, tried to turn back to regroup inside the terminal. Exhaustion, a B-grade movie director, heightened the scene. As I attempted to pivot the cart, it tipped. Eight bags slid, tumbled, skidded. A bevy of drivers rushed to help. Nadir. Now, years later, I know they really *were* trying to help—most of them. I didn't know that then. I seized my private property, tried to rebuild my pile; it refused to stack. I tried again, we retreated.

Twenty minutes later, with the help of a German diplomat (a veteran of Moscow) whom we had met on the plane and now reencountered in the terminal, we had picked out a pair of semi-official cab drivers (their cars had once been registered taxis, though the meters had been turned off with the advent of *perestroika*), had negotiated an (illegal) hard currency price, had split into two groups and were plummeting inside dented Zhigulis through the crazy submarine light of Moscow's nighttime highways, past the tank traps memorialising the furthest advance of Hitler's armies in 1941. We were dazed by the cavalcade of old battered cars and lumbering ancient trucks, the grimy unkempt buildings, and the hunched, demonic driving of our chauffeur—who was in all other respects a thoroughly pleasant man, his face visibly softened by my little boy's presence in his car. The love of Russians for children seems inversely proportional to their scarcity in Russian society.

Still, the other taxi careening through the Soviet night, through the faint illumination of its pothole-defined slalom course, did contain my wife and daughter, and I peered past the driver's shoulder out his cracked windshield to try to keep it in sight. I had the sensation we were fleeing something, or someone, that we were crossing the great plains of black-and-white Russian war movies winding to their ends. Punch drunk, or haunted. Part way in, the twenty-fifth hour of our day, with the tombstone high rises gradually giving way to the heavy eight-story brownstones of the post-war rebuilding, we saw some of the city's buses parked for the night along Leningradsky Prospekt, hundreds in a solid row, block after block, thousands of empty windows to give back our reflections (a U-turn would have brought us eventually to St. Petersburg—still Leningrad that night—six hundred kilometres to the north). The scale of life had been enlarged. The taxi drove on and on. We waited.

Stray pensioners, sturdy legged, shuffled the lonely sidewalks.

*

The cabbies had now become human beings, making a tough late-night buck on their cars' last legs in the death-gasps of the empire. They helped us with the bags. The lock accepted the key. We were inside an apartment. Ours. 3:00 a.m. It had been a full hour's drive. Some organ—part of the body, not the mind—was remembering all of this. We learned more about the word "home."

For now the suitcases stayed in a sentinel's row by the door. We found a room with two beds and gave Caitlin to one of them for sleep. One piece of luggage was a travel crib, unfolded by our fumbling brains and hands, a place for John.

Only later, six months, a year, would we be wise enough to understand that our trip from Ottawa to the apartment in Moscow's centre would be viewed far differently by Soviet eyes. What a smooth and comfortable journey! The first flight had boarded on time at an airport stocked with an unimaginable array of comforts: heat, calm lights, comfortable lounges that were scrubbed clean daily, message boards to advise us of flights, functioning PA systems, pleasant restaurants possessing all the items on their menus, scented washrooms that sparkled and gleamed, book stalls to allay boredom. Actual departure had been a mere four hours late—"on time" throughout much of the Imperium—and during the interval cheerful and apologetic airline staff had plied us with liquor, distributed clean pillows and blankets for the sleepy, and toys and colouring books for the children, then fed us a tasty meal with a choice of wines never seen by anyone below the uppermost tiers of the Party aristocracy. A 747 had glided across the Atlantic, had never needed to put down in, say, Maine, for the pilot to go out bartering for fuel to hop the pond. The toilets on the plane had not backed up, smokers had only smoked in the smoking sections, the galley had not run out of food or water. When we missed our connecting flight, no one at the airline information counter had scolded us for making inquiries and interrupting their personal space. The airport had more good shops than most post-Soviet nations. Someone had planned a new route for us without being browbeaten or bribed, and had been so kind and efficient as to deftly intercept our bags and divert them to our new itinerary. Flights to Frankfurt and on toward Russia had proceeded like veritable clockwork, some of the delays measured in mere parts of an hour rather than part of weeks, with fine food and good booze at regular intervals. None of the ceiling panels on the planes were broken, the seatbelts belted, there were never more people on the flight than seats, there were no crates of eggs, or spare tires, in the aisles. There were no fistfights. On arrival, our passports had been docilely accepted without an all-night interrogation or extra fees for the official involved.

A luggage cart had been provided by the gods free of charge. No one had stolen a single bag. Two polite taxi drivers had sped us efficiently to the very centre of town for the rough equivalent of one hour's salary, a trifle. We had not needed to maneuver our bags and children through any snowdrifts or on and off any packed buses or metro cars. The hallway of our apartment building was lit. Someone had removed the garbage. The elevator up had functioned. Inside the flat all the lights were working at the flick of a switch, and there was no smell of gas. It had been, indeed, a trip to write home about.

Teresa and I explored, far too exhausted for sleep. The apartment was small; that is, enormous by Soviet standards. Two bedrooms and a small den. Washer-dryer built in to a closet. An eat-in kitchen and one large combined living-room dining-room. We entered that last room in the dark. Before we could fumble for the switch we stopped short. Along the entire north wall ran a ledge at waist height, and above the ledge, all window. The city glowed softly, a few million tiny bulbs in the great hall of night. There, across the rooftops, was the Kremlin, a fairy tale gone wrong, all wrong, but beautiful anyway. Mandelshtam saw it over my shoulder:

> A wandering fire at a terrible height—
> Can it be a star shining like that?
> The dreams of earth blaze at a terrible height.

Even now, my breath is caught.

Journal Notes

All day it has poured. The chill feels like November. In the Russian folk calendar, it is the Lenten feast of Ivan Postny, or John the Baptist, during which the eating of anything round, reminiscent of heads, is to be avoided. We are less stunned now by Moscow's truly monumental greyness and shabbiness, by six-foot trees growing from the cement of crumbling balconies, by the never-cut grass in Gorky Park and in everybody's playgrounds, by streets that have no edges but instead blur gradually into dirt which crumbles against a fractured sidewalk. Yet the Sadovoye Kaltso below our window is a sight that still amazes each morning: a continuous rally of weary cars and hulking trucks at high speeds without lane markings, pitted with potholes that can and do break axles, strewn with the odd brick; interrupted by the occasional car stopped amid six lanes of traffic, jacked up, the driver lying underneath to have a look at the trouble. It had never before occurred to us to think of the local garage and the radio-dispatched tow-truck as two of the great achievements of urban civilisation, but it does now.

The city at its best looks swept but never washed, save by this endless rain that rivers the sidewalks. The sidewalks: there the human price is most visible. The faces all appear to me to have lived through a Dostoevsky novel.

*As the Polish journalist Ryszard Kapuscinski has written,
the Homo Sovieticus that Communism wished to create is
in reality "first and foremost an utterly exhausted man,
and one shouldn't be surprised if he doesn't have the
strength to rejoice in his newly won freedom." Not to mention the Soviet Woman. Communism combined with ferocious Russian patriarchy has destroyed the vast majority
by age fifty. A late-middle-aged or elderly woman who
does not look broken and beyond caring, trudging on sore
feet in bad boots, and carrying too many bags, is a rarity.
Of course there are few old men. The war and Stalinism's
camps thinned their ranks on an unimaginable scale. Now
Russian historians, in calculating deaths by non-natural
causes (a bad term, since we continue to prove that war
and murder are part of our nature) between the revolution
and the death of Stalin, suggest numbers like fifty-four
million (Sergei Maksundov) or a hundred and ten million
(I. Kurganov). And the survivors scorched, their psyches
like old leather. And their feet, every day on Moscow's
streets, dog tired. Not many adult Russians have living
fathers. Solzhenitsyn was not using mere metaphor when referring to the post-Soviet citizenry as the "progeny of ghosts."*

*Tired from waiting. These past days I flinched see-
ing my first great lines snaking out the door of a gastronom
(grocery store) or state liquor shop and winding down the
street. This sort of queue is pretty much a Soviet inven-
tion. It has nothing to do with poverty. There are relatively few lines in the world's poorest countries. The
ideology of the line is pretty simple: it's a thumb on the
nose, a sneer, pure contempt. I'm in control; I'll dole out
the goodies; you will wait. It is a relative of slavery. You*

38

see its distant cousins on the modern assembly line or the brief lineup at the time clock come quitting time in a Canadian factory. No social system breeds out all evils, and these are mere traces of the pure product, persisting partly because no one can figure out how to get rid of them entirely, partly because they have hard-truth meaning, producing as a trade-off for their dehumanisation more efficiently produced and thus cheaper goods, allowing more people to live better on fewer hours at work. The real thing, in Moscow, means one sales clerk doling out a new shipment of shoes, taking her own sweet time with each purchaser, as three hundred people spend their entire Saturday waiting to reach her counter, while a dozen other clerks staff empty counters with nothing to sell, buffing their nails. It means the duly authorised Guardian of Doors at the Bolshoi unlocking only one of a dozen exits after the ballet so Muscovites can pass twenty minutes pushing their way out of the lobby instead of doing whatever they *wanted to do with twenty minutes. These are the more banal versions of three-day waits for flights in Yerevan or twenty-year queues for apartments in Tomsk, but they are also more important because they take place every day, for almost everybody, and thus consume the most lives. Samuel Beckett showed most starkly that waiting is a human essence: we wait for death hoping we are waiting for meaning. The entire human enterprise, civilisation itself, has been to* add something *to that primal context, to render life more than a mere hovering between birth and extinction. On a far from trivial level, the life of the line is a demonstration of a society structured to tear away at this endeavour.*

But I am already learning that in Russia there is always a but. The but is a spark of energy, an infusion of initiative, a determination of grace or grit against the grey weight. It poured. But when it finally stopped, in late afternoon, I strolled the little streets behind our apartment block—ulitsa Donskaya, ulitsa Akademika Petrovskovo—detouring regularly around the great ponds on the broken sidewalks. But one man had found a more or less flat patch to spread a white sheet beside his decrepit yellow Lada. The price of an economy model was running at six times the average annual salary. Figure it out. He seemed to be doing major repairs, as a number of engine parts were carefully arrayed on the cloth. The water itself presented too good an opportunity to miss. The rain ran in torrents through the street beside his work station, and he crouched there, wrestling with a larger chunk of his automobile. Stooping, tilting, where the rain water thundered into a storm drain, he was flushing out his radiator.

And looking pretty pleased.

OCTOBER
The rouble is thirty to the dollar. Long-stemmed roses, on sale at the flower stands which crowd every metro entrance with unexpected colour, cost three roubles apiece, ten cents. The rouble tumbles, but prices so far remain fixed, some unchanged since the 1960s. In state stores we're millionaires. Vinyl records, extinct in Canada, are three or four roubles. On the "private" book tables outside the mammoth state-run Dom Knigi (House of Books), volumes mysteriously unavailable inside are a bit more expensive, but cheap for western vultures. Yesterday I found

40

a beautifully bound two volume complete Mandelshtam—
all his poetry, all his prose—for sixty roubles, two bucks.
The poets are on every stand, especially Mandelshtam and
Tsvetaeva right now, as are translations of third-rate
American sci-fi, an extraordinary amount of Alexander
Dumas, and any number of books to teach you English or
German. One had the non-confidence-inspiring title Ameri-
can Idiom's Dictionary.

In shaggy Gorky Park (both a massive green space
spanning hundreds of acres of central Moscow along the
river near our flat, and an amusement park) it is the 1950s.
Muscovites jam it on weekends however lousy the weather,
promenading en famille. *The teenaged girls wear dresses*
and panty hose and heels, their younger sisters have large
bows in long hair. There is music over the loudspeakers,
pony rides, paddle boats and ducks in the pond, two Ferris
wheels, ice-cream cones and Pepsi, perogis for a penny
each, and plenty of booths where you can throw balls at
pins or hoops at pegs and win a prize. This past Saturday
(the last warm day?) we stopped at one of the park's
shashlik stands for some of the saucy shishkabob served
on paper plates with black Russian bread. As I stood in
line, a modest line by local standards, I noticed the pro-
prietor back behind his booth barbecuing the meat. Near
him, his assistant was busily sawing the legs off an old
wooden chair to feed the fire.

NOVEMBER
As Yeltsin and the other republican leaders argue with
Gorbatchev (his relevance fading daily) about the future
of the clearly disintegrating Soviet Union, the situation

41

on the streets is worsening. The distribution network, lousy during what are already being seen as the good old days, is coming apart like rotten webbing in a lawn chair: there is no real private market in place, but the old mechanism of control—fear—is gone. Everyone knows price "liberalisation" (it sounds nicer than "shock") is coming, so anyone who controls goods at any level, from factory director to check-out clerk, is diverting, hoarding, stealing or bartering. I talked to one ethnic Russian who runs a co-op in Moldova near the Romanian border. Moldova is the sort of place right now, by all accounts, that makes people wish they lived in Moscow. His co-op makes fake marble countertops. When I asked about local conditions, he mentioned that gasoline was impossible to buy (none too easy to find even in the imperial capital these days). Ration coupons for forty litres a month were distributed, but they were useless. I commiserated: not being able to use your car is irritating at times. Oh, but he could always get gas he corrected off-handedly. He just swaps it for fake marble counter tops.

Last week was the anniversary of the Great October Revolution, and since nobody has got around to changing the official holidays yet, everyone had the day off. But with winter already weeks old—short dim days, zero degrees Celsius, bits of snow, twilight by 3:00 p.m.—nothing much was happening on the big day, save that the bread lines lengthened another notch. A small knot of loyalists milled in front of our local Lenin statue, whose pedestal was scattered with flowers. But they were a tired lot, and seldom numbered more than a dozen at any one time. One babushka ("grandmother") did find the energy

the following day to scold Caitlin for dancing and skip-
ping on the marble concourse flanking its base. Insuffi-
cient solemnity in the presence of ghosts, one supposes.

As Russia reverts toward the micro-markets of the
Dark Ages, a modern society's standard infrastructure for
delivering millions of items to thousands of shops daily,
giant ships feeding transports and trains handing off to
vans zipping to delivery doors is replaced in part by hu-
man biceps. One could easily write a treatise on Moscow
built around the word "lug." Today, I saw one iron filing
in this immense magnetic field of survival patterns, a wiz-
ened little man the size of a jockey weaving from one side
of the walk to the other, half-hidden beneath a huge and
filthy sack of potatoes. Had he bought them at some rynok
and was now lugging them home? Had he grown them in
a zealously cultivated and jealously guarded dacha plot
outside the city and was now lugging his way toward a
vending spot to slit open the burlap and dispense the treas-
ure one lucrative kilo at a time? Had someone a little less
penurious paid him a few roubles (today at forty-seven to
the dollar) to lug them as far as the metro?

The service industry takes practice, no doubt. On
our first trip to St. Petersburg this past weekend, where
the 2:00 p.m. sunsets and decades of neglect failed to
obscure the city's grace and irrefutable character, more
character than a planned capital has any right having,
we saw our first Russian ballet in the intimate splendour
of the Maly Kirov. At the (obligatory) coat check, the guard-
ians of the garments also rent opera glasses, for twenty
kopecks. Ours asked me if I wanted a pair. Please, I re-
plied. U minya nyet, *she retorted. I don't have any.*

43

2

THE LAST NIGHT OF THE SOVIET UNION

The weather continued monotonous through December, 1991, getting no colder after late October, getting no warmer, always cloudy; we watched the slow draining away of light. Never before had I so appreciated the need to celebrate the victory of the sun at the solstice.

The Soviet Union, during those darkening days, had only weeks to go in its seventy-year run. The death toll on behalf of dialectical materialism was titanic: to recite the names of the victims, at the rate of one every five seconds, would take ten years—if the *lower* estimates were used, if you counted only those actually killed, and if you could discover all the names. It would all officially end 31 December, 1991. The beginning of the end was harder to identify; many fulcrums could be pinpointed.

One choice might be an incident on December 15, 1986, an event replete with bathos, Soviet-Kafkaesque absurdity, tinges of hilarity, and profound moral courage. On that date, as Andrei Sakharov relates in his *Memoirs*, two electricians appeared at the apartment where he lived in exile in Gorky, accompanied by one of the KGB agents who had spent years sitting in the corridor outside his door.

They rang the bell late in the evening, as the great physicist and civil rights activist sat watching television with his wife, Yelena Bonner. The agent announced that they were installing a telephone. The one in the flat had been removed long ago to prevent contact with the outside world. Before going off to bed, Sakharov and Bonner ruminated about who was supposed to call. Some sort of media interview (carefully controlled, of course)? *Literaturnaya Gazeta* perhaps? The call, they were told, could be expected at ten the next morning.

The following day they stayed in until three in the afternoon, waiting. This pointless delay, with its personal inconvenience, is all-too symbolic, as is the installation of the telephone for a single call. Just before Sakharov gave up and went out to buy bread, it rang. A woman's voice was telling him that Mikhail Sergeyavich would speak to him.

Gorbatchev came on the line and informed Sakharov that he could return to Moscow and "continue his patriotic work." Sakharov, being Sakharov, said thank you and immediately pressed Gorbatchev to take action on a list of political prisoner files he had recently sent to him in protest. Like all saints (though he would hate the designation) Sakharov was nothing if not stubborn. Besides, it's not every day you have the General-Secretary on the phone.

Sakharov doesn't mention it, but one presumes that a few days later, with the packing underway, two electricians and a KGB man dutifully returned to disconnect the wires and take away the phone.

*

In the West the media empires seized selectively from the many available emblems of the collapse of Soviet communism and *its* empire. Ethnic tumult, tumbling statues, and ubiquitous bread queues were favourites. As they rapidly became shorthand clichés substituting for thought, many such symbols simplified what must surely have been one of the most complex social and political matrices the globe had ever seen. The structure of it all was fine and filamented and confusing to begin with, and was now racheted by panic. There were, for example, many lineups for many products, but it was not true—and never had been—that all stores had lines or that all lines were caused solely by shortages. The bread shop (yes, stores selling only bread—two kinds if you were lucky), across the street from us, for example, never had lines long enough to reach out the door. I had no idea why. The best thing about this store was that its entrance and its emerging patrons were visible from our ninth-floor kitchen window across Garden Ring Road, enabling us to know, in spite of its unpredictable hours, whether a) it was open, and b) it actually had bread.

One of the questions any observer, and all residents, had to ask themselves in that double-jointed time, was whether disintegration would presage real cultural change: that is, whether Communism was the cause or the result of the current Slavic "character." Many locals had no doubt about this. A Russian colleague, a large, joyous, emotional woman, assured me that one could shuffle the leaders all one liked, but since you could not change Russians, the quagmire was inescapable.

For myself, I hesitated to exculpate Lenin and his contempt for the rule of law and the fate of the individual, or to "contextualize" to even the slightest degree Stalin's singular cannibalism by blaming it all on some Russian "essence." "Soul," is the word the theoretically atheist Soviet-Russians prefer; the Russian soul, *Ruskaya dusha.* This mysterious entity—real enough, I believe, however hard to characterise—had also produced Tolstoy, Shostakovitch, Akhmatova, Pasternak, Sakharov, *and* had revered each and every one of them. To attribute such overwhelming historical force to a national strain of some sort would smack both of Hegelian political mysticism and of the idea that democracy in its various imperfect incarnations is merely a Western capitalist canard—a notion much loved by voracious dictators from Beijing to Zaire. It would also mark, ironically, a succumbing to the formidable depths of Russian fatalism.

Through the autumn, events on the political landscape moved fast—but not straight ahead. They were spasmodic and unpredictable, high level epilepsy in the world's biggest empire, an agglomeration of one hundred and four recognized "nationalities." On September 5th the Soviet legislature voted to give up power to the Russian republican government, which then immediately recognized the independence of the Baltics. On the one hand, the Congress of People's deputies voted itself out of existence, suggesting the Soviet Union was defunct. On the other hand, it concurrently created the State Council, a two-chambered Supreme Soviet chosen by the republics, and an Inter-Republican Economic Committee, suggesting it was still in business. About the same time, Yeltsin sparked concern verging on panic when he suggested Russia might review

47

its borders with any republic unilaterally seceding from the USSR. Subsequently his spokesmen announced he hadn't said it. Another week later, prominent reformer Anatoly Sobchak, mayor of Leningrad-St. Petersburg, stated bluntly during a visit to Kiev that "the old Union does not exist and there can be no return to it." Some who had been far from fast friends with the old regime were not impressed. Dissident historian Roy Medvedev accused Yeltsin and Gorbatchev of acting arbitrarily and illegally. He was right, but given the constitutional vacuum, it was hard to imagine what "legal" might mean.

The economic prospects were bitterly grim. In late September Gorbatchev was sealing his disastrously negative image in the public eye by sending urgent letters to Western governments begging for food and medicine to get through the coming winter. Through the month Georgia in the south descended into civil war. The central government in Moscow, still in theory running the place, did nothing about it. Opposition forces in Tblisi trying to overthrow duly elected but increasingly tyrannical President Zviad Gamsakhurdia seized the TV station, and the president barricaded himself in the legislature building. On Georgia's northern border a second civil war was brewing. Soviet Interior Ministry troops in the region of South Ossetia (North Ossetia was inside the Russian Federation) found themselves caught between Georgian irregulars and the local population of Muslim Ossetians, who argued that their ancestors had settled the area more than two hundred years ago. Georgians contended most of the Ossetians had been handed land in the area only in 1921 in return for supporting the Bolsheviks. Soon, refugees were streaming in all directions away from increasingly vicious fighting.

In October, Gorbatchev and eight republican presidents signed a treaty of Economic union (Azerbaidjan, Ukraine, Georgia, Moldova and the Baltics demurred). How this could be done without dissolving the Soviet Union first was barely discussed. In what was to prove an ominous portent, the "Russian" region of Checheno-Ingushetia declared independence—independence from *what* wasn't yet clear. Yeltsin made his first blunder in the region by declaring a state of emergency which—clearly unenforceable—was promptly rescinded by the Russian parliament. In November Gorbatchev, sounding more and more like something from a time capsule, went on national television to warn Ukrainians that a vote for independence would lead to mass war between the republics. Simultaneously, Yeltsin's Russian Republic was pledging immediate recognition of Ukraine and continuing its rapid take-over of the Kremlin's powers by absorbing the Soviet central bank. What was perhaps the first hint of post-Soviet political structures came about this time when Ukrainian foreign minister Anatoly Zlenko suggested that the leaders of Russia, Byelorussia, and Kazakhstan should meet with Ukrainian officials on the issue of controlling the orphaned Soviet nuclear arsenals.

Throughout December, the editors at Rand McNally pulled out their hair. Ukraine formally declared its independence, and was instantly recognized by Poland and Canada, ending centuries of domination and Russification. For the moment at least. History has plenty of victims, but few innocents. Long before Muscovite imperialism was starving Ukrainians in man-made famines, the Kievan princes of the tenth century counted dumpy little Moscow as part of *their* hegemony. The infant state in 1990s Kiev was led by Leonid Kravchuk, a fifty-seven-year-old onetime Communist mainstreamer who had acrobatically transformed himself into a partisan of Ukrainian nationalism and market economics. A week later, somewhat anticlimactically, Ukraine joined a new Commonwealth of Independent States whipped up on short notice in a hunting lodge by its president and those of Belarus and Russia. Gorbatchev was pointedly not invited to the get-together. Should all those who signed up be the same colour in the new atlas? Canadians agonise for decades on how to rejig the fiddlings of their constitutional flow charts. In the "Soviet Union," republican presidents, without breathing a word to their constituents, dissolved nations and cobbled together new ones over a quick cup of coffee and an icy vodka toast. Six more republics, after getting over their pique at not being invited to the hunting lodge, said "me too" a few days later.

The end of an era, no doubt. But any sense of the momentous was sapped by the almost comic murk and general air of improvisation. Belarus (still Byelorussia then) is as good an example as any. Although it would be an exaggeration to say there was no nationalist consciousness in this hybrid buffer state whose current territory had been swallowed and regurgitated over the years by Russian, Ukrainian, German, Polish, Lithuanian, and Prussian princes, not to mention the Teutonic Knights, it was extremely quiescent. What was left of distinctively Belarussian culture after Hitler's armies savaged it was diluted in the great flood of Bolshevism. It was generally the most conservative of the former republics; when I visited three years later the ponderous statue of a lecturing Lenin at his podium outside the legislature of the new state was still standing, and no one had gotten around to removing the hammers and sickles carved above the doorways. The government was busy trying to dump the collapsing new national currency—called "Bunnies" after the picture of a rabbit on the one-rouble note and in honour of its buying power—and get back into the Russian rouble zone, an idea the old imperialists in Moscow were equally busy resisting. When the Soviet Union was abruptly dissolved, Belarus was roughly in the position Manitoba or New Brunswick would be in if Canada were to be disbanded on twenty-four hours' notice—not ready, and eager to join any new group going.

For Russians, on the other hand, it was all ending with a whimpering sigh, rather like the career of Mikhail Gorbatchev. The territory controlled from Moscow was shrinking for the first time since the boyars of Ivan the Great overran Novgorod and its colonies on the upper Volga over five hundred years earlier. Only a minority was yet nostalgic for the empire, at least in its Soviet version. But the haphazard ending, the jerry-rigged new arrangements, and the general economic pessimism and political disgust had left the vast majority irritable, psychologically displaced, and wondering what they belonged to and what belonged to them. This was further complicated, in Moscow at least, by the cosmopolitan nature of the imperial capital. If Russians had mixed feelings, how did long-time ethnic Georgian or Ukrainian or Kazakh residents feel? But the West wanted to celebrate; and in a fit of misfiring congeniality it wanted Russians to celebrate too.

In spite of turmoil and plenty of human suffering in Moldova's Dneister region, in Georgia, Armenia, Azerbaidjan and Tadjikistan, it was all disassembling itself more peacefully than anyone had dared hope. Perhaps there *was* no better way to give birth to nations than through a muddle of awkward and unsatisfying negotiations, through just getting by: no heroes, no battles, no myths.

*

The year seemed to be ending quietly for us as well. The city felt muted in the darkness and snow. We were beginning to feel like Muscovites rather than tourists; a sensation of settling in, a quieting of an internal clangour. We had managed to find a Christmas tree, and parcels arriving from friends and family in Canada made us feel less and more lonely at the same time. More than one gift mailer, having watched their TV news carefully, killed two birds with one stone by padding parcels with rolls of toilet paper. We ferried the wrapped presents from inside the parcels to the tree to await Christmas morning; aptly John, almost two, decided to help out by placing a few rolls of White Swan beneath the boughs. I had also succeeded, on our "Boxing Day," in finding gas for the car for the first time in weeks. I cruised back to the department in a mood of elation and triumph: we had gas! We had wheels! In the final, briefest days, with heavier snow now, a sort of exhausted peace did seem to descend.

On New Year's Eve there was talk of celebrations on Red Square, so about eleven I bundled up and took the metro to Kropotkinskaya station, intentionally leaving myself a long walk in the crisp air around the graceful red brick battlements of the Kremlin. Along the Moskva embankment, snow was disappearing into the river on one side of me while on the other, above the soaring walls, the golden domes of the cathedrals inside the Kremlin were bathed in light. I have seen few sights more beautiful, few combining such powerful sensations of tranquillity and passion. The streets were deserted, utterly silent. As I rounded the final tower, St. Basil's leapt into view like a conjuror's finale, hovering at the top of the long slow rise from the river; such a fairy-tale construction, yet on such a vast scale, on such a silent night, made me feel for a moment the reality of the Russian soul we are far too sophisticated, and far too politically correct, to believe in. I have never since doubted its existence, or its corruptions.

As I plodded up toward Red Square, *Krasnaya Ploshchad*, it became increasingly clear that any celebrating was a combination of government edict and CNN wishful thinking. The cobblestones of the great expanse where, during a mass prayer meeting to send off Ivan the Terrible's armies to fight the Mongols, a ragged holy man named Basil had wandered the crowd warning of the curse Ivan's reign of terror would bring, were tonight being swept by a skin-numbing wind. Soviet stars, rich and ruby red, stood shining at each pinnacle of the Kremlin defences. Although awash in floodlights, the square was populated mainly by ghosts of various glorious and inglorious spectacles, from Ivan's send-off to the crowds booing Gorbatchev during

53

the last great Soviet parade—plus a few flesh-and-blood knots of drunken teenagers, and frozen Western camera crews huddled under plastic sheets. Clearly Muscovites were doing the sensible thing: surrounding food-laden tables with family, friends and glasses of vodka and champagne in snug apartments, watching the freezing idiots on TV.

The cachet of standing on Red Square, not a hundred yards from where Lenin's waxen corpse slept in his tacky underground tomb, as the last hour of the Soviet Union ticked away, was fading fast. The sentiment had turned out to be profoundly misplaced. Besides, my ears were about to drop off. I pushed my fists deeper into my pockets and trudged toward the nearest metro. The drunken teenagers were wearing jackets and jeans, or skirts one inch longer than not needing to bother at all.

Under a colonnade near the metro, where the gloom was darkest, the hardiest flower sellers were still working. They knew the lads in the jackets were apt to throw away plenty of roubles on roses for the short-short skirts. I thought of the numerous commentators of the late '80s and early '90s confidently forecasting that it would take a generation for the Soviet people to learn the art of making a dollar. In fact it took about two weeks. All fall I had assumed that with the advent of winter the flower-sellers would disappear. But to defeat the cold they had all placed their roses in portable wooden-framed glass boxes the size of bird cages, with lit candles within to keep the flowers from freezing. In the darkness, the row of tables was a shrine, the soft lights casting floral shadows and gently illuminating the tired faces of the vendors, recreating, by subconscious cultural instinct, the interior of an Orthodox church, here, in the underpass realm.

The metro cars were almost empty. Scattered passengers dozed, chins nodding gently against chests. I got home in time to watch the fireworks from our living-room windows. We put on the TV and woke up Caitlin to see the New Year in. CNN cut away live to Red Square. Their reporter, doing a stand-up in front of St. Basil's, was bravely lying through her teeth, intoning with forced awe in her voice that thousands of Russians were gathering on this historic spot to celebrate the birth of their new, democratic nation, and that they were even having *fireworks*, which were so *extremely* rare here. (In fact, Moscow will set off fireworks on almost any pretext.) Our four-year-old, feeling drowsy, sat on the back of the couch, her head pivoting, looking first out the window at the distant waterfalling colour, then at the image on the TV. Like most of us, in December, 1991, postmoderns all, she wasn't sure which was more real.

Journal Notes

Late in the month; Epiphany on the Orthodox calendar. Russian folklorists note that in honour of Christ's baptism, the feast day had as highlight the blessing of the water by chopping a hole in the ice of the village river or pond, followed by a church service around the steaming aperture. Those seeking purification concluded the rite with a frigid dip. In January, 1992, prices freed, the populace in a state of inflation shock that is making nonsense of their pensions and salaries and a laughingstock of their savings, the new peasantry seeks solace in a free meal for the table. On the Moskva River, in the centre of ecologically cavalier and heavily industrialised Moscow, the old men saw circles in the ice, peer into them like moons in the river's sky, drop in their lines. As long as no one does a chemical analysis of the fish on their plates that night, "epiphany" will be as good a word as any.

An English-language newspaper in Moscow recently carried an anecdote that seemed to capture, as well as anything, the mood of early 1992, as the now-former empire and its millions of symbols carved on boulevards and balustrades across a sixth of the planet begin to grow transparent, turning to ghosts. In contrast to the ferment of

1987-89, Muscovites seem now to be sleepwalking out of their role on history's centre stage, consumed by the difficulties of daily living. In the newspaper story, an ardent Russophile expat, having endured a typical day of gloomy skies, empty shelves, bad roads, crucial offices closed for tea, no gas at the pumps and no roubles at the bank, smirking traffic cops and muck splashed on a new coat, arrived at her late-afternoon Russian lesson seeking only one consolation: What, she begged of her instructor, is the Russian word for "frustration"? The teacher, confident of her command of English idioms, assured her that there was no precise equivalent. Good English-Russian dictionaries can do no better than the serpentine nyeyudovletvoryeonost, *but any equally good Russian-English dictionary will translate this as "dissatisfaction," which will certainly not do at the end of a bad Moscow day. (This story is unrelated to Ronald Reagan's idiotic claim that Russian has no word for "peace."* Mir *is the sort of baby-word Russian-language students learn in lesson three.)*

Unconvinced, and even more frustrated, the expat visited a distinguished philologist at his office in Moscow University to pose the same question. As his English was imperfect, he asked her to illustrate just what "frustration" meant. She described her strength-sapping, blood-pressure-building day in excruciating detail. Understanding slowly dawned on his face. He patted her arm, and smiled reassuringly. Of course we have a word for that, dear, he said. That's djisn *(life).*

This is a moderately amusing story to a Canadian. Recounted in bad Russian to a Russian, it induces chokes

57

of laughter, tears of delight, gaspings for air, and the eventual need to get a drink of water.

FEBRUARY

As the old system totters toward oblivion, and the street price of Soviet army caps (a favourite tourist purchase on the Arbat) plummets due to oversupply, the new Russian economy is certainly revving up. It is based principally on the ever-more ubiquitous kiosks, clustered glass and metal huts like oversized parking-lot booths that crowd metro entrances and squares, distributing both the basics (at the shoelace kiosk) and the bawdy (at the combo pirated-cassettes-and-Penthouse kiosk). Westerners have to rearrange their impressions of the "freeness" of their enterprise: It seems unlikely the innumerable book tables lining underpasses and sidewalks (at least twenty along my five-minute walk to the metro) would be tolerated in Vancouver or Toronto without outcries from bookstore owners: Yes, they create congestion; yes, they pay more in protection money than in taxes; yes, they have unfairly low overhead. Many set up shop with thirty titles and a plastic tarp on the very steps of Dom Knigi, the state bookstore.

But for those living in the sullen and dispirited capital, ethnic strife remains on the distant hinterlands of the lost empire, and lineups are an infuriating but familiar part of the cityscape. One symbol of Soviet Leninism and the modes of its demise that never becomes either subconscious or simplistic is the city's traffic system and street grid. Of course the city roads are in disrepair, but stretches of Manhattan are worse. Sure, the drivers are as truculent

58

as Montreal cabbies, and yes it fouls the air (much like Parisian buses). More pertinent is that this supposed facilitator of movement for a city of ten million is a modern, planned network that resembles Minos's labyrinth: full of artful cul-de-sacs and misleading turns, composed of an inefficient layout and confounding intersections, with the ferocious (yet ultimately vulnerable) Kremlin at its centre.

In Moscow, legal left turns are as rare as affordable meat, directional markers routinely forbid exiting in either direction or going straight on, road signs are commonly self-contradictory, construction sites unmarked to add exhilaration, and broken-down Ladas and Zhigulis (designed by the same planners?) turn the thoroughfares into motorised pinball. The system's perversities twist the route to a neighbourhood shop into a pretzel, tripling the distance. All of which makes life cheerier for the equally symbolic legions of traffic militia, resplendent in long black coats and bandying sneers and white batons: you are always guilty of something. The result: an abundance of regulations, no order, and more cops per square foot than Belfast.

Yet much as word-of-mouth wildfires serve as public rebuke to the state's don't-give-a-damn distribution network, unofficial U-turn zones have been established by silent but unanimous agreement to complement the rare "legal" ones, rendering the road grid, against its will, only half as obstructionist. How do you know where they are? How do you use them? Observation, tact, cunning. Anyone seeking barometers of progression or regression could do worse than study the evolution of Moscow traffic. Because the road layout is only incidentally a trans-

portation system. Its teleological identity is a large-scale diagram of the Brezhnevite brain.

I have read no better description of Moscow than an epigram by Martin Walker, former correspondent here for The Guardian: *"Tough as nails, and deeply sentimental."* The sheer physical labour of life for so many certainly explains the tough as nails part. This is the Darwinian race of those who have survived decades in various degrees of Gulag. Now, as if to try to finish them off, prices triple overnight then double again next week. When asking prices you are not surprised if the answer is either 20 or 200. What's a little zero here and there? Almost everyone feels abruptly paupered. Yet . . .

Today a madwoman appeared in the snow outside the embassy, wanting to go to Canada. It was impossible to determine why. Relatives? None. Children here? None. Husband? No. A voice had told her Canada would be best. She stood in the dirty drifts, occasionally singing, occasionally blessing a secretary who had come out to try to reason with her. She had come on the train from Minsk. Dear, our brood of immigration-section secretaries told her, you should go back to Minsk. She shrugged. She had no money. Besides, she was going to Canada. As darkness fell, and we began to close up, something needed to be done. When I inquired on my way out what had ever become of her (busy, having forgotten her) I learned the local staff had pooled together fifty-three roubles to get her a train ticket home. Fifty cents, to me, but I at least by now knew better than to try to reimburse what they had freely given.

3

NO ROOM FOR THE EARTH:
TO PEREDELKINO

Pilgrimage passes from the profane to the sacred. And the
sacred, an amalgam of ritual and therefore a part of human
intention, is most starkly composed through counterpoint.
And as there is little so profane as a Moscow winter, and
few Moscow winters so profane as the winter of 1991-92,
the truest journey to Pasternak's grave should begin there.
The sacred is a guttering thing, always about to go out. You
must pursue it when you glimpse it, and feed it fuel. In the
desperate hand-to-mouth years after the Revolution, Anna
Akhmatova wrote "Everything is plundered, betrayed, sold,"
then, a few lines later, "And the miraculous comes so close
/ To the ruined, dirty houses—." Did I say the sacred was
the product of human intention? Fine. But our intentions,
where do we find *them*? Why do they find us?

*

At twilight the swifts have no way
Of stemming the cool blue cascade.

61

It bursts from clamouring throats,
A torrent that cannot be stayed.

So: inhabit the winter first. Week after week, while prices—
the only buoyant things—soar upward, carrying away life
savings, hopes of progress, post-coup bravura, carrying
away the last dregs of energy from the exhausted woman
lugging her palm-creasing, elbow-bowing load. Week after
week while prices rise, the sun does not. Instead, an under-
the-blankets light murkily descends after nine o'clock each
morning; clouds, the colour of washing-machine lint, im-
merse the crumbling cornices and the grime-obscured buildings. The clouds can barely be distinguished from the grey
air, the grey air from the ashen snow-and-sand soup of the
streets, the foggy snow squalls from the thundering trucks
that cast off parts in passing and throw wraiths of exhaust
behind them. And at two-thirty, lunch barely tidied away,
the shade is perversely drawn down, and night falls abruptly
with a disheartening sense of finality. When a blue rent
does appear, two or three times a month, the citizenry stops
on the sidewalk to gape and point; the vision is as strange
as if Chagall had reached down from the empyrean with
his whimsy-and-colour laden brush and dabbed a bit, benign and a little sad.

Outside the *univermag*, near the metro station behind Lenin's giant back, long lines of recently impoverished people form gauntlets before the entrance: pensioners
selling their socks, professors their six lemons, nurses their
husbands' used cardigans, an engineer a table lamp without
a shade, a student two pints of *piva* and a decent-enough-
looking pair of shoes, anyone at all flogging the uniforms of

62

offices that have been abolished. A man staggers past under a thirty-kilo sack of onions. Two women heave a massive string-wrapped box onto the metro escalator, battering shins that happen to be in their way. They are old, broken nags; their value has been set at zero; they have a million twins.

Before the first World War, the twenty-two-year-old Boris Pasternak, at that time obsessed mainly by music—his pianist mother, Rosa Kaufman, had been a student of Artur Rubenstein, and Scriabin was a close family friend—journeyed to Marburg to study philosophy. Two years earlier he had accompanied his father, a brilliant portraitist, to Astapova, where the artist had been summoned to draw his friend Lev Tolstoy on his deathbed. All his life, the pure inner song Pasternak felt demanded his primary allegiance was a note he must try to hold amidst cataclysm. The war began when he was twenty-four, the Revolution three years later, followed by civil war, dislocation, purges, famines, and a far greater war. But he was not, it turned out, a musician. So, using words, of what can one compose a pure note? "To aspire to purity is natural," he wrote. It was 1919. A year (another year) of horror in Moscow. Some professors burned books to keep warm, as they would again in Armenia in 1992. The economy had completely collapsed; the chaos was almost complete. The poet Marina Tsvetaeva, alone in the city with her two daughters, her husband lost somewhere in the south with the White armies, worked for a single day in a registry office putting file cards in alphabetical order. When she lost that job the girls went hungry. At last she sent the youngest, Irina, to a state orphanage, hoping she would get food there. When she

63

died, of starvation, Tsvetaeva could not attend the funeral because her older daughter, all she had left, had dysentery and a temperature of forty degrees. The precocious patient, seven that year, wrote a poem: "Do not be ashamed, Russia, my country, / The angels always go barefoot." "To aspire to purity is natural," Pasternak wrote that year. "This is how we at last approach the pure essence of poetry. It is disturbing like the ominous turning of a dozen windmills on the edge of a barren field in a dark year of famine."

Wonderful Marburg, ancient and filled with warm cafés, where he had read Goethe and Leibniz. He saw it again in 1923. "What had happened in the world was presented to me in the most terrible foreshortening. It was the period of the occupation of the Ruhr. Germany was cold and starving, deceived about nothing and deceiving no one, her hand stretched out to the age like a beggar (a gesture not her own at all), and the entire country on crutches."

Like a second transparency of the air, his words describe this afternoon. Along the tiled underpass, in the dankness below darkness, a killing wet chill: a gypsy woman sets her toddler on the icy cement with a tam turned up on its lap to beg kopecks. She is multicoloured and filthy. She is not solely responsible for the child's inevitable early pneumonia, its early death, but she *is* responsible. Farther along, near the turnstiles, a veteran wearing his medals and beret balances on his single leg between worn crutches.

Dead the year I was born, Pasternak had written of Yuri Zhivago: "And in order to do good to others he would have needed, besides the principles which filled his mind, an unprincipled heart—the kind of heart that knows of no general cases and has the greatness of small actions." In other words, today pay attention to small details, the compilation of the tone of things.

*

Pasternak is respected and studied, in the manner of the other great novelists—Gogol, Turgenev, Tolstoy, Dostoevsky, Solzhenitsyn, Bulgakov—because of the career-long breadth of his canvas and because of his ability, so uncannily Russian, to write as if at the end of history out of one long eschatological exhalation, gathering the long skein of all that had gone before, what he called "a second universe created by humanity, with the aid of time and memory, in response to the fact of death." In Soviet times when a key craftsman was the airbrusher of photographs, this was an unavoidably ideological mindset even in the notoriously politics-allergic Pasternak. Despite Gorbatchev's many failings, the "return of historical memory," as one observer put it, was his unmitigated triumph. The present moment—each present moment—is a finale, the climactic note of the series of human cries which reveals the ultimate structure—however complex, however *created*—of this newly complete narrative. Each instant concludes a discrete history. The earth, life itself, was for Pasternak God's creation and thus to be honoured above all else. But second came history—the stuff of human hands. So, admired for this historical sensibility and for its maturation in *Doctor Zhivago*.

And loved as the Russians love only their poets. Russia is perhaps the last place on earth one can toss the names of the major modern poets with perfect confidence to anyone one meets. Love for his lyrical instrument of pathos and sentiment—not excluding sentimentality—for his abasement to the moment:

> At twilight the swifts have no way
> Of holding back, high overhead,
> Their clarion shouting: Oh triumph,
> Look, look, how the earth has fled!

*

Having outlasted the winter, from the cold fronts of early October to the final April flakes—thaw and freeze, rain and snow, mud and ice in between—I can appropriately approach May's end and the anniversary of Pasternak's death, looking into the 10:00 p.m. daylight of Moscow's late spring evening at what he called the city's "insatiable, fabulously leisurely sky," where swifts do indeed script the air above the unholy mix of lush greenery and grimy factory and industrial blocks, and consider heading for Peredelkino in the morning, May 30.

Winter, in this country of vast emotional, meteorological, and political oscillations, has been utterly vanquished, sent underground. This morning the sunlight hums against our curtains by 4:00 a.m. in a great blue wash, and the west will be a slow diluting of aquamarine and citrus until 11:00 p.m.—and the same tomorrow and tomorrow. It is a city of a half-dozen parks that could swallow Montreal's Mount Royal or Toronto's High Park whole, of boulevards hedged with doubled poplar borders and bastions of oak, of a blue sidewinding river, of the gold glory of the Kremlin cathedrals from my breakfast window. Are the people still lugging their bundles? Are the proletariat still tired, still bitter? Yes. Are they any happier? Oh yes, a little.

Pilgrimage passes via the profane to the sacred, so I descend first to the underworld. En route to the metro I traverse the gloom of the underpass where the breadth of Leninsky Prospekt, the road south toward Kiev, encounters the square-jawed, broad-browed gaze of monumental Lenin, glaring sternly at the future counterclockwise along the Ring Road. A low-ceilinged passage lined by pillars. Her back to one of them, seated on a campstool, a woman lives her life playing her subdued accordion, kerchiefed against the damp, her face geological. The same face sears photographs of the Great Patriotic War by the brilliant Dmitri Baltermans: a woman, lost somewhere on a vast plateau of a black-and-white world, a surreal tumult of clouds seething above her, digs a body from an endless harvest of mud to pile it with the others like cordwood on a wagon drawn achingly by human beasts across the fertile steppe. The wagon is full to toppling. I pass a three-rouble note into her brown hand. There is a shortage of large-denomination notes; I received packet after packet of devalued threes and fives at the exchange bank, pocket fodder. She stitches a cross in the air, blessing, absurdly, me.

Oktyabrskaya Metro's name is as yet unchanged in spite of the blatant allusion to *the* October. A bank of escalators ferries Saturday crowds deep into the earth (in Moscow, those with vertigo quail at the subway) to the every-minute trains accosting platforms wreathed with mosaics immortalising Socialist youth. Sturdy as East German discus champions, reaping the fruits of their labour,

67

they are the grace of ancient Athens—vines scrolling the borders—on a high starch diet. You can inspect them for signs of the artist's self-mockery, and never quite be sure. Inside the metro car, thundering through tunnels, the intercom recites the stops. At Kievskaya I flow out with the crowd and ride upward into May sunlight again.

And into one of Moscow's central meeting points, and one of the foci of Russia's new economy. Here three metro lines, a splay of suburban electric routes, and the intercity network for points south and south-west—Kiev, Kishiniev, Prague and Budapest and Bucharest, the Crimea and the Caucasus—all knot together. Along the sidewalks and on Ploschad Kievsky Vauxhall, the two dozen kiosks that sprang up like mushrooms last fall have sporulated to two hundred, specialising in mind-bending diversity, like IQ tests gone wild: shoelaces and cognac, blouses and cigarette lighters, Chanel Number Five and condoms, track shoes and tampons and bootleg cassettes, while even smaller micro-enterprises surround and engulf them, proprietors seated on one upturned crate with a second as display counter, or simply standing with their wares in both hands: a few bottles of watery beer, cucumbers, banks and banks of flowers—lilacs for five roubles, roses now twenty—jeans from China, a six-title book shop (Everyday English Grammar, Orthodox Church pamphlets, Sex Tips, Horoscopes for All, yet more Alexander Dumas), a sack of cabbage, Georgian bread, Fanta, men's dress shoes (one style suits all), Armenian cognac and Moldovan "champagne," more flowers, ice-cream bars steaming under dry ice, a small selection of CDs (Shostakovitch, Prokofiev, bootleg Sting and Leonard Cohen). Once sold out they will

reboard their trains to wherever they've come from to re-
stock. The crowd is dense and swirling. I keep my shoulders square and my wits about me.

At one of a series of small windows set into the
ponderous concrete face of the station, I settle into a
comfortable-sized queue and, eventually, buy return train
fare to Peredelkino for the rough equivalent of four Canadian cents.

The *elektrichka*, army green, suns itself outside the
station among a dozen others, the last car barely visible
down the platform. Crowded onto the hard benches is a
weekend-family-outing trainload, filling the facing seats,
knees jostling. They are, of course, *lugging*. Something,
anything. Treasures, modes of survival. Often two men
heft a single monumental bundle by a pair of handles, one
on each side. A woman has a songbird inside a rude cage,
like a heart. Bags of vegetables abound. Most of the adults
read as they await the first jostle and glide of the train
pulling out, deep in books or folding back one of Moscow's uncountable newspapers. After a while the train is
clicking and sliding past parks, factories, epic apartment
compounds—many of them half-built, paralysed dinosaurs.
Four or five stops—peering anxiously at dusty Cyrillic signposts—and we are entering the village realm of wooden
houses and picket fences that lurks nostalgically close at
hand on the very edge of the metropolis, like a model of
the Russian psyche. A sixth stop: Peredelkino. I step off
into (I know this is an exaggeration but write it down anyway, a sort of truth) heaven on earth.

*

69

It's not, of course. But the wooden platform gives onto agreeable mysterious pathways through densenesses of lilac and apple blossoms and low-boughed pine. A potpourri of scent, an antonym for Moscow. Fixing the eye, golden domes of the village church rest in the upper branches of deep green, burning.

Somewhere off to the right, I've read. Surely then, a small paved path will wind charmingly through this olfactory wonderland with just a bit of breeze to stir the sunlight under a soft blue sky—and there it is, wide enough only for strollers or bikes, curving down to take an arch-backed plank bridge over a trickle of brook. Climbing the other side, it nips under a copse or two and circles a gully, occasionally passing carved benches set out for musing before arriving at an avenue of mature timber dachas, ornate, gingerbreaded, almost hidden in apple yards of pink and white profusion, calm and complex as haiku behind eye-high picket fences painted dark green, breached by latched gates. I realize I haven't seen any graveyards and have no doubt come too far. A passer-by, strolling with a collie, does, of course, know the way. The directions are intricate though, and my Russian imperfect.

Doubling back, I glimpse through a gap in the trees one of the ubiquitous garden plots where Muscovites attempt to provision crucial winter larders: a thick grandmother in huge rubber boots and a floral dress; a ten-year-old galloping through the rising heat in white undershorts; a solitary cow grazing in a shadow; papa sweating in his boxers, a pale belly dumping over the waistband. Over my shoulder, a startling and enormous swath of highrises crowns a distant hill, home for tens of thousands, like a page glued in from another book.

Eventually I reach the gate of a graveyard and peer expectantly within. Nothing but Saturday families tending the plots. (Over the years I will learn that Russian graveyards are quiet but never empty. They are busy places, good for gardening and afternoon strolls; in the massive city cemeteries, weekends are crowded, with hawkers doing boom-business in flowers for the dead and ice-cream for the kids.) Each grave in the thickly wooded cemetery lies within a wrought-iron enclosure. Most include a short bench, and an elaborate stone with portrait or photograph of the deceased, and a small garden of perennials, blooming from the underworld. Here, I can see no notice boards about the famous poet, no arrows pointing the way. This can't be the place.

It is. Looking for publicity—signposts, come-hithers—betrays a barbaric mind; pilgrimages are best reserved for devotees, and devotees are most accurately identified by their persistence. At yet more forks in yet more roads I must choose blindly again. Over another stream (or the same one again?) and fifteen minutes farther on I come to a tranquil pine forest carpeted with needles. Here there are no low boughs. The trunks rise straight and clean, clearing away a quietude of shaded space. High above, the branches are radiating spokes, spindles holding up the dimness. I sense, amid this stateliness, that I am closer, although it is of course nonsense to think his geographical surroundings will mimic the movement of his verse. Official-looking gates appear between brick portals. A stolidly lettered Cyrillic suggestion about writers, national trusts, state committees, culture, and the building of socialism is posted on the wrought iron. Behind the fencing, huge two- and three-storied dachas lord over (state owned!) private acreages. Closed off, to me at least. I stroll under the canopy of scented green, rather hopelessly looking for clues. A taxi loaded with foreigners—Swedes, maybe—plummets to a stop, and the driver asks me the way to my own objective. I wander, and eventually choose the most picturesque of byways on the same dubious principle: a white gravel road descending through the glade and separated by a single file of pines from a field which, in turn, slopes to the tiny Setun River, affording another view of the sun-streaming onion domes that I only now realise I have been slowly orbiting. It proves the correct choice. I can see it now through the gap in the board fence: medium-sized, two stories plus loft or attic under gables, a distinctive curved front to create splendid bays on both floors under a steeply pitched roof, set well back behind vegetable and flower gardens—recalling a 1957 photograph of Pasternak in knee-high boots, rolled sleeves, and peaked cap squinting into the sun and camera. A little farther along there is a small sign and a small delegation of sprightly, striding, sixtyish women, who stop to point out what I have just discovered. *Y magilla?* I query. And the grave? Oh no, they respond. The museum first, the dacha first. That's the proper way. Then you need only follow others performing station two of the pilgrimage. You can't miss it.

So I enter the gate and walk a curving avenue of birch. Entry is by the side door. A scattering of visitors lounge near the front porch. Around back, in the pine grove, a young couple with two children and a friend squat and sit with a picnic of strawberries and melon and pepperoni with mustard. Inside, the elderly woman at a wooden table takes three roubles and, ruler carefully placed, tears off a paper ticket.

Making museums of the homes of writers and other artists is something of a Russian specialty. Moscow has dozens. For titans like Pushkin or Tolstoy there are three or four; residence in a flat for even a few months imparts holiness enough for a shrine. One can contrast extremes of style in the Mayakovsky museum across from the old KGB Lubyanka headquarters and torture chambers in Moscow— a deconstructivist bedlam built on a swirling ramp at all angles to capture the poet's society- and consciousness-exploding fervour (albeit with one calm little study in its midst, where he actually worked and slept)—and the stately home of Chekhov in Yalta in the new Ukraine, set amidst his beautiful semi-tropical gardens overlooking the Black Sea. The museum ladies in the latter, who loved their writer, were so excited to encounter a foreigner who tried to splutter a few play titles in Russian that, peering over each shoulder to make sure the coast was clear, they let down a chain blocking an out-of-bounds room and carefully lifted the yellowed original manuscript of *The Seagull* from a drawer for our veneration.

In 1992, even amidst the collapsing of state arts funding, yet one more apartment museum opened. At 6 Pismenova Ulitsa in Moscow, Marina Tsvetaeva lived, in dire poverty much of the time, from 1914 until leaving for the West in 1922. The building would have long been rubble except that during the Great Patriotic War against the Nazis, a battlefront surgeon named Nadezdha Katayeva-

Litkina was one day given a small volume containing the poetry of Tsvetaeva. She had been operating continuously for three days and had collapsed. A co-worker gave her the poems "for strength," and, in Katayeva-Litkina's own words, she carried "that book with me throughout the war." In a very Russian twist of fate, she was assigned a room after the war at 6 Pismenova Ulitsa. As the building decayed, the authorities made plans to demolish it as they had so much of the city's history. In 1980, when the bulldozers arrived, Kateyova-Litkina, with her generation's determination and apparent immunity to hardship, decided the home of Tsvetaeva would *not* fall. She stayed. The authorities tried to expel her. They threatened to arrest her. They turned off the water, then the gas, then the electricity. She stayed, alone in the dark and chill, for seven years. Gradually, she rallied Tsvetaeva's readers, until in 1987 they convinced the city to call off the bulldozers. The house was instead repaired, artifacts were gathered, and finally in 1992 the memorial to the poet opened to the public on the one hundredth anniversary of her birth.

Pasternak had been awarded this dacha—part of the writer's village carved from an old estate—in 1936, as the terrors of the great purges were accelerating, the terrors which were to dance around the margins of his life from that time on but always, mysteriously, to miss him. Not that he was unaffected. In one of those acts of simultaneous absurdity and cruelty that characterised Stalinism, the KGB arrested a pregnant Olga Ivinskaya (usually cited as the model for Lara in *Doctor Zhivago*) in 1949 and, following the birth of their child in Lubyanka prison, sentenced her to hard labour in the east for "close contact with persons suspected of espionage," that is, Pasternak himself, vilified as a British spy. She served three-and-a-half years of her sentence before being released after Stalin's death. *The spy himself was untouched.* (In the boom-town commercial nineties, Ivinskaya and the Pasternak family were aptly enough locked in a legal battle over ownership of the poet's archives.) Following the novel's publication and after turning down the Nobel Prize, Pasternak was viciously reviled in the press week after week. He awaited seemingly inevitable disaster. Peredelkino became his principal home, a beloved refuge upon which he became increasingly reliant. During those final, darkening months, when, as one of his poems put it, he felt his throat in a noose and longed "for one second" for "my tears to be wiped away by someone at my right hand," he carried poison with him at all times, afraid not so much of death, or even imprisonment, but of the fate of Solzhenitsyn and so many others—forced exile from Russia, exile from Peredelkino.

*

The rooms are elegant in an uncluttered, almost spartan manner. They have the cleanliness and casual sense of unforced order that, it occurs to me, I have often expected from my own life—later on, of course, when I am less harried, am settled down, have time to think. The light is generous on the wooden floors and tables, and on the flowers; the colours are clear but not luxuriant, Cézanne rather than Monet. The verse: its slender, unenjambed lines, its fixation on simplifying, on honing, and thus its author's

75

rejection of the celebrity-poet of his youth, Mayakovsky, and Pasternak's eventual distaste for much of his own youthful work. The walls are graced with small framed drawings and paintings by his father, Leonid Osipovitch, a portraitist of such emotional precision that the attributes of genius and craftsmanship seem indistinguishable in their presence. In the dining room, some of Leonid's illustrations for an edition of Tolstoy's *Resurrection*. A small grand piano, representing Pasternak's first passion, fills most of a back room. On the shelves his own compositions—piano preludes mainly—lie next to scores by Scriabin, hero of his youth. In another room, as understated shrine, a charcoal of the poet in his coffin stands on a small easel, with a handful of flowers brought by visitors laid on the varnished hardwood before it.

Up a narrow staircase I find the spacious study. The writing desk is near a wall of windows looking into the garden and, beyond, across the road and fields toward the stream. A cot stands in one corner. Against the near wall, bookcases are filled with Russian, French, English and German fiction, poetry and philosophy (the four languages he read most comfortably), including, a bit surprisingly, a complete set of Hogarth Press first editions of Virginia Woolf. The desk bears an angle of light perfect for writing—surely he has just taken a brief pause for tea or gardening, and will be back in a moment.

A tour guide stabs his finger passionately at a visiting group of school children and recites the incantatory and incomparably musical Russian verse, a bit too melodramatically. There are worse sins against a writer's memory.

From here they carried his open coffin to the grave on June 2nd, 1960, floating it on the sombre sea of a great crowd assembled via the traditional Russian word-of-mouth broadcasting of the officially ignored deaths of cultural icons. The funerals of Akhmatova six years later, and of seventies folksinger-actor-director-poet legend Vladimir Vyssotsky would prove the same. The unplumbable depth of Russian bitterness, so evident in 1992, is balanced by equally extreme summits of devotion. On the day of the poet's death a hand-written note was taped by a ticket window at Kievski Vauxhall, where I had purchased my own train ticket two hours earlier. It stated that "At 4:00 p.m. on Thursday, June 2nd, the last leave-taking of Boris Leonidovich Pasternak, the greatest poet of present-day Russia, will take place." According to one biographer, the note listed alternate train routes in case nervous officials shut down the Moscow-Peredelkino line. Torn down repeatedly by watchful militia, the note was repeatedly reposted over the next three days.

While he lay in the dacha, some of the country's best pianists, led by Sviatislav Richter, performed in tribute for several hours, until, as the dénouement of Chopin's *Marche funèbre* died away, the coffin was borne out. A Writer's Union offer of a hearse (the state writer's organisation had expelled him two years earlier) was hooted down, so that he would be carried the mile to the grave in the traditional manner, on the hands and shoulders of the mourners.

In a beautiful memoir, poet Andrei Voznesensky wrote that as the coffin moved slowly down the road, past "the grieving non-literary crowd—locals and out-of-towners, witnesses and neighbours of his days, sobbing students, the heroines of his poems . . . his features surfaced repeatedly on the face of his eldest son, Zhenya. . . . The trees came out from behind their fences, the melancholy dirt road, which he had taken so often to the station, bitterly threw up dust. Someone stepped on a red peony, fallen by the roadside. I did not return to the dacha. He was not there. He was not anywhere anymore."

*

He was not there for Voznesensky, who had known well this proud man of tangled emotional allegiances and extraordinary dignity. But for me, born the month after the funeral, the grave with its mourners (his readers) is a habitation more real. Doubling back toward the church's floating domes, I must inquire my way once or twice more, for no others happen to be en route. Near a small garbage dump I find a crystal spring in a pool no larger than a washtub, the edges tinged by the rust in its hard water, and, stopping, splash the cold over my face and neck before wading into the tangle of graves. I am at the bottom of the same cemetery skirted earlier, where the graves have spilled beyond the high iron fence to stand among the long grass and lilac and wild strawberries on a steep slope above the stream. A receding series of narrow paths lead dimly upward into the heart of the graveyard; each seems promising but inconclusive. I wander in a final fit of frustration. How, in such a conundrum, to locate a singularity?

The poetry saves me at last. Climbing to where the brush and undergrowth give way to a higher alley of pine and a less tangled shade, I hear a voice chanting, an odd, strangled sort of voice, calling out from a dream. I need merely draw closer, allow myself to be reeled in. 2:00 p.m. I emerge into a cool, more open space, a modest but definitely larger plot, a simple but weightier stone. A gathering of a dozen or more: six or eight seated on the single long bench in front of the grave—which is submerged under scores of bouquets—five or six others standing with hands behind backs or fingering caps, two or three walking forward to the smaller monuments of his children tucked into back corners of the clearing, one elderly woman fastidiously arranging the flowers. And one man, a worn seventy-five, is singing Pasternak out of his throat—loudly through long emphatic stanzas, then whispering exultantly to himself. He is quietly provided with lines he forgets by the others. Between poems he weeps his own griefs, on behalf, I somehow feel, of everyone assembled.

During the funeral here, KGB agents lurked under the three great pine trees which stand over the grave. Later, microphones tracked the visitors. I think of this, suddenly, of their ill-cut suits and short ties, their half-hearted attempts to conceal their insolence, and almost laugh out loud. The whole immense weight of Lenin's and Stalin's and Brezhnev's perverse, incompetent and murderous reigns floats up like a child's balloon, silly, lighter than air; the world's lens is flipped over like an optometrist's choices of vision: which is clearer, this, or this? The KGB turn so easily into obtuse school boys as I sit by the grave of Pasternak on May's most heavenly afternoon. All meanings, all beliefs, stand on a carpet effortlessly pulled from underfoot. (Yet, look again: they hold death casually in their pockets. In spite of clownish incompetence they can

take it out and hand it to you as simply as a business card.)
For now, I mentally address the chanter with a line from
the Irish poet Seamus Heaney: "Raise it again man, we still
believe what we hear."

*

On the train back I dozed off in the late afternoon sun that
baked the west windows and Peredelkino sank beneath the
waves. I woke with a start as we lurched to a halt in the
centre of Moscow, disoriented, stumbling off onto miles of
platforms. Electric lines ran overhead, harnessing the sky.
In the distance I could see Kievsky Vauxhall. I began to
walk, half lost in an old dream, so far down the tracks that
there were no crowds, everyone else having disembarked
before I had gathered myself.

In 1918 Dr. Yuri Zhivago, returning from the front
after both war and revolution, arrived in Moscow by train.
In the late afternoon he approached one of the city's main
squares. As I approached the throngs of the station, now
also a gigantic, variegated marketplace, the scene floated
toward me. Horrified, Zhivago reentered his dramatically
altered home town after a long absence.

> And it seemed to him that already he saw, shrinking
> against the walls, thin, decently dressed old men and
> women, who stood like a silent reproach to the passers-
> by, wordlessly offering what no one needed—artifi-
> cial flowers, coffee percolators with glass lids and
> whistles, black net evening dresses and uniforms of
> offices that had been abolished. . . .

But that was in another story, I thought. And each story is new? I walked ahead, on profane ground, wondering what came next.

Journal Notes

JUNE 1992

In Canada, where there is no aristocracy of the arts, the role of a Shostakovitch or Pasternak or Bulgakov in a society's sense of self-understanding—of its hopes for dignity and an inner calm out of which to create rather than destroy—can only be experienced vicariously, as a piece of cultural tourism. Our two countries' elites only overlap in the precinct of hockey.

The twentieth anniversary of the classic 1972 Canada-Russia series, so sadly unrepeatable, brought a CBC film crew to Moscow to do a documentary. At a reception hosted by the Canadian ambassador, members of both communities from military guards to senior diplomats turned out in large numbers. The elegant nineteenth-century rooms of the official residence were chock-a-block with oversized former Russian players going a bit soft. I found myself with drink in one hand and finger food in another suddenly next to Paul Henderson. Suavely, I had an overwhelming urge to tell him he was Paul Henderson. Swallowing that, I stumbled to other less than original conversation openers, like telling him where I was when he scored The Goal (a hallway of my elementary school where a big TV had been set up, watching with a few

*lingering students and the principal; I had just missed my
bus—it was amazing to me anyone got on it—and would
have to walk home to the farm). Henderson, an unprepos-
sessing, curly-haired, youthful-looking man now working
as a minister, didn't seem to mind. I asked him if the team
had still been optimistic in the dressing room after the
second period, down 5-3 with the series—life itself—in
the balance. No, he said, pointing across the room, because that fellow was in goal—a larger than expected
Vladislav Tretiak was chatting in the next group. Tretiak,
who would stop in regularly to pick up his visas in person
(and sign autographs) and knew all the staff by name, had
been only twenty at the time of the series, and still looked
about twenty-five: jet black hair, clean shaven, extremely
handsome, with huge hands.*

*Others lounged about—Yakushev, Shedrin, Mikhailov:
names stirring deep nostalgia for Canadians. We all in-
dulged ourselves in old emotion. Their eyes and minds
long since glazed over by a steady diet of government
ministers, premiers, and other big-wigs, the assembled
diplomats peered about, impressed. These were important
people. Miracle man Henderson. His foil, Tretiak. The
legendary skaters on the Soviet side of the seventies, year
in and year out the best hockey team in history. Ralph
Mellanby, producer of Hockey Night in Canada for eons.
And Alan Eagleson, overly-tanned, jaw like a Mulroney,
hyper-tailored thousand-dollar suit, jumping about, ex-
postulating, slapping backs like someone wanting to be
seen slapping backs. Finally, a sentimental speech by a
wild-haired old man bending over a walking-stick: Anatoli*

83

Tarasov himself, father of Soviet hockey. Eagleson in the end had to interrupt with a toast, otherwise the old gentleman, clearly revered by everyone present, would be philosophising still.

Summer in the softly sighing countryside near Moscow. Over a weekend at a dacha on the Volga River one hundred kilometres north of the city, we try to absorb what is distinct about the paysage of the Russian heartland. Certainly it evokes deep emotion in the Russian heart, best seen perhaps in the poetry of Yesinin. Subtle; no remarkable forms; it is neither steppe nor hills. Long slow slopes to the swift but broad grey river; the river like the final definition of the incline; wide sweeps of fields bordered, in the beginning of haze, by silent stands of birch and fir, white ghosts, green shadows. Avenues of trees along every road and everywhere the ornate wooden country houses, painted dark blue or pine green or chocolate, trimmed in brighter hues; village wells (rope and bucket and pulley) with little wooden roofs to mimic the houses; the weary women lugging water. As we speed past on the highway home, people glance up from their roadside pails of potatoes for sale, their three bottles of sour cream. Chickens scratch, huge roosters pose for effect; fruit trees suspend small clouds of blossoms behind the picket fences.

Has Communism weakened the pull toward the soil, in a nation that reveres nothing so much as the graves of its uncountable dead? The vegetable plot by the rude dacha, the fifty square feet garnered through luck or connections or impertinence next to some industrial zone—is it as vital to a family's winter larder, and to their inner spectres, as it was to their grandparents? A dozen chickens: three or four dozen eggs a week. That's one for the family, two to sell. . . . But the longer we live here, the less satisfying the mere economic explanation becomes.

By the Volga you can still find enough light to read outside past eleven o'clock, as the last fishermen are rowing in their boats.

AUGUST

This week the rouble crashed through the two hundred per dollar barrier. At least, that is the standard metaphor, currencies figured as weight, anvils breaking weak flooring to land with a great ding in the basement. But a genuinely collapsing currency (the other image of the journalists: money as a once solid old house eaten through by the termites of inflation and given a shove by the international bond markets) does not feel like that at all. The sensation is much more like watching a series of soap bubbles floating up and away, pop-popping as they go. Your mouth is a bit agape at the sight, a child with its first bubble wand. You had forgotten that money itself was a fragile, fictive thing, dependent on miniscule forces of tension and pressure; a mere convenient arrangement to avoid having to lug potatoes everywhere to swap for tampons, ferry timber to the next town to trade for toasters or vodka. The amount of carrying Muscovites are doing these days is one sign that the wad of notes in our wallets is becoming less holy by the day, that the suspension of disbelief is fading as the lights come up. Once agnosticism sets in, versions of transubstantiation get harder and harder to sell.

In the stores, the first Russian-language Harlequin Romances have appeared as Liubimi Romans, *Love Novels. The predicted market: one hundred million literate, sentimental women absolutely famished for Romance, apparently the more old-fashioned and male-dominated the better.*

The economy spins and dances on the head of a pin. At the Stanislavsky Musical Theatre (the city's "third" stage for opera and ballet, and superb), where the final duet between Onegin and Tatiana in Tchaikovsky's Evgeni Onegin *is spellbinding in any language, a glass of coke at intermission costs five times the price of two good seats.*

OCTOBER

All roads led to Rome, in the days when Rome controlled an empire covering the territory of thirty-five or so current UN members, give or take an Andorra. After the eternal city had been sacked and its treasures hauled off to the Rhine or Bulgaria, most of the best roads west of China were the networks the Romans laid out. Such was still the case a thousand years later. When an empire vanishes abruptly, like mist before wind, the infrastructure lags, anachronistically intact. I recently met a hydro engineer. He worked in an electricity grid control room in Moscow. The switches there could still turn off the lights in provin-

86

cial Russian cities—or in the capitals of half a dozen newly independent states.

The roads to the centre radiate inward even after the hub is no longer hub of anything more than an outdated encyclopedia entry. So Moscow is full of lost souls, cast up by cold war alliances, out-dated visa exemptions, imperial ventures of the ghost empire. And not only the Chechens and Georgians and Kazakhs who happened to have been working in Moscow when the Union's demise was announced, or who indeed had been born there. The Russian Federation government seems to have more or less accepted that those fleeing Afghanistan are to some extent its responsibility. Visas are apparently no problem; Pushtuns and Uzbeks and representatives of every other ethnic group of that fractured post-colonial horror show sit around in Moscow and St. Petersburg wondering if the road, having reached the old centre, still leads onward to anything at all, any sort of life.

One Afghan told me this week that he had been trained as a military doctor. He had left Afghanistan because he didn't want to be involved in killing people with his scalpel. After graduation in Kabul he had been ordered to a rural area. Under Najibullah's regime, he said, and under the one before that, political opponents were often killed or maimed in hospitals by surgeons operating under government edict. Unnecessary surgery would be performed. The amputation of limbs was a favourite. A four-hundred-bed hospital had been built by the Soviets, he claimed, primarily for the "treatment" of prisoners from various Mujahaddin factions. He guessed that once

87

in power the various warlords—fighting in the name of Islamic purity—would be unlikely to shut down such useful institutions.

Moscow and Kiev are also home to thousands of African students from regimes having fraternal socialist ties with the Soviet Union. Most of them spend their time starving or lining up outside their embassies begging for either a plane ticket home or an increase in their stipend. The Russian and Ukrainian governments have dealt with the "problem" by honouring the scholarships to the letter—so that the students still receive the three hundred and fifty rouble per month stipend agreed on in 1988 or 1989, at that time something close to an average Soviet salary, but now worthless. The Ethiopians are in a nasty spot. Most are military men on training at various naval or air force academies. The government has been overthrown back home and isn't kindly disposed toward them. If they are junior officers, possible Western asylum countries point out that they are in little danger at home. If they are senior staff, from what was a thoroughly ferocious regime, they are indeed in danger but no Western government will touch them. Some of them thoroughly deserve their fate. Others do not. Life in Moscow for Ethiopians and other Africans is not convivial.

Amazingly, even hundreds of Somalis have found their way here, generally living in very poor conditions—though some have plenty of money. Most have travelled from their homeland to Kenya on foot, then to Syria (which they could enter for a time without visas) by boat often via Yemen, then to Turkey by train and onward by Black Sea boats into Russia or Ukraine. They come here because they can get here, and think that it leads to somewhere else. But the stage at the heart of the antiquated Imperium seems to have more entrances than exits, and life there for most is an endless wait for visas to mythical freedoms.

4

KAZAKHSTAN:
ONE DESK, NO LEOPARD

I remember being alone with Chechanovski, who took
me out to a quiet corner in the corridor for a confi-
dential chat. . . . . A person sitting behind a desk
always inspired great respect. . . . If we wanted an
idea of someone's importance, we always asked:
"Does he have a desk?" Chechanovski had a desk
with drawers—a sure sign that our conversation in
the corridor would be one of moment.

Nadezdha Mandelshtam

—Are you resolved that I am being comprehensive?

Yes, Pavel, not to worry. You are understood. Twenty,
and hopelessly unemployed, Pavel, (an ethnic Russian living in Kazakhstan with a brand new diploma in Linguistics)
was anxious about his hard-won but rarely practised English. Inaccurately accented, littered with obsolete set-phrases
("I am honoured to make your acquaintance"), but under-
pinned by a capacious vocabulary, it proved perfectly serv-
iceable. Pavel was our interpreter. It was Thursday; I was

two days in town, and I was going to a turquoise lake fed by glaciers of the Tien-Shan mountains to search its shores for a snow leopard. Hardly the first Westerner to be lured by the vision: a white leopard. Leopard padded softly through my mind, stillness somehow moving, like not having to choose.

We needed a jeep. For forty dollars U.S.—or a satchel of roubles—I had engaged Alexander (owner and operator), Valeri (driver) and Pavel, along with the said vehicle. Alexander, who insisted on being called "Sasha," was trim and forty in a blue nylon track suit. His sleek black hair and broad features suggested Tatar or Kazakh blood mixed with the Slavic. He was a professional engineer who, like most post-Soviet professionals, was exploring a sideline to supplement the plummeting purchasing power of his salary. Valeri was fiftyish and heavy set; he walked as though carrying something on his shoulders. A long-time military man, he came to life only when I resorted to an infallible conversation starter: hockey, and my slight acquaintance with Vladislav Tretiak.

We squeezed into the jeep and made our way through Alma-Ata's dusty traffic—sagging beige Ladas, ponderous Zil limos, ancient trucks—toward the city limits. At intervals Sasha prodded Pavel to recite interesting facts about the TV tower, the sewage system, the 1905 earthquake (which had flattened everything except the "miraculous" Orthodox cathedral), the network of party bosses' dachas. We were soon onto rising slopes of apple groves. The city's name means "Father Apple," and those of the local variety rival grapefruit for heft. Following an above-ground pipeline, six feet in diameter, that funnelled glacier runoff into the taps and tubs of the city, the road narrowed to a single lane of blacktop, then to well-maintained gravel. The pacific groves gave way to increasingly arid cuts bottomed by twisting mountain streams. Around one more bend and the snowpeaks veered into view, staggering, distant, austere. Now I felt viscerally, spatially, what I had already known: that the Tien-Shan continued eastward for three thousand kilometres into central China; that its peaks surpassed by two *miles* straight up those of Banff or Interlaken. Closer to us, nearly vertical slopes of a tan shade I recognized from Kazakh paintings were superbly interrupted by deep green fir forests. Something tugged at my memory. Not the colour this time: the pitch of the slopes, the narrow triangles, the jagged approach to the sky, the summits two-thirds up the painting. From here the mental landscape led to China, ink brush on rice paper. Only here, it seemed, in the vertical, could a sense of standing calmly, of plateau— the sense of the snow leopard—be most perfectly approached.

Far away, yet only a middle ground because of the mountains' great receding, sheep scattered the steepnesses like grains of wheat on a drift of sand.

*

Two nights earlier I had entered Alma-Ata (recently renamed Almaty after the site's ancient settlement, destroyed by thirteenth-century Mongols and now capital of the ten-month-old nation of Kazakhstan), where I would spend a week working at the Canadian diplomatic office. A late October evening, balmy, clear. It had been sleeting for a week in Moscow; we had all been donning our stoicism in the face of early winter, our philosophy of slush. The Ilyushin 86 had been crammed, as cosmopolitan as the old empire: Moscow bureaucrats, Kazakh traders, a sprinkling of Chinese and Koreans, Uzbek politicians, French diplomats, American businessmen and born-agains, Russian and Kazakh families wise enough to have brought their own supper. People met by swapping language aptitudes, settling into pleasantries if a match were found. After the squalor of Moscow's Domodyedova airport—from which all flights for Asia departed—the city airport's arrival lounges were calm, mildly dented, and not even filthy. The car into town had plummeted down densely tree-lined streets behind dim headlights. Corners of buildings flashed into view, Cyrillic shop signs clearly from the same factory as those over every old state store from Magadan to Minsk. It looked pretty Soviet out there.

So that when morning dazzled the edges of the window blind, I was delighted (a blue gem of a day, and warm), unsurprised (a standard-issue Soviet town to all appearances, with dust stirred in; blocky buildings from an all-brown Lego set, overgrown non-lawns, tackiness all round), and disappointed: where were the mountains? Everyone had raved about the spectacular setting in a bowl of the snow-capped Tien-Shan and Ala-Tau. I scanned the horizon. From my eleventh-floor perch in the empty, cavernous Intourist hotel, I had clear sightlines through two hundred and seventy degrees. Nothing. Damn.

Then I looked up. Impossibly elevated crags hovered above blue slopes lost to view in early morning haze.

It turned out to be that kind of place, grim and splendid. It would require new tricks of balance. It would leave me with feelings without names.

Kazakhstan is a vast tableland, the centre of Central Asia, eight times the size of reunited Germany. Its capital is tucked in the south-east corner up against China and Kyrgystan, hundreds of miles from the Russian-speaking Siberian steppe of the new country's northern and western reaches. Alma-Ata is as distant from Moscow as Jerusalem. It had been one of the last lands consumed by the expansion of Russian empire, yet also one of the most reluctant to now abandon Moscow's orbit. It wasn't until the 1850s that Russian explorers reached the Tien-Shan mountains, perhaps the first Europeans on their (reputedly haunted) glaciers since Marco Polo had crossed them centuries earlier. The Kazakhs themselves were a dispersed and wandering nation. Their name may be from the Arabic *gazac*, "outlaw." They are closely linked, ethnically, with the Kyrgyz and Uzbeks. Distinguishing amongst them, and assigning each a republic, served Stalin's divide and weaken approach to empire management. The region had been literally decimated by the Golden Horde of Genghis Khan. The Russian advance, from what is now western Kazakhstan in the early seventeen hundreds to the establishment of a fort at Vierny, on the site of Alma-Ata, in 1854, splintered them again. Later still, hundreds of thousands fled into the Sinkiang-Uighur Autonomous Region of China in the wake of the Bolshevik revolution. Thousands live in modern Afghanistan, perhaps a hundred thousand in Mongolia, and a quarter million are scattered through the former USSR.

The czars defeated them with armies sent from Siberia. The brutality was remarkable, if not quite up to Genghis Khan's standards: "By 1870 the Kazakhs had lost an estimated one million people, a quarter of their population, in the wars, revolts, famines, and land grabbing by the settlers."

Large scale "settlement" of Slavs continued apace. By the time the revolution was complete, Kazakhs were a minority. Certainly, on the streets of Alma-Ata in November 1992 I heard Kazakh spoken only occasionally, even by ethnic Kazakhs. But a century and a half of living together in large numbers had created a relationship more complicated than one of coloniser and colonised, of master and servant. Kazakhstan's vast mineral wealth had created an economy inextricably woven into the Soviet central-planning web. The Kazakhs had never been profoundly Islamicized, so religious resentments were less acute than in Uzbekistan's great centres of Sufi culture and learning. Though the price had been terrible, the Russians *had* brought industrialisation, literacy, and sharply improved living standards.

Two institutions I visited showed variations on the symbiosis. A superb Russian language performance of Bulgakov's play *Heart of a Dog* at the local Lermontov Theatre seemed a somewhat sad foreign excrescence, put on in a half-empty, too-large auditorium by a company that one suspected might not long survive the loss of state subsidies. Of course the long-established local Russian intelligentsia would resent the implication. The production was top-notch, the play caustic and witty. But watching it after a day about town I could not escape the sensation that this was something like polo, lawn croquet, and tea on the terrace in the British Northwest Frontier Province (not so many miles away): well done, thoroughly civilised, but foreign, a weak graft. On the other hand, the capital's brand new *banya*—considered a must-see for visitors—combined Turkish- and Russian-style saunas with ornate central Asian architecture *and* standard issue babushkas out front selling birch branches. It was vast, busy, popular, loved: a steaming solace for weary citizens of all sorts. The Asian and European faces of the old Russian empire blended so seamlessly it was impossible to say which way the influences were flowing.

All of this, combined with level-headed non-nationalistic strongman Nazarbayev at the helm, led to an inclination toward continued integration in the critical year of 1991, an inclination in the end doomed by the powerful disintegrative forces at the end of the Gorbatchev era. The establishment by Yeltsin and the Ukrainian and Belarussian leaders of the new Commonwealth of Independent States with virtually no consultation, the abrupt announcement of the USSR's demise, was bitterly resented. Nationalist movements evolved with time in each new state, but in some cases they had to be started virtually from scratch by government edict. It was an ironic example of the former "colonies" being miffed at not being consulted about being set "free." Kazakhstan's leaders weren't stupid of course: given the lack of preparation, the economic, political and ethnic dislocations would prove severe, and would in turn threaten their own positions. Within a year Moscow would find itself criticised for "forcing" these independent countries to adopt their own currencies.

To add insult to injury the citizens of the new Kazakhstan would have to live with the irreducible exasperation quotient of the Soviet system for some time to come.

The day before ascending the Tien-Shan in Sasha's jeep, I went shopping for a desk. Our expedition was launched with ease. The hotel where our office was temporarily (we prayed) located, was demanding back the desk we had borrowed. Placing our sanity in the balance, we had resolved to effect the purchase of a standard-issue office utility. Flat surface, a couple of drawers, more or less wooden—we weren't fussy. Our secretary, Galina, an ethnic Ukrainian raised in Armenia (and prone to scatological comments on Ukrainian nationalism, sacrilege from Kiev to Calgary), had cadged a rendezvous after only three or four calls with a deputy director in the office desk division of State Furniture Factory Number Three (this did not imply, apparently, that there was a State Furniture Factory Number One or Two).

The entryway to the city's sole repository of office furnishings was dim, naturally, and decorated in oiled cinderblock. A large guard station squatted centrally, herding visitors into corners and against walls, where they stood in lines for futile telephones. In the spirit of the new era we tried the bored guard first, mentioning names, positions, job titles. He shook his head placidly. He had no such information. Could he call upstairs for us? Calling was not his profession. He gestured to the wall phones, with their apparently permanent patrons.

We made what nasty remarks were required by local etiquette, and trooped over to join them. The woman occupying the rearmost spot smiled toothlessly. Did we have a fifteen-kopeck piece? she asked. She would pay two roubles, over ten times face value. Galina was firm: no. She heard us speaking English, Galina whispered to me. Thinks we're stupid foreigners. Fifteen-kopeck pieces were in short supply. I nodded sagely. Phones were one index of the state of things. A few months later a Moscow magazine ran a statistical summary. The street price of fifteen-kopeck coins was ten roubles. Thirty-three percent of Russian pay phones worked. The leading cause of malfunction was vandalism. The leading cause of vandalism was theft of fifteen-kopeck coins. Well, one was tempted to muse, capitalism doesn't get much purer than that.

After a time we reached the front of the line and carefully inserted our precious coin. Galina dialled. The denizens of the line watched, grumpy as if in the waiting room of an overbooked dentist. The Assistant Deputy Chief of the Second Wood Furniture Division wasn't in her office. No, it wasn't known where she was. No, we could not be escorted up without an appointment. No, the clerk who had answered was not authorised to check the Assistant Deputy's calendar to confirm our appointment. She was not the Assistant Deputy's assistant. Yes, she did know who was. Her number was . . .

Galina began to plead shamelessly, loudly. Interest picked up in the entryway. *Could* the call be transferred without redialling? She didn't have another fifteen-kopeck piece. (The wiliest equipped themselves with a coin with a drilled hole, suspended on a string.) The secretary could not; she did not have a multi-line phone. These were still rare: bigwigs could instead be identified by the number of phone sets on their desk. But she was apparently willing to keep the line open while she called the Assistant Deputy's secretary on another phone. This secretary, exercising the proper authority, peeked at the chalkboard by her boss's door and confirmed our *bona fides*. The clerk Galina was talking to could not come down at the moment to guide us past the guard but could, with this confirmation, arrange to have a message left for our original contact, who would surely follow up promptly.

We were as good as in.

*

The jeep jerked and spurted up a winding ledge above precipitous drops, the snow caps lording over us, earth-brown slopes between, numerous magpies looking after our luck. A half-hour above the city we came to one of the many small hydroelectric stations that ran water from the pipelines through turbines to power Almaty. Communalnik, a small village of cinder-block houses, surrounded it, interlaced with an odd array of above-ground hot water pipes necessitating dozens of little footbridges to get from place to place. We got out and stretched our legs. Sasha beckoned me down the hill to a bit of meadow just above the river gorge. A few end-of-summer flowers were still unfaded in the grass.

—I'll show you the punishment cells, he called. I felt a psychic flinch. A fragment of the Gulag? Not exactly, I would learn, though part of the same spirit. Invisible from higher up, a turf-covered bunker. Around one side a heavy iron door, akimbo, set into the hillside. A small opening: five feet high, narrow.

Tucked into the green turf. History, most of it catastrophic, opens up suddenly in the old empire, a fold in the air, a cavity underfoot. Only a few weeks earlier back in Moscow I had fallen into conversation with a family visiting from Estonia. The woman's Scandinavian face—fair, open, lightly freckled—combined with her seemingly native Russian speech and her husband's more central European complexion (Lithuanian it turned out—well, sort of; his ancestors were Polish) had me wondering if she was Estonian, or simply a fair Slav. For that matter, maybe she was Finnish. Reluctant to betray my ignorance, I took a roundabout route by guiding the conversation to birth places. When childhood in Moscow was mentioned I took the opening and asked if she had been born there. No. Oh. Where had she been born?

—In prison.

—Pardon?

I thought I had misheard. A town name perhaps, a rhyme with Tallin.

—My mother was in prison. It was 1937, she added by way of explanation. The year when Stalin's slaughters peaked. For non-Russians, the rate of incarceration had been even higher. It was also the year my own mother had been born, on a southern Ontario dairy farm, in another universe.

Sasha pointed to a date scratched into a stone. 1951. He explained that German and Japanese prisoners had been kept here. According to locals, the last did not leave until 1956, eleven years after Hiroshima. The heart quailed once inside the child-sized entry. A single corridor twenty feet long, chalky, damp. Opening off to the left, four iron doors with grills no larger than cigarette packs, each rusting and crooked on its hinges. And the cells, each the length and width of a large desk, with ceilings high enough to permit only a school child to stand erect. I went into one. It was difficult to pass through the doorway; some sort of force pushed me away. It felt forbidden. Near the ceiling on the end wall of the cell, a vent the size of a postcard afforded a glimpse of a view worthy of *The Sound of Music* or a Beautiful British Columbia tourism poster. Pine, peak, snowcap; depths of mountain air to open the chest; wisps of cirrus in exalted blue. I crouched there, paused, for about thirty seconds. It was a long time, long enough to under-stand—or to sense, since it was an animal's inkling. Not the terror. Too common a sensation. Not the humiliation. That is survived—with its costs of diminishing and harden-ing. Here, the amputation of a human being.

*

We walked into the wood shop with the Assistant Deputy, a solid and slightly florid woman of fifty. The shop was an expansive, aircraft hanger-like space. Passing the chair zone, where thousands of seats were stacked or hung from raft-ers or jumbled in huge careless heaps like computer mod-els of randomness, we reached the country of desks. There they were, arrayed before us, just sitting there, as if, as if . . . as if you could just walk up and buy one. The Assistant Deputy was badly disillusioned when the two standard models—small, of maple-like wood, one shallow drawer

101

on the right; small, of maple-like wood, one shallow drawer on the left—failed to impress. I was thinking of something with twice the surface area, I explained, with at least a few good deep drawers. These models, I mused, might be useful as side tables, or to hold computers and printers when the Canadian office moved past the lap-top stage.

We wandered, cheered only by the sweet scent of sawn boards, the heady fumes of varnish (though no actual *producing* was visible). As the son of a carpenter-cum-farmer who could build or fix most anything and liked nothing better than the challenge of creating in his shop whatever seemed overpriced in the stores, I associated the smell and the white sleekness of new lumber with virtue itself, with enterprise. A few variant desks appeared amidst the acreage. Small still, no drawers at all. Two drawers, each large enough for one pen and three sheets of paper. Slightly larger, one centre drawer suitable for a modest selection of thumbtacks. At length we spotted it. A solid bear of a desk; at least eight feet long and four deep; tidily built; two drawers only, both on the right, but the second of decent depth; nicely finished, trimly varnished. It would be fine. I grinned.

—*Skolka stoyt?* I asked confidently. The rouble was still used as legal tender in Kazakhstan. With its collapse continuing, I could pay.

—Oh. No, I can't sell it to you.

—*Potchymu?*

—It's a special order. This is not a standard model.

Wow, I thought. *Someone's* got nerve. I wouldn't have dreamed of suggesting a custom job.

—So this one's taken? Can we order one like it?

A disturbing thought. No, it didn't seem possible.

102

—Potchymu nyet?

Galina and the Assistant Deputy began an earnest exploration of the question, delving like etymologists toward the root of the matter, going by common cultural consent through byways and in direction's I only half followed, sneaking up on the main point from behind.

We could not order a desk like this one because the Assistant Deputy could not authorise special orders. She did know who could, but there was no sense approaching him because this was the only special order ever, except from state organs. (Americans, I thought grimly, or the Chinese. Clearly this desk had been ordered by the embassy of a Great Power.) *However*, if we liked this desk, she recommended a model number seven, which was exactly the same except three inches shorter and in a different kind of wood. Only three inches? *Real* wood? Not veneer on pasteboard? Same drawers? Precisely. Could we see one? No, they didn't have any. Number sevens weren't made any more, but the model number hadn't been officially stricken. It wouldn't technically be a special order. So, we could order one? As a favour, yes: she was fully authorised to approve such an invoice.

I was wary, but desperate. Even since arriving in the Hades-like entryway my mind had at various points prepared to say "Fine, dammit, we'll go elsewhere." But there was no elsewhere, I knew, closer than Bishkek or Tashkent, another country, another nightmare.

How long would it take?

She ruminated. Two months.

Two *months*. It was out of the question. The hotel administration was reminding us daily of regulations, re-

103

calling past extensions, eyeing our desks with deep concern: all was not right with the hotel's world.

How could it take two months? The shop was flush with lovely lumber. I studied the equipment surrounding us, pictured lathes spinning, table saws churning, routers routing. Busy varnishing vats. Four hours tops, for veteran shop hands, and two days for the varnish to dry. Three days seemed lots. But there was no sense being crazy.

Could they do it in two weeks?

Weeks? Non-stock orders of less than two months were express orders.

And?

And she was not authorised to approve express orders.

My Russian was up to this. I slowed my words to the rate of water droplets in torture cells. Will you tell us who is? *Vuiy . . . gavaritye . . . nam . . . kto . . . mozhne?*

Yes.

Yes?

*

The jeep corkscrewed endlessly upward; the road drilled slowly into the sky through elegant pine groves intersected by nerve-wracking ravines thrown into relief—as if by stage machinery—by the glaring, thrusting peaks, now even higher, ever more unearthly and chill. Gravel gave way to dirt, dirt to a rough track with grass flourishing between the tire ruts. The occasional thunder of logging trucks terrified me on the hairpins. Here and there, last houses, last musterings of sheep. Even this high up, halfway to sky, the buildings were identifiably Soviet pre-fab. They might have been plucked by helicopters from the outskirts of Moscow or Minsk.

The pines sank gradually into dwarfs suitable for Christmas tinsel, then into shrubs; we emerged into Alpine uplands, ridges of gravel and snow. Over the crest of a rise, we rolled to a stop. I staggered out of the jeep, fumbling for my camera. Sasha grinned.

—Don't hurry, he advised. We're over three thousand meters. You'll get tired.

A broad lake hovered before us; in colour a dead ringer for Lake Louise in the Canadian Rockies, but on a stupendous scale; in today's sun an impossible turquoise; but, looking again, tilting the head, blue? purple? Lilac. A lilac lake. Behind it, miles away, sweeping regally upward to yet another unsuspected height, a great crag: Mount Pobyeda ("Victory") itself, over seventy-four hundred metres and unmistakably Himalayan. And from this fortress, a gleaming expanse of glacier, a river of light, descended toward a meeting with the far shore of the glorious lake. A stunning vista. But more: to the right a gracious, bowl-like sweep, a deceptively large valley lent texture by sturdy rock outcroppings, from which protruded the buildings and domes and upturned dishes of a large observatory. The stars, I thought, from here . . . And all around us, huge silence.

—*Krasivuiy, da?* It was Valeri, the driver, nodding happily.

—Not bad, I said, *Nye ochin ploha.* They laughed, delighted.

—About hundred metres of here, close, no? There— Sasha pointed, trying his English—at the, the—*Shore*, Pavel supplied—The shore, *gode nazadh,* last year, I see "snow leopard." This term he had clearly studied: as a nascent tourist operator, this English phrase was his bread and butter, and he knew it.

Of course, I thought, overwhelmed. What other spot on earth would merit your grace, your rarity, your deep calm?

*

Up a set of noisy stairs, past workshops, along a vinegary corridor we went, a little official parade. The correct door. A discrete, parade-master knock. Inside, a long table centred an absurdly narrow room. There seemed no space to push back the chairs. I wondered how those lining the table would ever get out. Perhaps it was an eternal meeting. The Assistant Deputy engaged the important someone at the table's head, who endured the interruption with stern benevolence. Galina and I stood outside the open door. I couldn't decide whether a pleasant and cooperative air, or a brusque and not-to-be-messed-with demeanour was the better tactic, and tried them by turns. Finally the table's head nodded, the trapped meeters tried to resurrect their interest, and we withdrew. Permission for an express order? In principle. We ploughed on. A secretary bearing a crucial ink stamp was approached. She was advised of the Head of the Table's verdict by the Assistant Deputy. Dubious. She lifted a robin's egg blue plastic phone and dialled. Confirmed. (The vectors of power seemed reliant upon the principle that everyone lied, pointlessly and routinely. Once this principle is accepted, procedural safeguards—normally needed only at those specific points were possibilities of theft or corruption exist—can, must, be tripled. Then everyone can have an "important" role in the network of check and countercheck. Important, so long as the founding principle isn't questioned. Everyone is part of the web, implicated in routinely demeaning their colleagues.) The secretary hefted her stamp and applied it precisely to a document bearing small print worthy of the best of Canadian mortgages. She unscrewed the obligatory fountain pen and signed across the seal. We found the stairs. We ascended.

On the fifth floor we located the accounting section. Our entry startled a gaggle of clerks perfecting their makeup. (These employees were mainly ethnic Russians. It may be an ethnic slur, but it is also undeniably true, that Russians consult mirrors more than anyone on earth. A quick visit to the coat-check zone before a performance at the Bolshoi is confirmation enough.) A menagerie of machinery sat on long desks: computers with oversized monitors (dust-laden), pocket calculators and typewriters (turned off), sets of abaci (their wooden beads polished with use). Here, the finish line in view, we encountered a final hurdle.

The Assistant Deputy deposited us with the Special Orders Accountant. She appeared a lesser adversary at first, early middle-aged, hair falling loosely about her collar, more wary than severe. Briefed by our departing Virgil, she selected a lengthy order form. Her pen began to crawl over the paper. Only time-lapse photography could have done justice to her prudence. Certain blanks on the form seemed to deplete her will; she would sigh, wrestle with inner demons. I caught myself feeling guilty for her trials then shook myself angrily. I was not a criminal! I simply wanted to buy a desk!

We waited, she scribed. She finished one form, launched into another. At length, its exigencies nearly exhausted, she stopped short. Galina, hovering nervously, asked the question which, once broached, was an invitation for fate, for bureaucracy, to crush you under its shoe.

—*Problyema?*

—Yes, today is the 27th. She shrugged.

—Yes . . .

—This is an express order. (Her lips curled in distaste.) All express orders must be paid in advance.

I was soothed.

—That's fine. We can pay now.

—You don't pay *me*. (I was obviously an imbecile.) You pay in the cashier section. That isn't the problem.

—What is the problem?

—An express order takes two weeks. Two weeks will be long after November 1st.

—And . . .

—On November 1st the prices will be raised. The rules are absolutely clear. You must pay the price in effect at the time of delivery.

—Really, its not a problem. We'll pay the higher price. We understand about the inflation. How much will it be?

—The prices for November haven't been set yet. Then, in case I would dash for an opening, And all express orders must be paid in advance.

I thought. My brain foundered. Then it hurt—especially because I was beginning to understand. I was beginning to accept the logic.

She had a point there.

*

A hundred feet above the radiant stained glass of the lake, Valeri pulled off the path. We got out and tossed a few snowballs. The trail twisted on up over a little hill and went into the side of a cloud. The jeep backed over spongy alpine turf to a flat spot overlooking both observatory and lake. The glacier shimmered. Bruised foreheads of thunderheads loomed. The snow leopard padded, somewhere. From the back of the jeep, like heavyweight Mary Poppins, the men unloaded more than the small compartment could possibly have held: a folding table, canvas chairs for all, a navy footlocker-sized hamper, plates, mugs, tablecloth, a feast of food. Soon we were seated, besweatered, in the lemony sunlight, preoccupied by the methodical Russian ritual of eating—slicing the salami and tomatoes and bread, passing the plates, opening the beer, unwrapping the cheese. Tins of cold Pilsner from Czechoslovakia. Fresh dark bread. Sausage Sasha distributed in thick hunks. The cheese, red tomatoes, grapes, gigantic local apples. A dog, from the last village I supposed, came by to be spoiled.

Finally we talked about something other than the scenery. Valeri's army pension was being ridiculed by one thousand percent annual inflation. His cut of the day's hard currency proceeds would help buy his wife overdue shoes. Sasha was trying to get this touring outfit up and running, though the tourist flow into Kazakhstan still left a lot to be desired. A planned new Lufthansa flight direct from Frankfurt had him scouring for German-speaking guides. He had a day job at an institute of some sort, where he showed up from time to time to collect his increasingly irrelevant salary. I promised to pass around his business cards back in Moscow. Certainly at that moment, with Czech beer in one hand and sweet bread topped with sliced tomatoes in the other, the lake and glacier before me, inhaling the transparency of the air, I would have recommended him to God. Pavel was the most vulnerable. The academies, the arts and culture organisations, the higher learning institutes were shutting in droves. As a recent graduate in the arts he relied on his English and his contacts to glimpse any prospect of a future.

The question of being Slavs in the new Kazakhstan was, for the moment, surprisingly muted, although they worried. (Nationalist rhetoric about protecting Russia's fellow "countrymen" in the "near abroad" was already starting to heat up inside the Russian Federation.) Stalin's creative boundary drawing had been designed with the imperatives of a Moscow dominated Soviet Union in mind: now that it no longer existed they were as transparently arbitrary—and as troublesome—as those in post-colonial Africa. Official international declarations on the question were tidily contradictory: "peoples" had a right to self-determination, but current borders were sacred—start fiddling and there would be no end to the chaos.

With a population split ethnically and linguistically down the middle, the government of the (relatively) benign autocrat Nursultan Nazarbayev was studiously pursuing conciliatory strategies, attempting to cool any Kazakh nationalist fervour without exactly losing Kazakh political support. Democracy, gone a bit wild in Moscow, should be cultivated only slowly, a long term project à la Singapore. One of the ironies of 1992 was watching former Soviet mouthpieces like *Izvestia* condemning totalitarianism in the new Central Asian states.

The moment's collision of cultures and empires was bewildering. The presence of Moscow still loomed large. Lenin frowned on every bank note. My Aeroflot ticket made reference only to Moscow time, even for the flight departing Alma-Ata, a city closer to Beijing than the Kremlin. The best restaurant in town was Chinese, but it operated on thoroughly Soviet principles: in spite of a reservation and a half-empty hall, I was only allowed to smell a caravan of redolent dishes passing me on their way out of the kitchen before being turfed. They *never* took reservations for single diners, was I mad? But the American empire was making fitful inroads, if by indirect routes. The U.S. dollar, impotent at the moment in Japan and Germany, was king of the heap in the Kazakh markets. And next door to the Intourist hotel a Korean magnate had opened an imitation McDonald's called "Shaggies." The restaurant seemed to have been designed by someone who had seen a McDonald's on TV, once. Visually, at first glance, it was familiar. But the food was sad—burnt two-ounce lumps of ground "beef" in an antique bun, sliced potatoes that had apparently been boiled—and the floor needed sweeping; there were huge stacks of pop-bottle empties next to the counter, and the place was full of hoods instead of chipper families.

So there was not, for Valeri, Sasha and Pavel, any simple sense of being outsiders itching to go "back" to Russia. They had been born here. Besides, finding housing would be impossible, never mind jobs. They hadn't much liked what they had seen of Moscow on short visits. Their abiding preoccupation turned out to be the newly visible, increasingly blatant corruption. Sure, they knew that the old days had been rotten to the core. But, by and large, the old guard had enjoyed its privileges in seclusion. The new *businessmeni* flaunted it in your face, day after day, when a man couldn't afford a bike for his kid, meat for supper, or tickets to the *banya*.

As they talked, I entered their hall of mirrors. In Kazakhstan, in the old empire, there was no place upon which to stand, nowhere to plant your lever against the crushing weight of graft and influence-peddling and the outright theft which too often proved the real outcome of "privatisation." Should the Communists expose the Democrats, or the opposition parties expose the newspapers, or the police expose the Reformers, or the Democrats expose the police, or the Nationalists expose the Communists?

The silence adopted us again. The leopard came to my mind, like an answer without a question. We wolfed the ripe tomatoes and tossed grapes to the dog and gazed down over the gravel and moss and snow to the lake, to the mountains, at our ease. Glacier, hard blue sky, grey of stone: I scanned slope and peak for movement, felt certain for a moment that I was in the stillness before motion. But there was nothing there.

*

It was all here, carefully negotiated, repeated, confirmed, put down in ink. We had a deal. It was a new era, right? We would lay out the current price now and sign an undertaking to pay the balance—reflecting the new price—upon delivery of the desk. This was a special favour. We understood that. This was not done for just anyone. We were appreciative. It was entirely unorthodox. We were deeply indebted.

Did the split lie between what was and what was not of the spirit? Or could the soul itself be a divided thing?

We had arrived at 10:00 a.m., and it was now barely after two. A mere four hours. True, the desk would arrive only later, after my departure from Alma-Ata; I couldn't touch it, lay my eyes upon it, put a file folder into one of its lovely deep drawers. But, with reasonable luck, the model I had ordered would be safely ensconced in the office in two (okay, probably three) weeks. Galina was unruffled. This had been a snap. But I was delighted with our inventiveness, our fortitude, our veteran-of-the-bureaucratic-wars savvy. It felt like a personal SALT II.

Taking out my wallet, I began to fish for hundred rouble notes. So where were the cashiers to be found? We were to take the requisition form provided by the accounting section to the number three cashier's window on the second floor. Not to worry: she doubted the line at that cashier was particularly long. Line? With perfect resignation, Galina gathered her things. But best to go now, the accountant added hastily. To get a good spot. The cash window would reopen right after the two to three o'clock break . . .

*

In the dream I am in the punishment cells for Japanese prisoners, underground, the sod flowering in sunlight over

113

my head. The clammy walls are six inches from each shoulder. Damp glistens on the ceiling below which I crouch, my back to the slab of iron in the door. I have my head twisted awkwardly to one side, and I am pushing my forehead into the well in the wall before the little grate.

In the outer air, that unfathomable expanse just beyond my skull, is a narrow rivet of green, all that I can see of the bank of grass across the streambed. As I watch, a snow leopard pads slowly along the ridge. The thick pelt of ghostly grey, the liquid shoulders, the black eyes that gaze into its calm, suspended world, a world always poised for a bolt of fire, for necessary speed. When it comes. Grace, I think with lightness in my chest, it moves with grace. In the dream the word seems a momentous insight. I want to tell Sasha, or Pavel, or someone, what I have seen. But in the way of dreams I turn for the door to find it has somehow gotten closed, jammed, and I realize that long before I manage to push and scrape and wrestle it aside—if it has not been locked?—the leopard will have vanished. And has it seen me looking, I wonder? Has it seen the man in a cage?

Journal Notes

Near Ismailova's great twenty-odd-square-kilometre swath of park and woodland on Moscow's north-east boundary, a phantasmagoric outdoor craft market is burgeoning in the new economic order and disorder. Literally hundreds of artisans—now joined by vendors of everything from kittens to plumbing supplies to auto parts—squat beside an array of paintings, handmade chess sets, a few trillion matryoshka *nesting dolls, fake or contraband Orthodox church icons, lacquer boxes and painted wooden eggs, sculptures, weavings, embroiderings. Kilometres of pathways, thousands of potential buyers. The creators sit on little stools or chat and smoke in small groups nearby. Many are college professors or office workers or engineers with hobbies they are now desperately trying to turn into a dollar or two via twelve-hour days in the slush and chill, where a single good sale for hard currency might equal a month's salary at their regular job.*

But at the centre of the circle in this weekends' smoky late-autumn air, there is a scene of enchantment. In a clearing in the throngs is a field with a few dozen apple trees, bare now, and a bit ghostly in the cold fog. Ropes have been strung between the trees, and scores of bright quilts have been hung, a hundred colours suspended in the mist.

For a weekend trip to Estonia's beautiful medieval capital of Tallin we had for the first time been required to get visas for travel inside the former USSR. The overnight train from Moscow reaches the new Estonian border at about 5:00 a.m. There are no exit controls yet around the core of what was once the world's largest prison. The Estonian guards board the train and bang loudly on the door of the compartment, but they aren't yet very good at arousing fear. The uniforms are brand new and look a bit stiff, and the brusque show of authority can't hide the bad skin and pale jaws of teenagers. It is a challenge for the new nations to staff sensitive positions with people untainted by association with the former imperial overlord. Half the Estonian cabinet, in fact, appears to have interrupted college studies to join the government.

The compact cobblestoned grace of Tallin is surprisingly cosmopolitan; both visually and in mood the city seems part of western Europe or Scandinavia, though in a country with a forty percent Russian ethnic "minority" this is certainly in part illusion. But in a bookstall, a dizzying number of nations and languages meet, in the best central European manner: spending the crisp new Estonian kroons—convertible, colourful, and stable!—I buy a biography of Marina Tsvetaeva. This book about a Russian poet who spent most of her adult life in Paris was written by a Czech (Maria Razumovsky) in German, then translated into French and published in Switzerland, before being purchased in Estonia by a Canadian living in Moscow.

New types of borders, new versions of division, appear weekly. As November closes I try to fly to Kiev. In dank Vnukova airport on a Sunday evening a ferocious battle-axe snarls at me when I try to present my ticket. No flight. Come tomorrow morning. Will there be a flight tomorrow morning? Who knows. After a few hours in mob scenes at the rail station unsuccessfully trying to get onto an overnight train (I have interviews booked for the entire week, beginning Monday morning, and many of the families will have travelled hundreds of miles to be there), I'm up at 6:00 a.m. to haunt the frigid lounges. Nowhere to buy even lousy coffee. A good time all round. No flight, though it takes three hours to find that out. Ukraine, it turns out, can't get its hands on any jet fuel, so that in 1992 the two great Slavic capitals, fifteen million people between them, are linked only by jammed trains doing fourteen-hour runs. A colleague at our embassy in Kiev had been to the airport to try to meet me. He reported that the domestic flight arrivals area (where passengers from Russia still disembark a year after Ukrainian independence) had been closed tight with a sign saying the next flight would arrive . . . in January.

The old masters never dreamed it would all end. In his memoirs Sakharov gives one of the most telling of chilling details. Presuming they would always be in charge, the party and KGB elite did not fear keeping careful records of the slaughter. In KGB files of those executed, there was one document stamped "To be preserved forever": an affidavit that the death sentence had been carried out, with the serial number of the pistol used.

DECEMBER

Just back from Kiev (by train), where the Russian economy looks good in comparison, where half the populace seems to have congregated on Kreshchatic Street—Ukraine's version of the Champs Élysées—to work under sandwich boards as money changers, swapping Ukrainian coupons for roubles, dollars and deutschemarks.

Here, we keep waiting for the bottoming out, the sense that there is some force other than gravity, some direction other than down, some force other than disintegration. But the country is chilled to the bone, and not only because in early December it is already minus fifteen: chilled by the tearing away of every fig leaf of normalcy, of the way people thought things worked, of what they thought was believed, what they thought had value. Last year saw the dissolution of political and ideological structures, saw new colours on the maps, new names on the plaques, empty pedestals and plinths. 1992 has been the year money itself turned into mere coloured paper, the year your kid made more washing cars than you made teaching at the university, the year three hard currency shops became three hundred, and hard currency apartheid became a fact of life, the year everything was displayed in the shops—at breathtaking prices. The year having your salary only doubled twice meant disaster, the year the latest Sting and Bryan Adams went on sale on CD at the state Melodia store priced at fifteen times the peerless string quartets of Shostakovich. The year foreigners snapped up Shostakovich and the kids washing cars snapped up Sting. The year Westerners explained condescendingly that this was how the market worked (though

118

in Toronto the same recording of the Shostakovich quartets cost double Sting's latest). The year kiosk owners made more than factory directors. The year industrial output dropped twice as fast as during the worst year of North America's Great Depression. The year the economic gurus nodded approvingly.

No one really knows what the inflation rate was for the year. Trusting government economic figures is as pointless as it was under Brezhnev, though for different reasons. (In the classic Soviet political joke about how the Union's various leaders deal with the fact their train has come to a stop in the middle of nowhere, Brezhnev's solution is to have the blinds pulled down and everyone on board rock back and forth to simulate movement.) Finance ministry officials are, more or less, trying to give snapshots of the precise total size of a thousand different blocks of ice in a thousand different frying pans. A few thousand percent. Twenty percent some months, sixty percent others. Percent of what no one is sure. The rouble is now four hundred and fifty to the U.S. dollar, or four to the Canadian penny.

Right-wing demonstrations continue—that is, left-wing demonstrations. Commies. Or perhaps Fascists. Or both. The extremes meet again, if they ever really parted, and do a confused dance in the shadow of our local Lenin monument in weekly ritual, waving faces of Stalin and the Tsar, hammers and sickles and double-headed imperial eagles, reviling democrats and Americans, "chornies" (darkies, meaning, roughly, those from the Caucasus) and Jews. The Congress, led by men who rallied around Yeltsin against the coup plotters sixteen months ago, meet to try

119

to savage his reform program, and the president, veering between stout bravery, formidable determination, and erratic lashings-out, tosses ministers overboard with abandon to try to keep the (trial) balloon aloft. It looks doubtful, from here, that the conservative forces (that is, the Socialists—sort of) have enough power to topple Yeltsin; and in any event they don't really seem eager to run the place.

Unfortunately, as one journalist wittily hit the nail on the head, the shock therapy program has so far been all shock and no therapy. The old command structure is still too intact for the freeing of prices and limited privatisation to generate actual production. The "laws" of supply and demand are little help when there is often still only one supplier, and when inflation-stunned buyers have no cash left with which to stimulate demand.

Personally, we are currency-apartheid beneficiaries, of course, and although we are far less wealthy in relative terms than we were early in the year (inflation is succeeding at outstripping the rouble's fall, slicing ten or fifteen percent off the dollar's buying power every month), it sets us and all Westerners into a different economic universe. This fall, with Teresa teaching at the Anglo-American school, we have been able to hire an energetic, warm young woman who is fully qualified as a kindergarten teacher to look after John (now almost three) during the day. He loves Katya and Katya loves him; she gives him more developmental stimulation than a bevy of daycares as she tries out all her training and skills on him. The U.S. dollars we pay her make her well off by local standards—in any event, with the dietsky sad *network in steep*

120

decline, she would otherwise be unemployed. We had hoped John would soon be speaking Russian, but instead he seems to be teaching Katya English. Which is, on sum, for the best, from her point of view. In Moscow right now, language skills mean access to foreigners, and foreigners mean money.

And this December the elevators are even working. Last year, Teresa had to leave the stroller downstairs to carry John up to the ninth floor through grimy, half-lit stairways. In an all bad news year, you take what you can get.

5

UPDIKE IN OKHA

*He doesn't know what to do, where to go, what
will happen, the thought that he doesn't know
seems to make him infinitely small and impossible to capture. Its smallness fills him like a
vastness.*

John Updike, *Rabbit, Run*

*[Sakhalin] seems to be the end of the world,
and there is nowhere left to go. . . . The most
common surname is Unremembered.*

Anton Chekhov

Sakhalin Island, clinging to the Pacific Coast of Russia north-
east of Vladivostok, shaped like a distended Italy and little
closer to Moscow than to Montreal, seems in the atlas an
insignificant slab of land, dwarfed by the mass of Asia. But
the vastness of Russia distorts one's perspective: Sakhalin
is a thousand kilometres north to south, and has more square
miles than Ireland.

Nevertheless, the island is undeniably a long way from the navel of the Russian literary world in the editorial offices of Moscow's "thick journals," the hefty, large-circulation, state-subsidised behemoths which throughout the Soviet era have been the vehicles—for both good and ill—of new writing. And if Sakhalin and its modest provincial capital at Yuzhno-Sakhalinsk (population 106,000) are not entirely obscure, Okha, it must be admitted, is. On a good map you can spot it, on the island's north-east tip; it stares across the Sea of Okhotsk toward Kamchatka's volcanoes and the Bering Strait, seven hundred kilometres north of the capital's few bookshops. A remote part of remoteness. The village does, however, boast three of the hundred and fifty thousand subscribers to *Inostranaya Literatura* ("Foreign Literature") magazine. Editor Vladimir V. Lakshyn, in time of economic collapse, knows this, and can't get them out of his head.

Inostranaya Literatura is one of those thick journals. The most famous is *Novy Mir* (The New World), renowned for throwing the flaming brand of Solzhenitsyn's *One Day in the Life of Ivan Denisovich* into the early days of the Khrushchev thaw. *Inostranaya Literatura* prints two hundred and fifty densely printed pages each month, translating into Russian contemporary writing from all over the world, with scores of lengthy reviews jostling delightfully in the back. The issue I pick up that day includes eighty pages of the great Austrian Robert Musil, his name looking strange in Cyrillic script, and other work from Spain, China, the U.S. and Poland.

1992. The year inflation is four digits, though which four is uncertain. In May we visit the magazine offices for the first time. On a day too cool for the season we are ushered into dim offices in a shabbily elegant four-story building on a street replete with such crumbling grandeurs, in an old neighbourhood tucked in the loop of the Moskva River. At the end of the street the gold domes of the Kremlin burn and shimmer as they do in any weather. We pass down a long, dim corridor guarded inconsequentially by an ancient woman on a wooden chair. A brass-haired secretary with a soft smile shows us from the cramped outer office heaped with books and magazines into a spacious sanctum.

Distinguished; passionate yet classical; sixtyish and neat, with glasses and silver moustache, old-fashioned suit and tie: the editor seats us around a low table and, after beckoning for tea, waves in a half-dozen senior members of the manifold full-time staff to join us. In spite of knowing some of the prices paid, it is impossible to quell envy entirely at the mere thought of it: a literary life—a *salaried* literary life—outside of the universities. And impossible to forget the tissue of complicities with, and resistances to, the old order that any such staff consists of. Someone, to pass the time before the meeting begins, points to a drawing hung on the far wall. A Picasso, they explain. A former editor knew him well, carted it back from Paris.

I remember a quiet and a weightlessness that is the beginning of one type of Russian hospitality, waiting for the emotional angle, for the intellectual radiants, that will join or divide: they will, by and large, either love you or despise you. Despise you if there turns out not to *be* any emotional tangent.

We settle into our chairs. Mr. Lakshyn tugs at his vest. He appears solemn unless you notice that his eyes twinkle continuously. Spring sunlight slants across the wood-panelled walls and highlights the Picasso while the secretary serves the tea, just drawn from the samovar perched in the outer office, in gilt and purple china cups. The journal is, begins the editor, as if mentioning some curious little tale, in the midst of economic catastrophe.

*

Five months later the weather has turned ominously winterish, though September is barely complete. Between the metro stop and the editorial offices half the storefronts are dusty and dark—it is always difficult to determine whether these old state shops are actually closed or simply growing dim and apathetic while awaiting resurrection in "private" form, most often meaning a former bureaucrat has cadged a monopoly or a duty free import "licence." The fact the shelves are empty doesn't mean a shop has formally stopped operating. This is a country where in recent years plenty of goods-less stores employed large idle staffs to harangue those who strayed in the front door.

The species is dying, but not yet extinct. The streets are bustling along Pyatnitskaya though; the sidewalks are congested by the numerous kiosks, boon and bane of Moscow's cowboy capitalism, with which the crowds must compete for space. These kiosks don't share the weariness of the storefronts, though they still offer a rather monotonous array of liquor and smokes, soft drinks and chocolate, with the first inroads of useful products—combs say, or pantyhose—just beginning to appear. The old buildings behind the metal-and-glass boxes of the kiosks are long and low, only two or three stories. Their plastered exteriors, mostly in the dark yellow-and-white of much of Moscow, crumble away here and there to reveal the wood and lathe innards of the walls. Between the embankment of the looping Moskva under the Kremlin walls and the Garden Ring Road a mile to the south, this is one of the relatively few intact historical districts. Remarkably, given a ninety-percent destruction rate during the Bolshevik era, a dozen seventeenth- and eighteenth-century churches survive in an area comfortably covered in an afternoon stroll. Kitty-corner from the metro, from where a lane leads west to the great (but under perpetual renovation) Tretyakov Gallery, is the Church of St. Clements, over two hundred years old. It has the Italian lightness and loft more common to St. Petersburg. The inevitable inactive scaffolding clings to its eroding cupola.

Inostranaya Literatura, a block south, is still surviving on accounting slights-of-hand. Today they are launching an all-U.S. issue. Their building is still unheated, though the babushkas on the street have donned kerchiefs and fifty-pound overcoats. The hallway is, at best, five or six degrees. The crowded main lounge is cosier due to body heat and the invigorating vision of tables laden with vodka, wine and cognac, bread, cheese and caviar, sausage and fruit, cakes and sweets. At the head of a long table Vladimir Lakshyn introduces the new issue. American novelist John Updike, not exactly a darling of the Brezhnev era *apparat*, is the main attraction in this month's pages. One tries to imagine even Mikhail Gorbatchev getting the point of Rabbit Angstrom. But the fact that *Inostranaya Literatura* is an institution does not mean it is stodgy. As early as 1990, editor Lakshyn could also be found writing an introduction to the novellas of Bulgakov, a particularly carnivalesque genius.

A cross-section of Moscow literati and a scattering of foreigners invited for the occasion follow his remarks with attention. This is clearly out of respect for Lakshyn himself. Graciousness: how firmly it persists amidst a brutalised, spectacularly rude and cynical populace, amidst economic, spiritual and physical violence. One attempts to define Russianness at great peril, but the unique mingling of formality, sentimentality, and ferocity is surely part of it.

Most laugh frequently at the editor's lines, eyes cheerful yet weary, many showing something approaching love. A few slouch, professionally cynical. A number of the magazine's editors and translators seem to be sixtyish women of straight bearing, kind faces, and silver-grey hair—when they later approach to welcome me back, they exude, if the word can be used in a classless sense, *gentility*. A late-arriving journalist noisily sets up his mike, so apologetic at interrupting that the intrusion is doubled. Lakshyn is recounting the evidently hilarious history of John Steinbeck's visit to Moscow in the 1930s. Although my Russian is not up to all of the jokes, I do catch one punch line. Apparently Steinbeck had mastered a single phrase of Russian for the occasion, hoping it would deal with all exigencies: "My name is John Steinbeck, the famous American writer," *Minya zavute John Steinbeck, isvestniy Amerikanski pisat'l.* One evening, separated through a series of misadventures from his hosts, lost in the dusty summer alleyways of Moscow, he has a run-in with the *militsia*. Surely a misunderstanding. Nothing to be done. A visit to the nearest station appears necessary. In indignation,

Steinbeck icily informs the policeman, *Minya zavute John Steinbeck, isvestniy Amerikanski pisat'l.* Tough, snaps the cop, I only read Hemingway.

Later, having retreated from a boisterous crowd unloading the tables (Muscovites prove that the heights of celebration are proportional to the depths of daily frustration), a few of us head to an upstairs office in search of cigarettes and a place to talk. The rooms are plain but comfortable, with two large desks per office, tea kettles and mugs and sugar bowls, glassed-in shelving overflowing with books and papers. Grigory, one of the younger members of the editorial collective, offers a local brand apologetically, scratches a match, and wants to know who the major Canadian poets are. I hesitate, make noises about its being a young country, that of course being abroad one wishes to take a positive viewpoint, to encourage . . . He fixes me with a friendly but corrective glare, expert by heritage at ignoring meaningless prose. You are an intellectual, the glare says (a serious accusation in Russia); of course you will tell me what you really think. I tell him I sadly feel we haven't yet been blessed with a major poet—though some good ones, some interesting ones—and quickly change the subject to fiction. Conveniently, Michael Ondaatje has just shared a Booker Prize, and my promise to loan a few choice Canadian novels beyond those they know (Atwood, Davies, Munro), including the prizewinner, fulfills my civic duty. (It turned out Grigory liked *The English Patient*, but he was in the non-fiction department: the fiction section never, to my knowledge, pursued a possible translation.)

So, I say, how *are* the finances since I was here in May? And by the way, how many staff *do* you have? (I

128

had been trying to count offices on the way through.) *Forty*, he replies, grimacing dramatically behind his short, thick beard. It is what we call invisible unemployment. Economically, it is a catastrophe.

*

As for every section of society, 1992 was for the arts a sort of apotheosis of crisis—following upon year after year of turmoil and overturned expectations since the mid-eighties. For writers, painters, theatre workers, filmmakers, dancers, musicians, 1992 added economic dislocation to the ideological ferment that had been both stimulating and unnerving creators and audiences since the advent of *perestroika* and *glasnost*. Most (but not all) had had little affection for the precepts of Communism and less for its practice; yet most were social democrats in instinct and hardly found what passed for capitalism here worth celebrating. Some (but not most) had resented the heavy hand of state censorship hedging their creative reveries; but the abrupt dissolution of all-Union structures combined with a sudden multiplication of possibilities was unnerving and exhausting. Many, all but a very few, had assumed that the Soviet Union itself, minus its East and Central European satellites, was indissoluble—a tiny percentage had understood that the Baltic states might, in the fullness of time, be reasonably permitted some autonomy.

For a brief period, a hard-to-define era that lasted perhaps six months, perhaps ten, a vast majority had their minds turned inside out and assumed that the Union's dismantling was as natural and inevitable as its permanence had seemed as late as 1990. That epoch also gone now, most thinkers had thoroughly mixed feelings on the subject. Only a minority had chafed at the relentlessly *structured* and bureaucratic but generous and reliable system of state funding for the arts, the cosy writers' unions, vast print runs, decent salaries, dachas, sanitoria, Black Sea retreats—the unquestioned *respect*—accorded to artists and the intelligentsia, however prescriptive those terms proved in practice. Even the few who had found the system claustrophobic now found themselves in the difficult free air of a sort of orphanhood. Before, the state had accorded artists the ultimate respect of deeming their ideas worth shooting them over; or, at least, in more recent decades, worth shipping them to the camps or dumping them on the tarmac of Western airports, stripped of their citizenship. Stalin had for example flicked Osip Mandelshtam into oblivion—an anonymous death sometime, somewhere; freezing in a half-built prison hut in desolate wasteland near Vladivostok—for a wittily nasty eight couplets about the "Kremlin mountaineer" ("He rolls the executions on his tongue like berries. / He wishes he could hug them like big friends from home") *that the poet never even published.*

Such a context gives words and images great weight. It also renders readers both starved for honest words and exquisitely sensitive to original thought. This accounts both for reams of stultifyingly dead art and, from the few artists immune to the virus of dictate, work of unsurpassed vitality and concentration. It also accounts for a barely suppressed envy in Western artists for the horrible and heroic lives of the Soviet martyrs. Certainly I myself was not immune to it, though long wades through the two volumes of

130

Mandelshtam's widow's memoirs taught that what it really meant was decades of acutely stressful, deadening, wearying, exhausting, *unpleasant* days in lousy housing with lousy food doing lousy jobs. Year after year after year.

But when, suddenly, everything is allowed, one worries that nothing matters. Just as post-Soviet shoppers were confronting the grim reality that whereas in the Gorbatchev era they had lots of money but nothing to buy, they now under Yeltsin had lots to buy but no money, artists could say what they liked but were worried no one was listening. Into this ferment and uncertainty, 1992 had stirred the financial crisis of withering state support and breathtaking inflation. Some sectors of the creative world had adapted better than others.

The great state-run ballet and opera companies, headlined by Moscow's Bolshoi (which in Russian simply means "Big") and St. Petersburg's Kirov (cum Mirinsky), faced huge challenges. With vast administrative structures, very large companies of dancers, singers, and musicians, and expensively aging buildings to maintain, they were hit hard by the steeply declining real value of their government subsidies. The plunge in the rouble meant middle-rank dancers were earning far less than nannies working for foreign families. Companies in the West lured away many of the stars with hard currency contracts. It was no longer necessary to defect and carry away your world in your suitcase while on tour in the West. You could plan your departure, get a passport and visas, and know you could jet back from Lisbon or Paris or L.A. whenever too much sunshine and superficial chit-chat made you long to be creatively gloomy in Mother Russia. Rock-bottom ticket prices that had made

131

even the Bolshoi accessible to everyone climbed steeply, though they remained a bargain and the seats remained full. Financially, the major companies had the advantage of being able to head abroad on tour and soon rake in enough from hundred-dollar seats at Carnegie to pay many of the bills during the rest of the year. As a result though, their great halls stood empty for long stretches while the companies were out of town. Even very fine companies in Minsk or Kiev had no such luxury. The market in the major Western venues was lucrative but narrow.

Creatively, the Bolshoi by general agreement continued to rest on past laurels, its superb productions of the classic repertoire getting stale, with no new stars to excite the demanding Russian audiences (who do not at all have the irritating habit of feeling standing ovations are necessary after every performance. If they find a performance routine, they clap twice and head for the coat check). St. Petersburg's company retained "Kirov" alongside the dusted-off "Mirinsky" for, ironically, commercial reasons (ironic given that Kirov was a Bolshevik hero)—the name Kirov sold tickets in Paris and London. Unlike the Bolshoi it had managed to maintain artistic freshness. The turmoil of 1990-93 seemed to heighten the company's daring, resulting in sparkling and dynamic new productions praised around the world.

The situation was much the same for classical music. Public support was rock-solid: deep, widespread, passionate, and well-deserved. But the best companies and conductors still needed to compensate for domestic economics with tours to Berlin and Vienna, London and New York. Many top performers fled West in search of a liveable paycheque, and the second-string companies—many of them in fact superb—were in dire straits all round. Rock music, far from leaping into the limelight in this new wide open era, was generally agreed to be in dismal shape—Russian rap was, for example, arguably the ugliest hybrid ever heard, with all the authenticity of, say, Jamaican polka. On the theatre scene, while all concerned moaned about impossible economics, and many of the largest companies seemed paralysed, activity actually boomed, with companies opening and closing weekly and the flamboyant staging of Russian directors coming to the fore, proving that anything from *War and Peace* to experimental musical dramas by Schnitke could be transported to the boards.

Visual arts proved particularly adaptable. More flexible, less reliant upon budgets and buildings, scores of new galleries opened, artists sold out of their lofts; outdoor art-marts full of both schlock and occasional treasures sprang up, mushroomed, exploded, and the large state galleries put on dazzling shows of long-absent masters such as Chagall and the Russian avant-garde of the twenties alongside a steady string of vivid, stimulating exhibitions by little-known newcomers. Entry fees remained miniscule, Russian families turned out en masse, and showing up at the wrong time often meant long queues at gallery ticket windows.

But when it came to putting words on paper, the golden age of the late eighties, when the giant state presses raided the desk drawers of dissidents and printed long forbidden masterpieces from Bulgakov through Pasternak to Solzhenitsyn in mammoth print runs, seemed to have collapsed, both economically and artistically. Magazines that had provided sizeable royalty cheques and large readerships went bankrupt as once-subsidised paper prices skyrocketed. The effect was even more dramatic in some of the former republics whose economies were weaker still, and who had become totally dependent on Moscow in various ways. In Kyrgystan the newspaper industry virtually died overnight in 1992 as the price of a ton of newsprint, all of which was imported from Russia, rose from eight hundred and thirty to twenty-two thousand roubles. The leading Kyrgyz language daily chopped its circulation by sixty percent. The Writers' Union of Kyrgystan published one hundred and fifty new books in 1991, zero in 1992.

The dissolving of the Soviet Union had been replicated in splits and fierce infighting in the old writers' organisations, once trusty lapdogs of the state and always ready to pulp a planned edition of Akhmatova or turf out a Pasternak when the master's voice commanded. In June 1992, two factions of the obsolete but not quite moribund Soviet Writers Union—a reformist "Commonwealth Union of Writers" and an old-guard "Russian Writers' Union"—gathered at a final congress to do battle over the question of who would inherit the property of the old organisation: a mansion which had played a major part in *War and Peace* (ancestral home of the Rostovs), a now pricey restaurant savagely satirised in *The Master and Margarita*, a publishing house, various dachas and retreats, a medical clinic, contracts, contacts, and clout. Yevgeny Yevtushenko, arena-poet darling of the sixties, was burned in effigy in the Union's courtyard by the conservatives; the liberals threatened boycott and sent folk singer-poet Bulat Okudzhava to negotiate prior to launching lawsuits; and still other writers suggested that any sort of union was an outmoded idea (Stalin was, after all the founder, in 1932), and that "everyone should stay home and write."

The cynicism of the era (that is, the "era" of the early nineties) reached some sort of nadir when, in American journalist David Remnick's account, the world famous gadfly Yevtushenko scurried around the Hall of the Soviet Congress buffet the day after Andrei Sakharov's death had stunned the nation, "handing out to [foreign] correspondents (in Russian and English) a copy of the poem he had written instantly, in honour of Sakharov. 'Maybe you will print it on your editorial page?'"

*

A catastrophe, Vladimir Lakshyn continues, in May, as we sip our tea. We have a circulation of 150,000, with half a million readers. Each copy now costs twenty-two roubles to produce, but we receive, due to subscription contracts signed a year ago, 3.75 roubles per copy.

Unfortunately for post-Soviet journals, the practice in the Soviet Union is to renew all subscriptions at the same time each year, in somewhat the same way Canadians subscribe to concert or theatre seasons.

The math isn't complicated. The journal is bleeding three million roubles a month, roughly equivalent to thirty annual salaries. Like virtually all publishers in the old Union this year, the more *Inostranaya Literatura*'s sells, the bigger its losses.

He explains that after considerable debate the journal's staff has decided to honour its subscriptions. These are, he feels, undertakings, promises. In a country where all certainties, including constitutions and borders, live on borrowed time, it is clear the editor takes pleasure in this act of suicidal honour. They are now busily looking for sponsors. The French Embassy, as always, has a big arts budget, and the Germans seem interested. Where else can your country's writers find a cool half-million new readers? (The Canadian Embassy's arts promotion budget, needless to say, is invisible.) This way the magazine might just stay afloat until year's end and the arrival of revenue from a new subscription campaign at saner (but less affordable) rates.

Somehow, he insists, they must keep going. Recently he has asked the subscription department to prepare a breakdown of the journal's readers, who they are, where they live. He discovers a bit to his surprise that they have six hundred subscribers on Sakhalin Island, with three hundred in the capital and the rest scattered, including three— he holds up fingers—three in a place called Okha. He has looked it up on a map; on the northern coast, an arctic place; a fleck on the map of obscurity, hundreds of kilometres from book stores.

When the great playwright and fiction writer Anton Chekhov had taken his epic journey to Sakhalin by train and riverboat in 1890, a voyage to a place *east* of Tokyo, it had been a world of quiet fishing villages and sadistic penal colonies, where workers ate rotten wood "while the czar's ministers sold the island's salmon and caviar abroad." In 1992 it had already been governed for two years by an economics professor obsessed with the idea of turning Sakhalin into a Russian Hong Kong. Once the Communist Party was turned out of its headquarters, an international business centre had been installed to host "delegations of Japanese businessmen, American oil men, and World Bank economists eager to observe the 'Sakhalin experiment.'" Given that the highly militarised island had been closed even to non-resident Soviets until 1989, this was progress. But already the capitalist revolution was wearing thin as the majority took note of their impoverishment and sky-rocketing corruption. Local officials continued to complain that Moscow bureaucrats were calling all the shots. In 1995 a tragic earthquake would add to local miseries. There is nothing here to reassure editor Lakshyn about the fate of his readers in Okha.

He continues. Who *are* these people? he asks himself. A schoolteacher? A retired army colonel who has always regretted giving up his own promising verses? The village doctor? He doesn't know. But even there, once a month, *Inostranaya Literatura* arrives with the best of contemporary writing, the pitch of the imagination, from all over the globe—Graham Greene, Garcia Marquez, Nadine Gordimer, Spanish poets and Hungarian playwrights and Korean novelists. How, he demands, flinging his arms into the air, how can we just *leave* them there?

In the twin Russian habits of idealistic sentimentality and ferocious despair, there is a good deal of willful blindness. Was this was a *soupçon* of the former? Perhaps. I chose though, as a respite from the pummelling bad news that is the daily bread of Moscow life, to believe in Vladimir Yakovlich Lakshyn, and make of Okha, soon to be musing its way through Updike's urbanities, at least one of the symbols of this Russian year.

*

In August 1993 I had just arrived back in Moscow after a holiday home when a secretary stepped into my office with news, a bit teary-eyed. Did I know that Gospodin (choosing the archaic, formal mode of address) Lakshyn had died?

I had last seen him a month earlier. In the interval I had become one of *Inostranaya Literatura*'s authors—a surprise, unannounced. One of my poems had been translated by poet Bella Akhmadulina, who had major star quality on the literary scene, with records in the shops and appearances on TV. I suspected the magazine was more intent on publishing one of Akhmadulina's rare translations than one of my originals, but they had in any event commissioned two more translations to go with the star piece. Tickled to think of the poems wending their way to Okha and elsewhere, I queried friends as to how they read in Russian. I myself could do little more than puzzle out which line was which; I had no sense of their tone or colour. Upon receiving my copies, I had a call asking me to stop by the office for my payment—in cash of course, in the country without cheques. An owlish elderly woman had politely hauled down a Dickensian ledger, ruled a line under the last entry, and carefully written in my name and the amount of my royalties with a fountain pen before counting the roubles into my hand. The payment was, by local standards, substantial.

Hearing I was in the building, Mr. Lakshyn had passed a message for me to stop by, and we chatted in his dim office for five minutes, alternating between his rusty but

138

correct French and my half-baked Russian. We talked about the weather, poetry, the price of things.

Grigory later told me Mr. Lakshyn was in good health to the end. It was a shock. He was sixty. He had looked older. The heart.

Grigory was by then acting Deputy Editor. The staff went on to hold elections in December to replace Vladimir Lakshyn. When he died, *Inostranaya Literatura* was still appearing on schedule, the staff were all finding second jobs and fellowship stints in England or Japan to supplement inflation-ravaged salaries, and copies of the journal could now be found for sale between the vodka and the ketchup in the kiosks by the metro.

Journal Notes

Last night we saw a dazzlingly staged version of Mikhail Bulgakov's masterpiece, The Master and Margarita. *Written in one of those acts of artistic insanity that continually astonish those approaching the works of the imagination of the Soviet era, the novel was utterly unpublishable throughout the twelve years Bulgakov laboured over it, and did not appear in print until twenty-six years after his death. The story of—well, the story of what? Of Satan himself come to visit Moscow one hot spring afternoon in the heyday of Stalin (who is never mentioned, directly), in the company of a slick, vicious, huge cat named Behemoth (a character now evocative of 1993* businessmeni *sporting shiny suits and bad shaves); of his effect on the worthies of the Writer's Union of the day; of the brilliant and lonely genius known only as the Master writing his perfect book in his flat; of the woman the Master loves in the way he loves his own despair; of a not quite familiar story of Pontius Pilate, his headache, and his tormented encounter with Yeshua Ha-Nozri in sun-fevered Yershalayim. A novel that swings wildly between stony realism and surrealistic abandon, between dark comedy and gay tragedy, all of it prefaced by a haunting quotation from Goethe's Faust:*

"Who art thou, then?"

"Part of that Power which eternally wills evil and eternally works good."

The quote thereby standing as Bulgakov's simultaneous utter condemnation of Stalinist evil and his faith in evil's ultimate helplessness.

Settings range from a cuttingly accurate evocation of Moscow cityscapes in its opening at Patriarch's Pond (a charming square in spite of the decapitation which ends Bulgakov's scene, with a fine outdoor skating rink our kids loved), to midnight flights to the moon. One thing I would have said for certain: it could not possibly be staged.

But in honour of a writer many also consider the best Soviet playwright of his era, it had been done, pioneered by Taganka genius Yuri Liubimov in the eighties, whose work was an ancestor of the present production. And done in such a way as to not only rivet us to our seats for over three hours, but to miraculously encompass the novel's grand oscillations.

In the main hall of the Taganka Theatre the seats were full. The Russian script was flung out at a frenetic pace, as swirling as the staging and difficult to follow. But the fertile athleticism and rich visual symbols in the end generated a strangely moving stillness within the madcap pace and grotesque finale. Throughout the play a morose Pilate watched events from extreme stage-right, from what seemed a cross between an ornate picture frame and a theatre box, occasionally conversing with a lean and calmly suffering Christ who would appear abruptly at his side. A large, sail-like (and shroud-like) black curtain spun on a pivot at stage centre, sweeping scenes and actors on and off like the grim reaper. On stage-left sat a mockup of an old-style Moscow apartment block, where the Master chatted quietly in the madhouse moonlight with a temporarily deranged critic named Ivan Ponyrov and dreamt of Margarita and his lost genius. A giant pendulum-cum-clock hung always at centre-front; characters leapt upon it at times to effect Tarzan-like swinging exits. The brooding Pilate and the lost and crazy Master, sharing our role as spectators, generated a wistful, almost unbearable pathos to help suffuse the gymnastic magic realism and sparkling satire of much of the play with epic grandeur and *an intimate humanity. Not to all tastes. I was bowled over.*

After the last of many curtain calls, the actors had one more level to plumb. The curtain again parted, but this time the stage was bare, and a red brick back wall was exposed. Each member of the cast walked back and picked up different poster-sized photos of Bulgakov which were lying face down on the stage. They leaned them against the bricks to form an instant gallery of black-and-white images of the real Master. Turning their backs to the still-applauding audience, they faced the photos, and began to clap . . .

MARCH

On Novy Arbat, a broad thoroughfare gouged through an ancient Moscow neighbourhood in the 1960s, amidst a mile-long parade of identical kiosks (a retail mode be-

coming increasingly regimented as mafias buy up kiosk empires and city governments regulate appearance—to match a model manufactured by a company owned by city officials...), I saw for the first time a brand new Coca-Cola kiosk. It was in the shape of a giant Coke can, and painted to match.

Westernisation? Hmm. Maybe. Inside the gleaming tube sat a grumpy looking woman with two products on offer: Coke, and long purple coils of kolbassa, Russian sausage.

Today, as the vernal equinox approaches and we begin to think of the possibility of spring, the political crisis—a "crisis" of unrelenting paralysis—seems to be coming to a head. The evening news had Yeltsin's announcement that he will attempt to resolve his long-standing power struggle with Congress by ignoring them, and ruling by decree. Congress is meeting tonight in emergency session; crowds have gathered on Red Square and around the White House (where Congress sits); there is talk of resolutions to impeach the president; there is speculation about the army's loyalties; there are the first grim mutterings about civil war. We check the news more often; we check out the window to gauge the normalcy of traffic flow, to see whether anything looks any different above the Kremlin domes.

My own instinct, tonight at least, is that although Yeltsin's popularity has certainly dimmed (as will the popularity of anyone running Russia this decade), the popular support for the Congress will prove feeble indeed, and this will in the end dissuade all but rhetorical action. I might change my mind tomorrow.

143

Two days later (March 22), there are hints of compromise from the Constitutional Court. It has deemed Yeltsin's actions illegal, without addressing the constitutionality of the 1990 elections that reserved many seats for the Communist Party and led to the Congress's present make-up. But there is no give at all from Ruslan Khasbulatov, the genuinely despicable character who chairs the Congress. I don't think it an exaggeration to say that for Khasbulatov to gain power would be an enormous setback—for Russia, its former satellites, even for the West. But talk of civil war does seem to have receded. General opinion around town is that Congress may well vote to impeach Yeltsin but that Yeltsin will shrug, and there won't be much Congress can do about it—knock on wood—before Yeltsin's planned April referendum. Of course, the various military attachés in the Western embassies may have the wrong contacts inside the army, but I doubt it—all seem sure the high command is determined to stay out of it. But there are moderate-sized demonstrations in the White House neighbourhood, and since the school where Teresa teaches is nearby we are in no danger of becoming smug. Otherwise the city is unchanged; the streets and shops are as busy as ever. Some Russian friends see no reason to doubt apocalyptic possibilities, but interestingly the mocking of Yeltsin by the opposition may be backfiring, leading many who are none too pleased with the president to turn against them.

29 March. Yeltsin narrowly avoided impeachment. Sixty thousand people gathered below St. Basil's, just off Red Square, and waited all through the day while Congress was in session. Yeltsin and Khasbulatov compromised: instead of Yeltsin's plebiscite, fall elections. Congress then in rapid succession proceeded incoherently to: 1) vote against the compromise, 2) fail to impeach Yeltsin, 3) vote not to fire Khasbulatov, 4) pass a resolution in favour of (Yeltsin's?) plebiscite but adding a question to it concerning fall elections . . .

APRIL

There was a dispute over proper change today in the line in front of me at the gastronom's *check-out. A woman has purchased bread, cheese, and four or five cans of unidentifiable vegetables. The cashier rings it up, but the shopper disagrees with the change she receives (change now means hundred-rouble notes—kopecks are as extinct as Czarist bonds). With a dramatic sigh, the cashier totals it again on the cash register. Still, the woman is unconvinced. She holds up tattered roubles, points at the food; the cashier points at her register tape, at the bills in the woman's hand. The argument grows heated, and the woman in line between me and the disputing party begins to contribute* her *calculation of the sums. As far as I can tell she disagrees with both of them.*

Finally the manager arrives with an abacus. He slaps it onto the counter between the combatants. The large wooden beads, about the size of checkers, click back and forth, slapped up and down the wires, all eyes on them. There. The answer is evident. You can see it. The shopper departs immediately, content.

Today, the first real scents and signs of spring. In few places can they be more welcome than here, after six months of steel-wool skies and bitter air and grime. A watery sunlight floated the last snow in swelling puddles. Rivers of melt-water to delight a six-year-old's heart, and mine, coursed into drains. On the long slope of the Ring Road down toward Gorky Park, the sidewalks were crowded with striding Muscovites intent on wading the last slush and first mud in the park's long walkways with a candy floss in their child's hand and a few roubles in their pocket for a glass of Coca-Cola or a bottle of beer. Heavy coats were hanging open. The hardy young women, currently wearing the world's shortest skirts, were displaying new leather jackets above the world's longest legs. There was a rumour the Ferris wheel had been started. Today, almost anything was possible. On the Russian folk calendar this first week of April marks the Orthodox feast of the Annunciation. The custom to celebrate the day "that spring overcame the winter and set about its business" was to buy caged birds in the town market—and set them free.

MAY

On May Day the workers of the world may not be uniting, but, with Yeltsin having won his referendum against the parliament (never quite as stupid as every analyst is convinced he is—they having already forgotten that a month ago they caustically gave him no chance), the hard-liners of all stripes are in a foul mood in spite of the splendid spring weather. In the most violent clash in our almost two years in Moscow, over a hundred people were hurt as

146

marchers battled police lines while trying to advance to Red Square. There are reports of a policeman being killed.

From our windows we watched through the morning as little bands marched up from all directions behind fluttering red banners to congregate under Lenin's gaze on Oktyabrskaya Ploschad, and then march en masse south toward Gagarin Square. While they were gone a massive police presence moved in: they were obviously expecting the marchers to return. In rows six deep, their riot shields flashed in the sun. When we ventured out for fresh air, we discovered truckloads of troops on quiet side streets, sitting tight under canvas. This discreet presence seemed to us far more ominous than the rows of shields. We felt a new kind of shiver. We decided to pass up the rest of our planned morning outing, but cursed a bit: sunshine was a rare commodity in Moscow; to waste it was a sin.

When the demonstrators returned, the sense of menace dissipated. They came back a small and not very lively bunch, perhaps one thousand. Nothing happened. The police had their route north, toward the Kremlin, rather impressively blockaded. They made speeches. The militia watched, with their batons and helmets and shields, getting bored. I got bored too, on a balcony of our apartment block, and went down for a look. On the square a group of teenagers in uniform, clearly conscripts, lounged near their water cannon, watching the strollers with their dogs playing in the park on the edges of the grumbling mob. Most of these passers-by, I realized, did not even glance at the demonstration. They had no opinion. They were pointedly uninterested. It was a lovely May day. May might not have another. Go to Gorky Park and buy a balloon.

147

Ride to Kievskaya on the metro and take an electric train into the countryside. Sit in the sunshine and do nothing.

It felt odd to feel so pleased with the troops. A sports-fan sort of partisanship had snuck up on me. Way to go guys. Stay cool. Solid play. But the Communists and Fascists and Anti-Semites now seemed such a disorganised lot that this felt like cheering for the top dogs, hoping the defending champs would win another Stanley Cup, cheering against the no-hopers. On the other hand, the police and soldiers out here today were, more or less, under instructions from a more or less democratic government, and the government's approach to the events this weekend seemed reasonable even by Western standards, never mind those prevalent in Russia during the previous millennium: let the Leninists and Stalinists and Ultra-Nationalists march, let them make speeches till the elderly doze off, but make clear where they can and cannot go, make clear who is in charge.

I could buy that. The speakers, pathetic as they seemed at this moment, addressed a crowd carrying icon-like pictures of butchers. And had the speakers been commanding the troops there would be no demonstrators. That could be stated with certainty. The power displayed against the protesters was undoubtedly power: crack Interior Ministry troops, the OMON, could be seen here and there, and plenty of those lads had blood on their hands. Legendary for efficiency and brutality, a unit of black-bereted OMON troops had unwittingly spurred the mass movement for Lithuanian independence by gunning down at least a dozen people in Vilnius in 1990. Nowadays OMON colonels say all the right things about democracy. And it is far from okay that OMON murderers serve no time just because they haven't killed lately and are now working on keeping the even more murderous pent up on the square.

Someday, somewhere, raw power—busily corrupting, without doubt, those basically decent people wielding the reins of Russian government in May 1993—might be wished away. But not here, not on this square, not today, at least for all of us less than saints. Give these Stalinist ravers freedom of speech—but grudgingly, and hedge it with the hard men and their sun-dancing riot shields.

This was a surprising set speech from a voice inside me. New characters wanted on stage. They weren't all pretty. But they appeared to be me. I walked back to the apartment. How, after all this time in Russia, could this rather banal glimpse of the iceberg tip of Soviet horror still shock me? I knew better. This wasn't Kansas, Toto, and it wasn't a theme park. For the first time I began to suspect, as they sing in the old Eagles song, that once you've been here you can never really leave.

6

A CLEAN, WARM, WELL-LIGHTED PLACE

She only made it to Moscow once, by chance. In a taxi, scared stiff, she zoomed along the nighttime streets squeaking with frost; she gazed up at the enormous buildings—rearing black chests of drawers, the gloomy castles of vanished titans, gigantic honeycombs crowned with bloody embers standing guard. And in the morning she looked out of the hotel window onto a hushed thaw, the soft, grey day, the jumble of little two-story yellow buildings and annexes pierced by morning lights—muslin is draw back from a small window, a kettle whistles, a grandmother in felt boots entertains her grandson with white rolls—sweet, soft, Russian Moscow!

Tatyana Tolstaya

CINNAMON IN ST. PETERSBURG

Bleary-eyed, faces unwashed and teeth unbrushed, we hovered on a street corner outside the train station and peered down the epic swath of Nevsky Prospekt. St. Petersburg's

150

storied main drag, at eight o'clock on a November morning in 1991, was a dirty, cold, ill-lit place. This it shared with most of the former Soviet Union.

Somehow though, the Communist interregnum had failed to create a uniformly nasty place. Its attempt, via the elimination of as much beauty as possible, via the eradication of those unregenerate purveyors of convenience—small businesses—, via the crushing of variety in buildings, newspapers, theatres, novels, apartments, streets, shops, factories, parks, public statuary, magazines, cars, toothpaste, ties, shoes, speeches, elections, sausage, bookstores, sports stadia, holiday resorts, restaurants, trains, panty hose, suit jackets, chocolate, champagne, bread, and, nowhere near last and nowhere near least, the extermination of the sidewalk café—its attempt to stifle each of life's little pleasures (explaining its odd puritanism) was both the most thorough undertaking of its sort in recorded history and, in the end, hopelessly incomplete. Soul respites, heart redoubts: people had preserved them, like childhood songs giving solace to old age. And because uniformity and continuity starve the human animal, which is stirred by contrast (the less expected the better), the clean, warm, well-lighted places of the end-of-Soviet world are enchantments stronger than any available to citizens of Paris or Vancouver or Hong Kong.

It was our first trip to the masterpiece of planned capitals. An earlier attempt to come up by plane had been thwarted by domestic Aeroflot rules forbidding taking off when it is foggy at the airport of destination. Now it was November; we consoled ourselves with the thought that the lack of *light* at sixty degrees north—the same latitude

151

as the boundary between the Canadian prairie provinces and the Northwest Territories—would be balanced by having the tourist haunts all to ourselves.

We had reached Moscow's Leningradsky Vauxhall by metro just before midnight, kids in tow and accompanied by our friend Milly, a Canadian on temporary work assignment in Moscow. The approaches to the intercity train platforms rose out of the night like one of the darker visions of Dickens. At the metro exit we pushed through crowds of broken and decrepit vendors sitting gloomily on wooden crates before the rotting remains of cabbages or single bottles of beer. It was slick underfoot, a stir of mud and garbage. Two gap-toothed senior citizens in kerchiefs flapped newsprint publications featuring grainy black-and-white photos of snarling naked women in dog collars.

Past this initial gauntlet a broad Sisyphean ramp led up to the trains. In the yellow light of crackling overhead arc lights, dense crowds of exhausted travellers pushed and pulled carts, dragged massive bundles, shuffled up the incline against their own mirror images struggling down. It looked like wartime, refugees on the move, carrying their lives on their backs. We stepped around drunks—probably not corpses—sprawled face down on the concrete, and over gypsy children sitting in bright rags in the slop; we dodged reeling youths demented by vodka, passed ancient women and weary young mothers combatting gravity while buoyant twenty-somethings sauntered past in leather jackets, lighting up Marlboroughs. It was a wet, dark bough. The petals were lost in the mud underfoot. Another fin-de-siècle.

Along the platforms a dozen trains, each a mile long, were filling, emptying, trains arriving from or destined for Yaroslavl, Novgorod, Kirov, Perm, or Archangelsk, thirty-six hours north on the White Sea. Families heaved at outrageous suitcases the size of navy footlockers. Flanges screeched, air breaks hissed, the dim lights spat, the night hung over us and over all of Russia. We trudged down the platform past car after car, deeper into the darkness, until only a thin silent stream of walkers accompanied us. We found our *wagon* (pronounced in the French manner), proffered tickets to its guardian, passed kids over the gap and heaved open the sliding door of our compartment. Clean enough, quiet enough. We sat on the bunks and chatted, bedded down the children as the train slid off its mooring into the night sea and rolled through the suburbs into the pitch countryside, then turned in ourselves, rocked to sleep as we clicked faster and faster north and west.

Now in the grey light of not-yet-morning, with a bitter November wind sailing down Nevsky Prospekt, lugging our bags, we were exhausted. Foolish in the excitement of our first arrival in St. Petersburg, we had consulted maps and guidebooks and deemed the hotel a pleasant walk from the station: why not see a bit of the city along the way, get a real feel for the place? We were glum, starving, needing coffee and a hot shower. Sure, it was six or seven blocks. But we were beginning to understand St. Petersburg's epic scale: each block was an endurance test, five times the length of a Canadian one, lined by closed grey storefronts in the land without corner stores, without cafés, without diners and delis.

When you live in Russia there are various things about Canada you miss all the time. Corner gas stations, *The Globe and Mail*, Montreal bagels and croissants, CBC radio, pedestrian crossings, mown lawns, painted trim, fresh milk in handy cartons. But other deprivations lurk unnoted in dim corners of the brain, waiting to be switched on by an unexpected catalyst.

As we walked, carrying bags and kids, ducking our heads into the stiff wind which was reminding us how close we were to the Gulf of Finland, secretly wishing we had taken a cab and forgone this "experience," we pulled up short. We turned our heads left and right. Looked at each other suspiciously, unwilling to admit possible insanity. Finally we had to admit it, more or less simultaneously. We could smell—did olfactory mirages exist?—wafted on the wind, the unmistakable aroma of *fresh cinnamon buns and strong black coffee.*

A moderately stale plain roll and tepid weak tea would have been more than welcome at that moment, in that place, not that we would have dreamed of finding any to hand even on the main street of a city of four million. But we had not once smelled a cinnamon bun—and this smelled outlandishly like *warm* cinnamon buns just out of the oven— during our months in Moscow. And the sort of places that might be offering cinnamon buns to a chilly November populace did not exist in our mental landscape. It was as unexpected as seeing a palm tree, or a giraffe crossing the street.

A tiny women bent double with age, her back parallel to the ground, swept the dirt of the sidewalk with agonising slowness onto the dirty street, using a short twig broom. A dozen paces ahead of her a man turned, pulled open a door, and disappeared. As the door swung open, the aroma washed over us anew. We salivated.

There, breathed Milly, arm rigid as a good bird dog. *There.*

Our shock deepened. We had *not* stumbled across the entrance to a new five-star Swiss hotel with breakfast-café off the lobby at street level. The door was old, wooden, worn, smoothed by a million hands, a bit grimy. Above it was a standard-issue state store sign, *Buffyet*. I had ducked my head into a dozen such establishments and ducked it rapidly out again. They were normally filthy, hostile, and smelling of last month's sausage and backed-up toilets. This was *strange*. A quick glance in as a patron came out confirmed both that this was the source, and that it was, not surprisingly, packed with customers. Teresa and Milly stayed outside with the kids, given the crowds. I went in. There had to be a catch. Too good to be true.

The establishment had two halves. In one end, a small set of stand-up tables were crowded with folk downing small coffees and devouring cinnamon buns. Closer to me, a cashier's station with a snaking but fast-moving line— almost as if the cashier wanted to serve as many people as possible!—divided the tables from two counters, one selling plump golden cinnamon buns, the other equally splendid-looking cinnamon cake. Between them, with another hefty queue, a woman was preparing coffee by pouring syrup into tiny cups and banking them in trays of sand heated from beneath until they perked to individual perfection. My God, I kept saying to myself, my God.

155

I had been in the Soviet Union long enough to know miracles are transient things—I should move fast. I noted the price on a little card propped beside the buns and nipped to the back of the cashier line. After paying, receipt slip in hand, I moved to the queue where the buns were dispensed. A pleasant woman with powerful red forearms and her hair tied in a checked cloth cut the buns apart with a spatula as each customer came up, and set them onto sheets of paper with tongs. I could actually see the prism of warm air floating above them. When I was second in line, there were eight buns left. The woman in front of me bought them all.

At such crucial moments mental toughness is required, and a careful assessment of the odds. I took a chance; I headed straight to the cinnamon cakes without returning to the cashier queue to turn in my receipt and pay what might be needed to ensure my ticket reflected the exact price of a given number of cakes. I knew full well there was a chance the clerk at the cake counter would refuse to have anything to do with me. The cinnamon cakes were bigger. I wouldn't need five. I calculated. Three would cost just barely less than the price I had paid out for five buns. Often such irregularities provoked fury from clerks. But everyone here looked bizarrely cheerful. And why not? Somehow this state *buffyet* number whatever was *enjoying* its work; somehow someone who cared about quality had accidentally ended up running the place, someone who had fresh cinnamon buns baked every morning using all the ingredients of a good recipe (and not diverting the butter onto the black market, not chintzing on the sugar) for adoring locals. *Tre'e, puzhal'sta*, I said carelessly, as if I were a regular picking up my normal order, taking the soft steaming cakes as I handed over the receipt. The seller frowned. I smiled and shrugged idiotically. I'm a stupid foreigner; have mercy. She shrugged too, spiked the slip of paper onto the nail in front of her, served the next customer.

Hardly believing my luck, hands full, I did a cost-benefit analysis on the cooling of cakes, the length of the cashier queue and coffee line, and the weariness of us all. There was no sense tempting the fates. Just the smell of the caffeine had revivified. I headed out the door.

Later on that trip, and on five or six subsequent visits, we would walk the dazzling thousand rooms of the Winter Palace and its ten thousand masterpieces of world art; explore the dramatic yet intricate squares and archways and canals of Peter's capital; ride hydrofoils out the Gulf to disembark at the sea entrance to Peterdvorets, an imperial palace with hundreds of acres of paths and fountains and statues; find my way through narrow back alleys to the apartment where poet Anna Akhmatova lived in poverty and domestic dismay through the long years of her enforced silence, her "Home on the Fontanka"; stroll past the scores of sculptures amid the trees of the Summer Gardens at midnight as the white June light hovered and held and hovered. But these would have to wait, and these would fade faster in the memory and retain less vivid colours than standing on damp and depressing Nevsky Prospekt with the sun still trying to get up, munching soft, warm, sweet cinnamon cake as slowly as we possibly could.

MARCH IN MINSK

By the time I found myself picking a path between over-flowing garbage dumpsters and a rusted-out car shell half sunk in slush in the decrepit alley leading to 12 Skaryniy Ulitsa and the apartment of Leonid Levin, I was sullen. I had been in Minsk for two days. I was having trouble even trying to do justice to the capital of the new country of Belarus, successor to the Belarussian Soviet Socialist Republic. Drawing closer to the building, I noted a doorway imperfectly filled by a battered rectangle of wood inclining on one hinge and covered with multiple lumpy coats of dark green paint. I peered inside: dim and grimy, it smelled of urine. I wasn't surprised.

There may have been a tourist visiting Minsk for the sheer fun of it in March, 1994, but if so our paths didn't cross. The only other non-staff people I noticed at the almost new but already decaying Belarus Hotel were the leather-jacket set changing money in the lobby, the leather-skirt set pleading to "service" me (for U.S. dollars only—they wanted to say "serve" and were telling the truth only by accident) and a set of short people in track suits in the breakfast room who I eventually learned were Bulgarians and Texans in town for a key international amateur wrestling meet.

At this point, one had to admit, the new nation wasn't off to a flying start. Its populace as a whole did not exactly see the foundering of the USSR as a historical opportunity to be seized. On the contrary, recent polls showed fifty-five percent in favour of putting the old Soviet Union back together. The top priority of those currently in power was to abandon their new currency and join in fraternal rouble union with Moscow. Inflation was so high you had to mentally add a zero to the digits on your bank notes when spending them. If a price tag said five hundred, it meant five thousand—the printing presses couldn't keep up with prices, so a special government decree was issued announcing an invisible zero. Western media, especially *The Economist* and *Time*, routinely cited such polls and such negotiations on lists of incidents proving neo-imperialism in Moscow, but this was doing the Russians too much credit: they had neither the energy nor the desire at this point to scheme against Belarus sovereignty. More important, ethnic nationalism here was an ambiguous and only faintly developed force, and would perhaps be satisfied simply by the subtle name change from Belarussian (that is, White Russian, suggesting a subset of the folk in Russia) to Belarus (White Rus, more accurately denominating a separate branch of the northern Slavs whose early Rus princedoms in places like Kiev and Suzdal were, ethnically and linguistically, a common ancestor). In an era witness to the charms of post-Communist nativism from Bosnia to Georgia to Afghanistan, it was hard to see this as a bad thing; but of course post-Communism in this part of the world was also post-imperialism, so that a perceived lack of local forcefulness easily blended into accusations of craving the overlordship of Big Brother next door. Our flight to Minsk had departed Moscow's Sheremetyeva Airport from a "domestic" gate, and thirty months after independence Belarus passports existed only as gleaming samples passed about at the Ministry of Foreign Affairs.

Ideologically, Belarus was also showing a certain unwillingness to give up on the bad old days. The building housing the parliament bore fresco hammers and sickles above the entrances, and no one had bothered to take down the mammoth Lenin standing out front. This particular statue was one of the most offensive specimens of the sub-genre. The great leader, twenty-five feet tall, was represented leaning slightly forward against a podium, glaring down, bull chest and neck even more exaggerated than usual, apparently haranguing the silly Belarussians for some sin or other and telling the little folk not to be naughty. The calling cards of government officials I met still carried inscriptions like "Deputy Chairman, Executive Committee of the Minsk City Soviet of People's Deputies," or "Committee on National Policy, Supreme Soviet of the Republic of Belarus."

The country *was* in a tough spot. A nation of ten million, it sat on the western edge of the old USSR, sharing borders with a volatile and unpredictable Russian Federation having fifteen times its population, with economically collapsing Ukraine, with newly conservative Lithuania (the first former East Bloc nation to re-elect Communists), and with a Poland undergoing an ambitious and controversial program of economic shock therapy. Since Belarus wasn't causing anybody any problems, and seemed eager to give up its nuclear weapons, it was being studiously ignored. Historically, the Belarussians were northern Slavs who due to geography and history had spent just enough time under non-Slavic, non-Orthodox suzerainty (Polish and Lithuanian mainly) to develop a distinct cultural and linguistic personality before being forcibly reintegrated into the Russian sphere and then subjected to seventy Soviet years of intense Russification. Eighty percent of the population was ethnically Belarussian, and, according to official figures, most of these spoke the language as a mother tongue. But in fact, according to one cultural activist I met, less than one in three actually used Belarussian at home.

Hitler's armies crossed Belarus twice, and the country spent three years behind enemy lines. The devastation was mind-numbing. Estimates vary, but somewhere between one-fifth and one-third of the population was killed during the war. Yet by the time of the USSR's demise it had the highest standard of living in the union, fueled by a plethora of heavy industry exemplified by the famous Belarus tractor. (The tractor factory, which has its own metro stop and thirty thousand workers, contains an assembly line which is quite simply one of the biggest *things*, of any sort, I have ever laid eyes on.) This industrial base was, however, woven into the Soviet and COMECOM web, so that now, from a marketing point of view, it was having to more or less start from scratch. The Chernobyl disaster had dealt another ill-timed blow. Known internationally as a Ukrainian catastrophe, the nuclear plant's rupture had actually deposited a high percentage of its fallout immediately downwind, in Belarus. Almost twenty percent of the country's farmland, and two million of its people, had been affected.

During its first two years of independence, Belarus had suffered a less severe economic decline than most of the former Soviet Union, mainly because it clung zealously to the old ways and their comforting assurance of mere stagnation. But lack of reform, when combined with the disappearance of both its old markets and subsidised raw materials from Russia and Soviet central Asia, was catching up fast with Belarus. Industrial output was plunging, both official and hidden unemployment were rising ominously, inflation was taking off toward hyperinflation, the currency was halving in value monthly.

And the weather, that week, was obscene. The mercury hovered on zero. The entire city—levelled by the Germans and finished off by post-war Soviet architects: there are virtually no tolerable buildings—was composed of grey, poorly built concrete slabs. Fog made it hard to see further than two or three grey buildings away. Grey slush covered streets and sidewalks and parks where grey statues of poets and bloodthirsty dictators stood ghostly above the slushy benches. The line where the fog from the sky and the slush from the ground met was hard to pick out. Each morning when I peered out my hotel window I saw nothing but the insides of clouds. The ground was lost. A damp wind induced suffering from the bones out, but never managed to sweep the shrouding mists away. Occasionally sleet fell, with a cold drizzle for variety at midday.

The hotel had two restaurants. One closed at five, before I was hungry, the other opened at eight-thirty, long after I began to starve. I knew from earlier baptisms into Soviet rites that the latter's hours in practice meant hors d'oeuvres to nibble by nine if you were lucky, and entrees around ten. So just before five I forced myself to eat reheated "beefshteak" and (cold, hard) mushrooms in sour cream—a staple dish which even the most Brezhnevite of restaurants can usually make tolerable—and let myself into my room at five-thirty, with the *deshurnaya,* the floor lady, another Soviet institution the Belarussians were apparently keeping for old times' sake, keeping a keen watch from her desk near the elevators.

Inside it was freezing. I went over to the radiator. By pressing my fingertips firmly against the very bottom of the pipes I could detect a slight warmth. Not enough, however,

162

to perceptibly alter the air temperature anywhere in the room. The TV, a huge bulbous object, gave a flickering single channel: a parliamentary debate, in Minsk, being conducted in Russian. I hoped for some classical music on the radio, but it too was fixed on a solitary station which at the moment was offering military band selections interrupted by long banterings in Belarussian which I could not follow. As even this, the flagship hotel of the capital, had not a single foreign newspaper or magazine on sale, I took a novel from my suitcase, stripped a blanket off my bed to wrap around my legs, propped myself on the couch, and tried to read, with the radio voices on low to ward off the silence. After a while, chilled through, I checked my watch: it was six o'clock, and getting dark.

The other restaurant might have heat, but it wouldn't open for more than two hours. I had earlier checked out the roof-top bar and found it was closed for renovations and appeared to have been for some time; there were a few hopeful hookers outside anyway. There was nowhere but here. I kicked myself for not having picked up one of the astonishingly cheap bottles of vodka I had seen on sale earlier in the day in both of the mezzanine level's two shops. A shot or two might at least have warded off hypothermia. I got up and put on my coat, a heavy calf-length garment suitable for blizzards and, it turned out, for Minsk hotels. I read. Finally, by eight o'clock, I was too cold to continue. I went to bed, after washing up with the ice water coming out of the bathroom taps. I discovered I had forgotten to put soap in my shaving kit; there was none in the room; the shops downstairs sold only the vodka and Snickers bars. I could find only one extra blanket in the cup-

163

board. It would have to do. Perhaps if I lay very still. What a great town.

In the night, I woke up stiff with cold. I wondered if anyone had actually frozen to death in Minsk's best hotel. I leapt out, grabbed the coat, and pulled it down over the blankets as I slid back in. In the morning I was still alive.

Leonid Levin's daughter was accompanying me to their home. I had originally arranged to talk with Mr. Levin, architect and community leader, at the offices of the Belarus Jewish Federation, but as he had been ill the meeting had been switched to the apartment. His daughter had met me and my interpreter Alexander (government issue, but very pleasant) at the Ministry of Foreign Affairs. The apartment was within walking distance, so we sloshed our way through the city the colour of slush to that wasteland alley, and carefully opened the dangling door and went inside. It was dark. The stairwell was utterly unlit. Like the stairwell of every apartment building I had seen in Moscow, it exhaled gloom with the intensity of Kafka: floor of filthy, scarred linoleum, walls of bare, streaked concrete (sometimes dark grey peeling paint was preferred), perhaps an extinct radiator under a decade of dust, wooden stairs warped and cracked with a bannister bearing—without fear of exaggeration—a dozen coats of some irrecoverable dark shade.

We clumped up the stairs, our eyes adjusting but with nothing to see. Not a trace of colour. Not a painting, a plant, a colourful mat, a toy, a bicycle in sight. A cinder bin and a broom leaned against a wall, the prevailing spirits of the place. On the first landing we came to the lift. Elena Levin tapped on the buttons in a perfunctory way, listened

164

for a second, shrugged apologetically at the closed gate, and gestured us on up the stairs, eventually to the fifth floor. All the way up, every inch of wall and ceiling and floor, riser and bannister, was blank, grey, dirty. Litter lay here and there. The whole monstrosity was, I knew, invisible to most eyes here, and was growing invisible even to mine. Such sights gradually made no impression on the conscious mind. They did, however, slowly lay sediments on the heart.

Fifth floor. Elena let us in.

Inside was the soft glow of old lamps. Inside it was warm. Inside, someone was baking, the elevating scent wafting from a hidden kitchen. Inside it was spotless; shoes sat in tidy pairs on a wooden rack just inside the door; the floors appeared to have been polished five minutes earlier.

Leonid Levin was dressed in dark trousers, with a comfortably worn cardigan over a white shirt; slippers on his feet attested perhaps to his illness, or to the perfection of the floors, or both. He shook my hand, and Alexander's, and welcomed us, quite formally, to his home. In his late sixties, Mr. Levin was a man of medium height and slender build, with a strong high forehead and intent, focused eyes shadowed under bushy brows. But his face blended this intensity with a profound inwardness, as if he could combine conversation and contemplation; it was a face that made clear a depth of personal history. Afterward I would remember mainly this, and, more mundanely, his hands: large for his size but with very slender fingers. They rose and fell, sighed and expostulated, throughout our discussion.

The apartment was haven, family museum, nest of comfort, site for hospitality, locus for creativity. Ironically, the Soviet compression of living space into small flats, combined with the near impossibility of moving, of choosing where you might want to reside, could often produce, when combined with a lifetime devoted to family and culture, apartments of extraordinary density, of richness having nothing to do with money. (This is not a general phenomenon: Soviet society was malnourished in ethical, aesthetic, and many cultural spheres. Many apartments are as barren of individuality and taste as Canadian suburbia.) Although large by Soviet standards, being in an older building, the Levin's apartment had, at a guess, only seventy or so square metres. The entrance hall led to an unusually expansive and sunny salon. A narrow kitchen, and, it seemed, one or two small bedrooms lay tucked at the other end of the corridor, to our right as we came in. (Most Soviet families did not have the luxury of rooms serving only as bedrooms—each space had to be multifunctional.) The hallway was a gallery of framed family photographs going back to the last century, of small oil paintings in old frames, of an ornately carved walking stick in a corner, of a tall wooden clock with brass movement.

We passed into the salon—it seemed the only right word—where we were invited to sit on an old, overstuffed couch covered with a crocheted afghan, while Leonid Levin eased himself into an armchair of the sort of comfortableness only thirty years of use can give. (He did not seem to sink down into it, though: his posture, and attention, were buoyant.) While Elena and her mother brought tea and small homemade cookies, we exchanged pleasant-

166

ries, daylight coming in though the wide windows, and I gazed around the beautiful room.

The centre of the floor was covered by a very large, very old Persian carpet, dulled by many years of passage, and no doubt in need of a reconditioning no one in Minsk knew how to give. On two long walls, glass-doored wooden cabinets with gleaming handles and hinges held a library of thousands of books; the shelves within were pleasantly cluttered, the collection of a family that liked to organise their books but was prevented by regular new additions, and by continuous reading and rummaging, from maintaining perfect order. Oil paintings were crowded into every available spot in the European manner, even above the doorways. Lining all four walls, on a high shelf mounted two feet from the ceiling, was a formidable collection of plates: fine china, ceramic, stoneware, some painted, some plain but richly coloured and textured, most classic, some avant-garde. One I noticed, a black square with narrow red rectangles, wouldn't have looked out of place in a Kandinsky exhibit. Many appeared very old.

Near one wall stood an upright piano, its top heaped with scores. Dark instrument cases—a violin, a viola, perhaps a French horn?—leaned in the shadows beside it. Centring the space was a very large, somewhat low table in a light coloured wood, perhaps pine, that gave airiness to the whole room. Here was where the architect worked when he was at home. Large sheets were laid out; blueprints lay in long mauve rolls; heavy books were piled at one end. But someone in the family also painted: I noted one of the wonderful portable easels with attached paint box that can be found in any Soviet art shop set on one of the chairs, with sketch pads and crinkled tubes of oils on the table in front of it.

Leonid Levin was lighting a pipe and gazing over my head out the window and talking about his work, his community, the latest government, about nationalism and unemployment, new synagogues and emigration, Israel, Sognut (the organisation assisting and promoting emigration to Israel, a group generating mixed feelings in Jews of the Soviet successor states), multiculturalism, the arts, Communism, capitalism. We sipped our milky tea and nibbled home baking. This was a home, a culture, centuries deep and steeped in hospitality, music, religion, art, architecture, literature.

But Leonid Levin was well acquainted with horror. The heart of the Pale of Settlement under the Tsars, Minsk was from the fifteenth to the twentieth centuries home to one of the largest, wealthiest, most prolific Jewish communities in the world. The population was at least one third Jewish; the city of Minsk alone had over one hundred synagogues. Anti-Semitism was mild, at least by the standards of Europe. This community was murdered en masse in the German Holocaust; perhaps seventy percent died in the camps. Stalin repressed those who were left: at one time not a single synagogue remained open; now there was one.

Hitler's armies inflicted uncountable atrocities. Eventually, a partisan guerilla movement arose, trying in small ways to strike back. In reprisal the Germans doubled their ferocity, particularly in the countryside, where it was assumed the underground was given cover. At least a hundred and eighty-six Belarus villages were torched. Most, like the village of Khatyn just outside Minsk, were completely destroyed, the inhabitants burned in their homes, every house gone. In Khatyn's smouldering ruins, all that remained standing were a few stones, a few skeletal chimneys of vanished cottages. In a Minsk apartment, I tried to think about removing a village from the face of the earth. A village is like a tree, growing for centuries, tied to the earth, complex yet one entity. Making certain that every single house of a village was destroyed represented, as well as anything, the spirits of both Hitler and Stalin.

After the war, it was decided to create a memorial at Khatyn for all the annihilated villages of Belarus. (This decision was not without controversy: some contend the choice of Khatyn was designed to blur the public memory of unmemorialised *Katyn*, where Stalin's KGB slaughtered thousands of Polish army officers.) Mercifully, a sword-bearing statue of Victory, a triumphant monolith such as stands in Tblisi, Kiev and other Soviet cities, was not deemed appropriate. Here, there was only loss. Instead, the memorial's designer instructed that stones be gathered, laid one on top of the other. The charred remains were cleared away. The wind was left to moan in a small forest of forlorn chimneys having no houses in which to give warmth, among half-built walls of blackened stones with no yards to enclose. Ashes from the hundred and eighty-six burned villages were brought from all over the country and scattered on the soil. Bells were set upon the stone columns; the wind tolls them endlessly.

A man who made a home for phantoms, the designer of the Khatyn memorial, talked on from his worn chair about community councils, the future of Belarus Judaism, of State Ministries of Nationalism, about his optimism, about

Vladimir Zhironovsky. Leonid Levin wanted to know if we needed more tea, if we could stay a little longer. We could. We did.

LITHUANIAN HEAT

In March 1992 it was invigorating to be in Vilnius, the charming, upbeat, and history-soaked capital of a newly independent yet ancient nation. But it was freezing. Lithuania had paid one brutally simple price for its pivotal role in the crumbling of Gorbatchev's power and his Soviet empire: indomitable but impecunious, with little hard currency in reserve, and with a giant Russian neighbour now little inclined to subsidise the standoffish Baltic states with cut-rate rouble oil, the pipeline taps had been turned off. Luckily, the blankets on the beds on our Intourist hotel room near Gediminas Square at the city centre were thick and insulating. We sat on the couch with them wrapped around our knees, cocooned for survival.

It was just after lunch. Out for a late morning stroll through the seven-hundred-year-old streets of the city's medieval quarter—its narrow cobbled lanes and half-timbered houses constitute, along with beautiful walled Tallin, the best preserved district from that period in the Soviet Union—we had gotten thoroughly chilled in a two-degree wind that felt as though it had come straight off the Baltic Sea a hundred miles east. We had taken to carrying the children not so much because they were foot weary as for the benefits of combined body heat. In search of thawing, we had checked the doorways of a few restaurants. The interiors seemed only a degree or two warmer than the exteriors. They were mostly empty, and gloomy. Finally we settled on a cavernous Soviet-style eatery and sat numbly through lunch with our hands around our borscht bowls to get the feeling back. Hurrying to the hotel, with a few flakes sifting out of leaden skies, we found our room a balmy five or six degrees. We tucked both kids into one bed for a nap, heaped them with covers, grabbed some more blankets for ourselves, and sat hip to hip on the sofa, awkwardly trying to hold the travel guides we were looking through outside the blankets without letting too much draft in.

There was lots to read about. The city had splendid medieval, Romanesque, Baroque, and classical Enlightenment buildings, all of which an energetic and friendly populace seemed to be busily cleaning and painting and repairing. Perhaps the most astonishing was the monumental high-Baroque church of Saints Peter and Paul, one of the few Catholic churches that had not been converted into a museum or warehouse—or simply demolished—during the long Soviet occupation. This church had a stucco interior, but that is common enough in the Mitteleuropa that Lithuania was at one time very much culturally a part of—for me, at least, the church prompted flashbacks to Salzburg. It was the scale and intricacy of that interior that made it one of a kind: the inner space of Saints Peter and Paul enacts a cosmos in dazzling white stucco on a scale with that sculpted into the stone of the Gothic cathedrals of France and England. One writer inventively described the effect as transportation "into the heart of a perfectly iced wedding cake," but this fails to capture both the grandeur and the vast high-realism canvas of divinity and humanity that its *two thousand* plaster sculptures compose.

History, that is disaster, had visited Vilnius all too frequently during its many centuries—though the high-wire act of gaining independence in the preceding twenty-four months had, for once, constituted history without catastrophe, if not entirely without bloodshed. Now a compact and gracious capital of six hundred thousand, with the dreary Soviet apartment blocks relegated for the most part to the periphery, Vilnius was at least a thousand years old, and had been an important city for over seven hundred. The dramatic town square at the centre, dominated by the fourteenth-century castle that looms on a steep overlooking hill, is named for the Grand Duke Gediminas, who first made the city a capital in 1323. This capital was destroyed by the Teutonic Knights in 1377, annexed by the Poles in 1579, occupied by the Russians in 1655, stormed and overrun by Sweden in 1702 and 1706, given back to the Tsars in a treaty of 1795, occupied by Napoleon's *Grande Armée* in 1812, smothered by the armies of the Kaiser in World War One and Hitler in World War Two, and ceded to Poland between the wars. Its university was closed for eighty years after 1830, following a nationalist uprising, and its language banned from use in the 1860s. In the intervals between these events it merely had the standard allotment of fires and plagues. It had also, especially during the fifteenth and sixteenth centuries, become a leading centre of printing, and of Lithuanian, Belarussian, and Polish culture in general. For much of the century preceding the Soviet occupation, the city had again become synonymous with arts, scholarship, and a vibrant intelligentsia—such as one sees in some of the poems of the Polish Nobel Laureate, Czeslaw Milosz.

The movement for independence, never far below the surface, had gathered steam in earnest through 1987 and 1988, as it became increasingly clear that Gorbatchev was losing control of the *perestroika* and *glasnost* whirlwind he had unleashed. By spring 1989, the republic's parliament had declared Lithuania "sovereign" (as had Estonia and Latvia), though this was a somewhat ambiguous act given that the Soviet constitution said more or less the same thing. Though Lithuania would be, in 1994, the first Soviet Bloc country to democratically put Communists back into power, by 1989 there were no popular politicians left willing to associate themselves with the Party in Moscow; the popular front Sajudis was gaining momentum daily.

The progression to freedom was calm, non-violent, and scrupulously well-timed. As one journalist pointed out, the movement's most effective tactic was quoting Gorbatchevian rhetoric back at the Kremlin and putting the content of his fine speeches into practice. This drove Gorbatchev crazy.

In 1991, with the great reformer losing his grip and beginning to lash out like the trapped bear he was, the Kremlin made a last clumsy attempt to strangle the infant nation in its cradle. The propaganda and intimidation campaign the KGB had run throughout 1990 in an attempt to discredit Sajudis—arresting draft dodgers, seizing public buildings, sowing anti-nationalist fear amongst the Russian, Polish and Jewish minorities (in fact, once independent, Lithuania would prove a model of inter-ethnic tolerance)— had failed. So on January 13, 1991, a KGB storefront group called the National Salvation Committee tried to take control, with Interior Ministry tanks in support. At the central television tower, which they had occupied in a foreshadowing of the October 1993 events to come in Moscow, the KGB and OMON Interior Ministry black berets shot into the crowds and crushed other protesters under tanks, killing at least fourteen and injuring hundreds.

But as in the coup attempt against Gorbatchev later that same year, the old guard no longer seemed to know how to run a terror show. Gorbatchev's reforms had created too many loose threads for any one authority to gather them quickly up again. Pro-Sajudis newspapers continued to publish. The TV station in Lithuania's second city, Kaunus, boosted its signal strength and broadcast CNN and BBC footage of the thuggery to the entire republic. The newly independent media in Moscow were doing the same thing, while reformist deputies in the Soviet congress were screaming at Gorbatchev to call off the dogs in Vilnius. The *Moscow News* ran a front page editorial referring to "criminal acts" in Lithuania, and nobody touched its printing presses or its editors. (Those who rightly condemn Gorbatchev for allowing the Lithuanian bloodshed need also to remember this clear evidence of his non-totalitarian instincts.)

The Lithuanian independence drive was put on pause—though with thousands of patient demonstrators camped out around a parliament and TV tower now guarded by frightened Red Army conscripts, it was difficult to say who was imprisoning whom—but only, as it turned out, for a few months. By autumn Lithuania would be an independent state already mapping out strategies to place it back into a Europe which it felt, historically, to be its natural home. In time, it hoped, it would join the European Union, maybe even NATO.

When the children woke we decided we had to get moving again to generate warmth. The university seemed as good a destination as any. During the sixteenth century, Vilnius had been a cultural centre whose influence was felt throughout the region. One of the earliest printing presses east of Prussia was set up in 1525. Among other texts, the first book printed in the Belarussian language was produced there. Toward the end of the century, with the city under Polish rule, Jesuits established the early foundations of what would become its famous university, still operating today, in its fifth century.

We bundled John into the stroller, scarved and booted and mittened all four of us, and went out into the dimming midafternoon light. It had been sleeting; now, with the temperature dropping further, the streets were white with ice, the buildings highlighted with hoarfrost. We walked as quickly as we could given the slick footing. Although it was barely below zero, if felt much colder. The air was damp. Rather than emerging toasty from a warm interior, we were chilled through in advance. Our route, although only a dozen blocks, took us past streets of three or four different centuries, of three or four distinct cultural epochs. The ornate geometry of gracious classical facades, with their stress on extension, on elongation, the repetition of the elements—windows, portcullis, identical elevations on each of three stories, sculpted window bays, intricate cornices—drew the eye along the street to the next facade with its own repeated variations: a stately pacing of thought, human scale intimations of an orderly infinity. Given Lithuanian history, such buildings held a certain brave (or foolish?) pathos.

Here, without the frost, we might have been in Italy—or in St. Petersburg's back streets.

Around the corner, colder still, stamping our feet and clapping our arms, it was the seventeenth century: Baroque, almost (but not exactly) Germanic, in amazing combinations of red brickwork, browned by centuries. The effect was of a fertile inventiveness of *facets*—how many ways can you lay a brick—but retained an elemental squareness of overall structure, within which the bricked walls and bays and innumerable ornamentations were executed by the turning and trimming and halving and quartering of brick faces. Solidness, with humour for the gaze, for a gaze not going anywhere, settled in place, uplifted but crafty and patient, a textured body with time and energy of a slow-burning variety. The street, in this block, was suitably cobbled.

Down the next alleyway there was first an anomalous two-story wood and plaster building in ochre-tinged yellow with white trim, a Moscowish nineteenth-century import. But then, past a crook in the narrowing lane, we met the Middle Ages: small houses and shop fronts with walls painted in dark green, half-timbered rich oak doors and shuttered narrow windows, overhanging second floors; arched doorways between buildings leading into ancient courtyards.

On a slender plinth at the meeting of two lanes, there was a small modern sculpture of Mercury—balanced on one toe, febrile, about to dash off. His graceful energy and naked limbs only served to counterpoint the leaden chill pulling on our heavy feet. Once tired, the winter tourist's natural response of *Let's head back* came into our heads; we had to remind ourselves that "back" was a veritable icebox. Onward.

176

We found the first ancient buildings of the university. Penetrating into the quadrangles, we forgot the cold for a few minutes while we focused on the intricacy of the buildings and used signboard maps to identify the various faculties. At one point a low archway of age-blackened stone took us out onto a busy street of nineteenth-century buildings climbing a steep slope. We seemed to have left the late Middle Ages, and the university. A thick pablum of slush covered the sidewalks here; pushing the stroller was a bit like negotiating a beach. Dubious, we gazed glumly up the hill. Unfortunately, behind us the street was a cul-de-sac, and retracing our steps would have felt like giving up.

The cold was inside our coats, moving up and down our sleeves, next to our skin, in our bones. While shops were a little warmer than it was outside, inside the shops you couldn't keep moving. The hotel room was hopeless. I picked up Caitlin again, who was concluding, rightly, that her parents had abandoned common sense.

About halfway up a man coming down the street toward us turned left, climbed two steep steps, pulled open an old wooden door and disappeared inside. The door swung shut slowly behind him as we drew level with the doorway. We went on a few steps before stopping, before what we had seen and felt sunk in. We had been given a glimpse of muted, pleasant lighting, as of candles or a hearth, perhaps of wood and tapestries; and we had smelled coffee—and was that chocolate? and beer? And had we heard, unless it was masochistic imagination embellishing old memories, cups clinking, a scrape of chairs on wood, and felt a great gush of warm air . . .

I turned back and examined a small newly painted sign set into a niche of the stonework beside the door. Lithuanian nationalism, unfortunately for me at this moment, was starting to eliminate Russian. Two lines of text in Lithuanian. A private club? Faculty lounge of the university? Did the sign say "Members Only"? Having little in common with the authors of travel books, who seem never to experience doubt, hesitation, shyness, or a certain WASPish reserve, my reflex was to shrug and turn away, plod on. But Teresa had the look of a feverish marathoner seeing relief swim into view. I raised my eyebrows. With eminently sound reasoning—if based on desperation—she said: The worst they can do is ask us to leave. And, I added, we will just smile brightly and troop out like stupid tourists. Which we were.

As North Americans, we had to consciously remind ourselves to seize the day, had to keep the phrase on hand to balance off our pampered senses, which by training saw no reason to get excited most of the time. The former Soviet Union was in this respect improving our living skills.

Within was a student coffeehouse, a coffeehouse that would have been perfectly at home in Heidelberg or Vienna. In a city with harshly rationed electricity, gas, and oil, the first remarkable feature of this place of wonder was a large multihooked coat stand shaggy with garments. People were *taking off their coats.* It was pleasantly, cheerfully, cosily *warm.* It gradually became clear why. The coffeehouse, with rich velour drapes in front of its tiny-paned windows, with dark floral wallpaper above wooden wainscotting, with low oak-beamed ceilings and tiffany lamps, consisted of two snug rooms filled with patrons.

Between them, in front of us, was the bar, with a barman in dark trousers and white shirt, currently percolating coffee and getting sweets onto plates for the waitress (who turned to smile at us!). He was backed by an array of bottles—liqueurs mostly, and vodka. The rooms' small size, their densely clustered wooden tables bearing multiple candles in bowls, allowed the open spaces to be warmed by the crowd itself. The smells, the textures, the friendliness, the warmth, were all heavenly, the seventh heaven of the Unexpected Blessing.

We had to wait for a table. As if we minded. This was a Warm Place. We would stay as long as decently possible, try to defrost our muscles. After a little while a pleasant waitress stooped to greet the children, found us a place, took an order, scrounged up an extra chair for Caitlin. Even the kids would not grow impatient here, as it turned out, while mom and dad lingered over a second cup of coffee: They had discovered that the place sold *chocolate bars.* Students and professors came and went, doffing scarves and heavy sweaters in the little warm rooms, chatting economics and politics and whose girlfriend was standing up whose boyfriend, sometimes in Lithuanian, sometimes in Russian. We stayed a long time. I think I am a little warmer to this day.

THE TRAIN FROM KIEV

The first time I had visited Ukraine, a few months after independence in March 1992, the vast dining room of Kiev's Intourist hotel had hired four musicians—equipped with synthesisers, electric pianos and a peroxide blonde with a short, tight skirt and heavy thighs—to recreate live ver-

179

sions of muzak elevator hits. They were good at it. The attempts of stereo designers over many decades to capture the sensation of live musical performances in electronic reproduction had now come full circle: we had piped-in music in-house, our very own authentic muzak in the flesh, for our dining pleasure.

After dinner, alone in my room looking out over the light-scattered hills of the city, I put on the radio's pre-set single station. Frank Sinatra was singing "Chicago, My Kind of Town."

Even though I subsequently learned to like Kiev (pro-nounced *Keev* by locals)—its steep streets climbing up and down the lush hills on the banks of the Dnieper; its thou-sands of chestnut trees with their millions of candelabra blooms in spring; its delightful collection of truly eccentric buildings specialising in howling gargoyles, Grecian lads holding up the roofs, and fairy-tale cornices; St. Sophia Lavra's nineteen gold cupolas and ancient iron floor, the interior almost unchanged since its eleventh-century per-fecting by craftsmen from Byzantium as Prince Vladimir was mass-baptising his subjects in the river below—on this occasion, my fourth visit, I just wanted to get out.

The week's work had been thrown into disarray from the start when, on the Sunday evening back in Moscow, I had learned my flight was cancelled, as were, it would turn out, most flights to Kiev for an entire month. The country had exhausted its supplies of jet fuel. I obtained a ticket for the Monday night train, meaning to squeeze five days of appointments into four—but that came with the territory. More ominously, only a one way ticket could be arranged.

But if in the post-splintering era transport links had been badly gnarled, they had generally not completely fallen apart, and I was by now used to worrying about return tickets after arrival.

Yet attempts to procure one were failing as the week wore on. An embassy staffer had put through phone calls for an overnight berth to Moscow: confidently on Tuesday, with determination throughout Wednesday, with stern Soviet-era persistence on Thursday. There were no tickets. In exasperation—I missed the family and had no desire to spend the weekend—I fumed *Fine, if I have to stay over until Saturday I have to.* The secretary shook her head sadly. There were no deluxe berths for Friday night; there were no standard ("hard") berths either; or for Saturday; or for as far ahead as the ticket office was taking bookings. There were no tickets. Period. With the flights cancelled, the four huge trains per night were full. Invoking diplomatic necessity had failed. Besides, my official accreditation to Ukraine was a thing of the past. There were no tickets.

A Moscow embassy truck bringing in technicians and supplies was heading back on Sunday. If need be I could spend an extra two nights at my beloved Intourist and be squeezed into an already full cab. For a mere sixteen-hour drive. By all accounts the roads were even tolerable in some regions.

First, however, I was advised to talk to Misha, the embassy messenger. Official channels had failed. But Misha, it was suggested, knew the workings of Kiev like a Swiss watchmaker knows spindles and hairsprings. He could get anything, given time and a small hard-currency stake.

When I tracked him down, Misha shrugged like Pierre Trudeau. Of course he could get me a ticket; did he look like an imbecile? It was in pursuing such shrugs, in the untying of knots, that one earned enchantments—or at least the pleasures of making do—in the old Imperium. It was also an insight into the structure of existence: participating in it did not necessarily give pleasure, although the truly expert could find that too. Rather, it earned a sensation of oneness with fate's whimsy. It was existential; it was the opposite of alienation. Therefore it was dangerous, hard to change, addictive. It was the way the ancient Greeks felt when they had outwitted a sleepy god.

Where on earth could he get tickets? On the steps of such and such a building, on street Z, there was a little *rynok*, a ticket market. No one in their right mind, these days, would try to get a train ticket at the ticket office. Out of the question. Not with the planes grounded and the trains full to begin with. Deluxe berths were not do-able. It wasn't like his wife's brother was in parliament or something. But if one spot in a four-berther was acceptable, he would be happy to pick it up for me.

Then he warned, solemnly, that it would be expensive, would require hard currency. The Ukrainian coupon was worth only a fraction of the nearly worthless rouble.

Given that I was no longer accredited to Ukraine and was paying standard foreigner rip-off rates of two hundred U.S. a night at the Intourist, whatever I paid would be a bargain for the taxpayer. I gave him a hundred-dollar bill and said *pay what it takes.* He held the note like an insulting letter. I didn't maybe have a ten?

A damp dark was falling when I arrived at the train station Friday evening. Though I was accustomed to the endurance tests of Soviet and post-Soviet existence, of the weariness of those trapped on that particular stage, the sight that greeted me still shook me to the core. With no flights to anywhere, and hopelessly overbooked trains, the station had the look of a wartime exodus with no transport, of a refugee camp with no Red Cross. The great central hall was paralysed with blockaded queues. Families were camped out on every inch of floor. Many had clearly been there for days; trunks had become benches, a dirty blanket a bed. The ill or deranged or weak, pushed out of better locales, slept stretched out on the broad staircase leading to the upper walkways over the tracks, a thousand feet stepping over their oblivious heads. Their facelessness was profound. Mothers nursed infants while husbands with toddlers in tow foraged for cabbage pies. Vendors had set up bread sales on the bannisters. Lines hundreds of people deep receded from a ticket office wicket that appeared to have been boarded up since Brezhnev. Some sort of rumour, no doubt, had swept the crowd suggesting it would open tomorrow, or next week.

But I had dollars, so I had a ticket. With enough time I could get through the dense lethargic mob, step over the prone bodies on the stairs, and, on the overhead walkways, find a few square feet of bare cement in the near complete darkness—few lights were working—to await the arrival of my train. It was very late coming. I stood, then sat on my bag in fifteen-minute turns, crammed between a pair of elderly women speaking a country Russian I could barely follow, and a six-year-old sleeping on her father's knee—her head kept flopping against my thigh, her father kept apologising, I kept saying *neechivo,* no matter. In that brief bracket of time my legs began to cramp, my patience to fray, my spirits to founder. I was a true amateur.

When the train pulled in and the hordes attacked it, I grew nervous in spite of myself. One had to travel with cash here, and I had four hundred U.S. in my wallet, a good annual salary in Ukraine at the moment. Although my old grey overcoat was moderately shabby by Canadian standards—a state I was pleased with in the context—my nice tweed cap and solid boots made me stick out like a sore thumb, and of course as soon as I opened my mouth I would be a foreigner, and foreigners were rich. Stories of robberies on trains were legion, and I was about to be locked in with three random berthmates for a twelve-hour over-night trip. It would be fine, I kept telling myself. I could take a top bunk, cocoon myself in the bedroll, put on the little reading lamp, and keep to my nest until we were on our way, then try to sleep.

My travelling companions in *coupye* number six, *vagon* five, would, it turned out, have none of this. I was the second—well, third—to arrive: a slender young woman was seated on one of the bottom bunks with her five-year-old perched beside her, heels swinging back and forth, munching on a biscuit.

—*Vsdrasvyutiya,* I said.

—*Vsdraz,* she smiled, and elbowed the child, who quickly piped her own hello.

I heaved my suitcase onto the bunk above her head, shed my overcoat and swung it after the suitcase, then hauled myself up. I was still trying to arrange myself in the narrow space between wall and edge, mattress and ceiling, when the young woman stood up.

—*Mina zavut Elena.* She then held up the grinning girl with blonde pigtails. *Yeyo zavut Maria.* She was speaking Russian, not Ukrainian.

—*Mina zavut David. Ochin rad paznakomitis.*

—*Veuiy v' Anglia?*

—England? *Nyet. V Kanadye.*

Was I hungry? Did I want a cookie? No, really, I was fine. Thanks.

Elena looked about nineteen, but I supposed she was at least a few years older. Her thin blonde-brown hair fell onto her shoulders; her face was open and pale, her green eyes lively, a smile always about to appear. She was wearing a hooded sweat-top and blue jeans, and both she and her daughter had shed their boots and donned knitted slippers. I noticed that Maria was holding up a soggy cookie in my direction. I smiled and shook my head. The offer-of-food as key to social interaction had been cemented into place early.

The compartment door lurched open with an exuberant bang. Two young men entered, at a guess twenty or twenty-two, no doubt students at one of Kiev's numerous universities or polytechnics. They were both of average height, with sandy brown hair. Igor, as the self-evident leader of the pair, soon introduced himself. He had a self-confident air: you would like him, he would like you, probably you could do each other a favour or two. It turned out Igor and Pavlo were brothers, though apart from their hair it was clear Igor had inherited his broad brown face, and Pavlo his narrower gaze with skin prone to acne, from

185

opposite sides of the family. They tickled Maria, bantered with Elena about the child's beauty, slung their bags onto their bunks, arranged their things, stripped off leather jackets. Igor and Pavlo spoke Ukrainian between themselves, Russian with Elena. These choices may have corresponded to ethnicity, but I was far from sufficiently expert to be sure: Russians and Ukrainians may be able to distinguish each other by appearance, most of the time, but then no doubt Danes have no problem identifying a visiting Swede. They were delighted to meet a Canadian I was assured, and once it was established that my poor Russian exceeded their few words of English and non-existent French, Russian became the lingua franca of *coupye* number six. Ukraine suffered one more small colonization.

I got out my book as the train gathered speed on the long bridge spanning the Dnieper. With everyone trying to preserve power, the scattering of lights was dim and yellow on the high bluffs above the river, like campfires in the woods, as if Kiev had in the past two years slipped back a bit into its fifteen-century history. The city's legends insist, quite reasonably, that these lush and dramatic hills were responsible for the origins of the ancient town, sometime in the fifth century, when the three brothers Kiy, Shchev and Khoriv, travelling along the Dnieper with their sister Lybed, were so taken with the beauty of the wooded slopes that they landed and decided to settle there. The gigantic statue of Victory, in memory of the liberation of the city in 1943 after a two-year occupation, could be seen in silhouette from the train windows, crowning the hilltop.

With the trip underway, Elena and Igor, who had first met fifteen minutes earlier, set about making the *coupye* a

home, working in tandem as if the trip had been exten-
sively pre-planned.

—Come down, David, said Elena, while Igor put up
his hand to assist. It's time to eat.

Eat? It was eleven o'clock. Thank you very much,
it's not necessary, I'm fine. They ignored my words, got
me down, sat me on the bunk next to Elena and Maria, and
began to scrounge in rucksacks. They were so reassuring
about the quality of my Russian, and so scathing about
their own English, that they soon had me half-convinced I
had the eloquence of Pushkin. It is difficult to say what I
actually said, horrid to speculate what precisely my declen-
sions implied my nouns were doing, what exactly my verbs
of motion—in Russian, nightmarish tangles of multiple con-
jugations and triplicate aspects with replicating nuances—
suggested about my comings and goings. But they continued
to nod agreeably, laugh uproariously, assure me they understood perfectly.

Elena spread what appeared to be a tea-towel on the
small table fixed to the wall under the window. Chinking
plates emerged from Pavlo's bag, while Igor produced a
huge knife that would have pleased a butcher. Elena had
tomatoes and cucumbers and a golden crusted loaf of white
bread. These were welcomed by all, but Elena and Maria
positively clapped their hands with delight when a grinning
Igor pulled a thick foot-long coil of *kolbassa* (sausage) and
a block of cheese from his bag. I was feeling a bit like the
rich man in the New Testament parable: there was certainly a moral in this story, and it was pointed directly at
me. The others seemed oblivious to such considerations
though, and it soon became apparent that the only way I

could fail utterly was to have anything less than a wonderful time in the living room of their hospitality. I noticed that no one was saying "help yourself." Elena had not offered to share her tomatoes with Pavlo and Igor, and Igor had not suggested Maria have some *kolbassa.* It was all self-evident, sedimented in a layer of the subconscious I did not possess. I had underestimated Jung. Hospitality of this sort exists among British-stock Canadians, but it functions at the level of deliberation, and is dependent on mood, convenience, contexts of "feeling comfortable" with someone, of intimacies, friendships, family ties.

—*Borgia moy,* Pavlo was saying with disgust, as he continued to rummage in his Adidas gym bag. He looked up, defeated.

—*Problyem?* I asked, hoping I could help.

—*Stakan nyet.*

No glass. I didn't have a spare one on me. I hadn't as yet noticed anything to put *into* a glass, but Igor was at this moment standing two crystalline bottles of *Stolichnaya* on the table. All that was needed was to light a candle. I noted there were two bottles of vodka and only four adults, one being me. The mathematics were daunting. Well, a few sips wouldn't kill me if they insisted.

Igor was not discouraged for long by the forgotten tumbler. The resolving of such situations was crucial to his self-identity, given his age and gender and race. He was not about to reduce us all to swigging from a bottle: that was no way to ingest the elixir of the gods. Jerking open the door, he left the compartment to forage up and down the car for a loaner. In a few minutes he was back with a smallish glass, about six ounces or so. Now preparations could begin in earnest.

Mysteriously, there were enough plates for everyone, though I didn't see how my presence could have been anticipated. These were laid out, half on top of one another on the tiny table. Tomatoes were quartered. Cucumbers were sliced, without being peeled, in the local manner. Bread was sawn. Pavlo worked on the cheese and *kolbassa*, he and Elena taking turns with the knife. Whenever Maria grew impatient, a disc of cucumber was popped into her complaining mouth. I understood that protesting I had already eaten a big supper, wasn't really all that hungry, would have been ignored and perhaps misinterpreted, so I restricted myself to multiple *spasiba*s when my heaped plate was presented to me. I had nothing else to offer.

But I did! It said something not very complimentary about my culture, or perhaps just about me, that my brain in such a situation had not automatically done an inventory of my suitcases for possible contributions to the *fête*. I got up so fast, with such an enthusiastic expression, that the others were startled, apprehensive. Wait—wait—I managed. Don't start. Just a second. I climbed up, and with my feet dangling down in their faces searched my bag. Yes. I thought so. One large apple, from Kiev's Bessarabia Market, one granola bar from a hard currency shop back in Moscow, and one Snickers from a Kreshchatic Street kiosk (they were still a novelty in Kiev).

Pavlo slapped me on the arm as if I had produced a smoked sturgeon from a top-hat. Maria's eyes went from the Snickers bar—fifty cents for me, a labourer's day's salary in Kiev—up to her mother's face, and back to the chocolate. The apple was sliced in half with Igor's sabre and added to Elena and Maria's plates, the chocolate bar was soon melting in Maria's mouth and hands, and the granola bar—a curious object—was tucked into Elena's bag against future hunger pangs. We ate.

Between mouthfuls I answered a dozen questions about my work, about Canada, about what I thought of Kiev, how I would compare it with Moscow, about the odds of a visa since they would certainly like to visit Canada some day, and, from an intent Igor, about what I had seen of computers, printers, diskettes, modems, and software in Moscow shops. My inability to quote prices, brands, and store addresses seemed to diminish me a little in his eyes, but since he was essentially kindhearted he was already forgiving me this shortcoming. My Russian in dire need of a rest, I managed to divert the subject of the conversation to them.

Elena, it turned out, was from Moscow—sort of. She had grown up there, although she had been born in Crimea during her father's navy service—he was Russian, her mother a Russian-speaking Ukrainian. Her parents were now divorced. (Broken families are sadly rampant in the former Soviet Union, a product of overstressed two- or three-job families, miniscule apartments to exacerbate tensions and magnify incompatibilities, quick and easy divorce laws, alcoholism, general social decay, an exhausting and misery-inducing economic system, and other causes too subtle to guess at.) Her mother had moved back to Kiev, where her parents lived, and remarried. Elena's in-laws had an unusually good (four room!) apartment in Moscow, and Elena and Maria lived with them now. Her husband

Sergei was still working as a chemical lab technician at a research institute in Novosibirsk, an industrial and transportation centre two-thousand-odd kilometres east of Moscow. With the economy of that region in steep decline, and living conditions worse than ever, they were planning on abandoning the city where they had lived since their marriage. Elena had come back to Moscow and was looking for work while her mother-in-law looked after Maria. Sergei tried to find a cheap ticket on the two-day train ride to Moscow once every month or two. This was not, by Soviet or post-Soviet standards, a particularly severe hardship, however much it horrified me (Maria was the same age as Caitlin, and I found a week away difficult—I tried to imagine such a life, my children slowly forgetting what I looked like), and the main point Elena seemed to want me to understand was just how lucky they were that Maria's *babushka* and *deyedushka* had such a wonderful apartment, allowing them all to live there once Maria had a job and Sergei could chance resigning and come to join them.

Igor declared it time to open the vodka. Elena thoughtfully gave the borrowed *stakan* a wipe and polish with the corner of her impromptu tablecloth. Twisting off the cap, Igor sniffed at the mouth of the bottle then peered inside. Apparently happy with what he smelled and saw, he took the glass and began to pour the clear, light-filled liquid slowly down its side, as if a rough ride to the bottom might allow some flavour to escape. More likely, I felt, he just enjoyed pouring; and besides, it lent ritual to the occasion. If I had expected he would attempt to approximate a standard (standard in some world or other) one ounce shot, I was badly mistaken. He gradually tilted the slanted glass back to an upright position to enable him to fill it to the brim. Damn, I thought.

He presented it to me, and tried his English.

—Vor our vrent, David!

I enjoy a beer now and again, and wine with a meal. With harder stuff I prefer sipping: Scotch, bourbon, cognac after coffee. But straight vodka, here, was not a sipping drink. Vodka was a throwing drink. Drunk as cold as possible, preferably stored in the freezer, it was tossed to the back of the throat. Official duties had necessitated a few such tosses, and I knew that good vodka had a clean taste and hit with a pleasant fiery rush, with no sting or bitter burning. This, however, was not a shot, it was six ounces.

Of course silly pride was involved. Male pride to boot. Not that these three cheerful young ex-Soviets would have objected to a sip here, a half-toss there, a few minutes to get it down. They would have laughed, reminded me how much they loved Canada, waited patiently for the glass to come back. But the spirit of camaraderie, and the spirit of something even deeper—the necessity of taking on the disaster of this place with relish when the possibility of relish presented itself—and other existential angles, not the less real for having a comical edge—made the spirit seize the moment. I braced myself, nipped off the top half-inch with a quick tilting gulp to give myself space for a good throw (Pavlo seemed pleased with the strategy—hospitality had caused Igor to over-fill), then threw a great splash in, kept my head back, kept pouring, found the bottom. A completely involuntary gasp escaped as I set it down, eliciting pleased chuckles. There. That seemed okay. Nothing seemed to be happening. I gave the glass back. Everyone was too polite to make a to-do, but the energy level of the party stepped higher. Five seconds later, while Elena was specifying a half-glass and nipping it neatly, a sweeping wave of heady heat passed through my brain.

I was just settling back, pleased to have survived intact, nibbling *kolbassa*, when I realized the glass had already finished one circuit. The glass in fact now reappeared in my hand, full again of the clear liquid. Pavlo was unscrewing the second bottle. Again? Why not? It was only four feet, albeit straight up, to my bed, and it was still ten hours to Moscow. Cheers. A second wave came through, or we came through it; the compartment *did* seem a bit submarine now, like the inside of an aquarium. So when, after a little more eating, a little more tossing—the second bottle was being disposed of more prudently—and after Maria had dozed off and been angled down onto the pillow behind me, Pavlo produced cigarettes, an expedition to the smoking lounge seemed a fine idea to all concerned, smokers or not.

On Soviet trains the smoking lounge was the jolting, freezing dead zone between cars. As we worked our way down the corridor the train walls kept jumping back and forth at us, and the floor sometimes refused to come up to meet our feet in the normal way. Between the cars, with the metal plates grinding and lurching, and a glimpse of rail rushing past through a gap in the flooring like film through an old-style projector, Igor told me his plans as he passed around the cigarettes.

He had scoured Kiev thoroughly. It was virtually impossible to buy computer supplies: diskettes, printer ribbons and cartridges, connector cables, paper holders, mouse pads, basic software. One store claimed to carry them, but over a two-month period they had actually had almost nothing available for sale: diskettes for a week, mouse pads once, outdated DOS packages, not a cable or patch cord in sight. Yet all the new *businessmeni*, and the scattering of embassies and western firms, were shipping in PCs and laptops and laser printers like crazy from North America, Germany, the new shops in Moscow. Some were even coming in from China. A friend who earned a hard currency salary had loaned him his stake in return for one quarter of the proceeds from the venture he then outlined. He had $500 U.S. in his pocket. (And *I* had worried about getting robbed . . .) He was going to spend it all on brand-name computer supplies in Moscow. Nothing cheap, nothing pirated. If he was going to find a niche, he wanted a quality niche. In Kiev another friend had arranged with the manager of the shoe store where he worked to sell the supplies out of one of the shop's display cases. He didn't have enough shoes to fill them anyway. If Igor proved it could be profitable, the arrangement could be made permanent. He wasn't even insisting on a cut the first go-round.

What did I think? I was from the West; I understood economics. I must have an opinion on the feasibility of all this. Igor's harsh local cigarettes seemed to me as sweet as wood smoke on an Ontario autumn day. It seemed reasonable to me, I said. Supply and demand. Demand; no supply. That was good, from what I read in the papers, though I had to point out I had never studied economics, not even for a single semester. Really? Honest.

Pavlo just listened, smoking happily, allowing the swaying and jolting of the train to rock him; he was the second son, but also the one, I suspected, who would absorb lessons from his brother's pioneering, and might someday show the persistence to find a way through the social and economic morass—a way through for himself, at least. Elena wished them luck. Her eyes were half closed as she blew out a thin stream of smoke, tired, content. Her father-in-law knew *everybody* in Moscow. Would Igor and Pavlo like to meet him? He could probably help out.

Back in the warm compartment, the soft glow of one lamp encompassing us, I leaned back in one corner of the bottom bunk and closed my eyes. Maria slept soundly, her toes not far from my legs. Elena was half lying beside her daughter, on one elbow, her slippers dangling at the edge near my knees. I listened to them, planning and talking and laughing, seeming to understand their rapid Russian with little effort. Maybe I was making up their lines, maybe I was making their lives a free translation. I really should, I supposed, climb up to my own space, but it was really pretty nice right here, with the great overarching despair of post-Soviet life impossible to detect in their voices.

Journal Notes

Saturday in the park—in our building's bit of beaten dirt and weeds—playing with John, now three years old. Then a stroll in the lanes behind our apartment building to splash in the puddles. For children in their puddle-splashing years, Moscow provides an endless supply. At one of them, two Russian boys play with an old grey tennis ball, flinging it against the surface of the water to make as big a splash as they can. They are laughing loudly, delighting in the smack of the ball and the flying water. Walking past, John comments casually, "Those Russian boys laugh in the same language as us."

The latest on the sidewalk book tables is the finally finished Russian translation of James Joyce's Ulysses. *I once wrote a Master's thesis on the book, and am convinced Russians would be delighted by Bloom's blend of level-headed domesticity and dreamy romantic yearnings; that is, if any translator could capture the tone. Newspapers quoting sidewalk vendors (the only places you could buy it) report that sales of the fifty-one-thousand-copy print run are brisk. The hardback's price varies depending on location, but is in the two-thousand rouble range, about two dollars at the going rate. It has been a long time*

196

coming. *Excerpts appeared back in 1925, during the New Economic Program's era of relative freedom of expression. But in the early thirties Joyce was condemned as unsuitable for socialist readers because, according to premier ideologist Karl Radek, "His naturalism reaches the clinical stage and his romanticism and symbolism are close to delirium." This is finely put, and I'm certain Joyce would have taken it as a compliment. Besides, he was no stranger to censorship. A series of letters with his first publisher (of his story suite* Dubliners*) revolved around whether or not the word "bloody" could appear in print in Ireland. Radek, however, did not mean to praise, and the translators of* Ulysses *were arrested and sent to their death in the camps. Only forty years later did Victor Hinkis, well-known for his translations of Faulkner, begin to work on a new version. No publisher would touch it, so he laboured on, unpaid, for a decade. His colleague, Sergei Khoruzhy, took over the project after Hinkis' death in 1981, and the book appeared at last, lightly bowdlerised, in twelve consecutive issues of* Inostranaya Literatura *in 1989. Now everyone can pick up the complete text in one handy but hefty volume on their way to work in the morning. I like to think Joyce is somewhere keeping tabs, chuckling about that.*

In 1974, a young man about the same age as my cabin companions on the train from Kiev was arrested at the apartment where he lived with his parents in the city of Yaroslavl, a historic centre of medieval Russian culture on the upper Volga River. It was just before his nineteenth birthday. He was a Jew; it is not clear whether that fact

197

played a role in what happened. Almost twenty years later, having become a chemical engineer in St. Petersburg, he showed me a document. At the time of the arrest and trial, Stalin was two decades in his grave, but the reflex of totalitarianism which Lenin had so ironically adopted from the Tsars was still alive, if in a less murderous form. The document was unbearably specific, unrelentingly individual—small pedestrian phrases, little cogs of the great grinding wheels.

His was a small rebellion, though the reservoirs of courage required still staggered me, knowing full well I did not possess them. The leaflets which the court mentions but—in a curious, revelatory reticence—declines to describe, had accused the Soviet Communist Party of being undemocratic . . . In the eyes of the state, the crime was relatively minor. The sentence given was, by the standards of these things, mild. A commonplace; yes, a banality. Which tore a gaping hole in one man's youth. Here is part of what he showed me, in the stilted "official translation." I have altered details only enough to safeguard privacy:

Having considered the materials of the case, the Judicial Board has found the defendant's guilt in the fact that in April 1974 being at home at the address: City of Yaroslavl, 23 Revolution Drive, build. 6, app. 75, using his own typewriter he has typed around 20 leaflets containing deliberately false figments defaming the Soviet State and Social System, which he has distributed by way of sticking them during the nighttime from 14-th to 15-th April, 1974 in different districts of Yaroslavl.

The defendant KOGAN, ANDREI MIKHAILOVICH has admitted his guilt.

The Judicial Board, having analysed evidence being collected in connection with this case, has come to the conclusion that the guilt of KOGAN, ANDREI MIKHAILOVICH, besides his pleading guilty, is proved by:

the testimony of the eye witness RUBLEV, who has detained KOGAN, ANDREI MIKHAILOVICH at the moment of the leaflet's sticking and brought him to the local militia office;

the fact of confiscation of leaflets that had been put into KOGAN'S paper-case at the moment of his detention (sheet 8);

the testimony of the witness YAKUNINA about the fact that coming by the route pointed out by RUBLEV they have discovered several leaflets being sticked by KOGAN, ANDREI MIKHAILOVICH;

the decision of a commission of experts establishing that all the leaflets confiscated from KOGAN, ANDREI MIKHAILOVICH as well as those that have been found sticked to the walls of the buildings and in other places were typed on the typewriter that was confiscated during the search of the KOGANS' apartment;

the testimony of the witness VSEVOLOZHSKAYA about the fact that according to the KOGAN, ANDREI MIKHAILOVICH's words uttered by him on 14.04.74 she was informed that he had made (typed) leaflets which he was going to stick in different places in Yaroslavl:

From the text of leaflets that are added to the case (as material evidence), that were confiscated from him and distributed by him around the city, it is seen that the leaflets contain deliberately false figments defaming the Soviet State and Social System.

The Judicial Board considers that the defendant KOGAN, ANDREI MIKHAILOVICH has committed by his actions the crime provisioned by Article 190-1 of the Criminal Code of the RSFSR.

When determining the punishment the Judicial Board has taken into consideration that KOGAN, ANDREI MIKHAILOVICH was never convicted before, that when he committed the crime he was under aged and that he has admitted his guilt and repented of his deeds, and that he is characterised positively in his behaviour and study, but taking into account the social dangers of his deeds, the punishment of KOGAN, ANDREI MIKHAILOVICH has to be connected with imprisonment.

Taking into consideration KOGAN, ANDREI MIKHAILOVICH's deeds, the state of his health, the

Judicial Board considers that imprisonment of KOGAN, ANDREI MIKHAILOVICH should not be a long one.

Being directed by the articles 301, 303, 315 of the Criminal Procedural Code of the RSFSR, the Judicial Board:

SENTENCED:

YAKUNIN, N.V. brings in a verdict of guilty by the article 190-1 of the Criminal Code of the RSFSR;

determine as punishment to KOGAN, ANDREI MIKHAILOVICH in accordance with article 190-1 of the Criminal Code of the RSFSR, the imprisonment of two years with serving at reformatory labour colony of general regime;

not to change the measures of suppression for KOGAN, ANDREI MIKHAILOVICH, and to keep him under arrest.

The imprisonment before trial since April 15, 1974 is to be reckoned to KOGAN, ANDREI MIKHAILOVICH in account of sentenced imprisonment.

Material evidence which are kept with the case—the paper-case and tube of glue—to be obliterated;

typewriter—to confiscate;

the wrist watch deposited to the chamber of material evidence of Yaroslavl KGB Office on the receipt of 176427—to be returned to the defendant's mother KOGAN, LILYA ALEXANDROVNA.

As the solstice approaches, at the dacha on the Volga north of Moscow, it is dim but far from pitch dark even at midnight on clear evenings. The air's great clarity slowly fills with darkness, a process so gradual you think at times the clarity is winning. This goes on hour after hour. The lightly corrugated Volga, a mile across, is full of pink and orange and mauve. Dimming yet clear. A suspension. A sense of time dominating space. This brutal, ugly country is so beautiful; the haunting is so irreparable.

JULY 1993

The political climate grows more polarised and poisoned each week, the government's grasp of governance less firm each day. Totalitarianism breeds one kind of fear. I have never experienced its full force, but have caught a scent of it in phrases, faces, frames of mind. Building a political culture almost from scratch, with a government internally divided and clumsily administered, control spinning off into the independent fiefdoms of crime and anarchy and fascism, creates a dread and dismay every bit as real as that fear. Even foreigners, even diplomats, cannot escape the sensation: chaos, like Bolshevism, allows freedom only for the few.

Yesterday another fiasco of governmental self-contradiction, of auto-cannibalism, played itself out. The cen-

202

*tral bank announced out of the blue that all pre-1993 rou-
ble notes were no longer valid. If your bills had Lenin's
bald pate on the front, they were henceforth useful only as
bookmarks. No warning, but the policy makers in their
wisdom allotted a generous two-week period to turn in
anything up to thirty-five thousand roubles (this seemingly specifically designed to provoke panicked assaults
on bank counters and allow Russians to participate in
their national sport of jousting in unruly outdoor lineups
in the rain). Any amount above that could be deposited in
a government savings account for six months. At current
inflation rates, citizens correctly felt the bank notes were
better mulched and used as fertiliser.*

    *Of course there was immediate panic—and outrage.
Congress speaker Khasbulatov denounced the policy, conveniently forgetting it was the hard-line parliament, not
Yeltsin's government, that controlled the Central Bank,
and that it was the spectre of hyperinflation sparked by a
parliamentary plan to* triple *the deficit that had spurred
the bank to take the steps it did. Bureaucrats and politicians from deputy bank director up to the president took a
quick measure of public opinion (this at least was a sort
of progress over Communist times—public opinion existed), and denied knowing anything about the policy or
having been consulted on the matter. The Minister of Finance flew home from a trip to the U.S. apoplectic with
rage against all concerned. He appeared sincere. On the
other hand, Prime Minister Chernomydrin, in whose cabinet he served, seemed to have supported the move, though
he was now making noises about "adjustments." Returning from one of his frequent holidays, Yeltsin issued a*

decree increasing the refundable amount to one hundred thousand roubles and extending the deadline to the end of August. The other nations of the former Union still using the rouble (most of them) were understandably livid, as there had apparently been zero consultation. Such were the hazards of using a currency printed by another country's central bank.

Ironically, in the end it will all make very little difference to anybody, outside of causing lots of queue hours, irritation, and inconvenience, since pre-1993 notes are all of small denomination by current standards. Five thousand rouble notes are now common, and tens are on the way. Few people, if any, would have one hundred thousand roubles in small bills. It did manage, though, to devastate confidence in the recently stabilising and even strengthening currency at a crucial moment in Russia's post-Communist economic adventure, and chase many nervous citizens back into U.S. dollars.

AUGUST

Russians are obsessed with the making of memorials to keep the ghosts of history alive. It is perhaps this very attentiveness to the past that made the Bolsheviks both capable of and inclined to such a thorough propagandising of historical memory. The Russian love of honouring and maintaining memorials has one unexpected consequence. The present is turned into History very quickly; the contemporary is injected into the past, rapidly resetting it in the company of the other chronicles of the country's vast collective memory-hoard.

In the immediate present, while the struggle between Yeltsin and parliament intensified, the outcome less and less predictable, the rhetoric more and more explosive, we took advantage of a rare sunny Sunday to get away from all that, heading to Vagankovskoye Cemetery to look for the grave of poet-bard-actor-director and sixties rebel-legend Vladimir Vyssotsky, the epitome of a man no system, no party could contain. In the newly advertisement-bedecked metro cars, two come-ons seemed to sum up the era. One was for automatic washing machines—here a cutting edge consumer luxury. The other was that of a bank advertising two hundred percent interest on its savings accounts, and bragging that this special new rate was three times higher than previously offered. Given inflation at twenty percent a month, this was, if my shaky grasp of compounding interest was accurate, a terrible deal. But it sounded good. In this economic climate convincing someone to leave their cash sitting in a bank, rather than buying something—anything—is a daunting task.

On the subway platform, as we got off, a fiftyish man in filthy blue clothes sprawled unconscious on the cement, arms and legs stilled in an attitude of reaching out, as if still trying to move on when the haze overcame him, or as if trying to grasp the earth itself. We walked past. I first thought that it was too bad my children had to see this; but then I decided this was the wrong attitude. Still, the parental notion that children may as well see reality is easier to champion in the abstract. And there are many kinds of reality. But that correction of my own Canadian tidiness was itself immediately superseded by a blunter truth: this was old-hat to them and they paid little attention. So were they getting a realistic view of the prevalence of human misery in rough-around-all-the-edges Moscow, or simply growing calluses at a tender age? Russian families for the most part tsked slightly. Then, one of the much maligned (including by me) metro guardians— fierce sixtyish women, kerchiefed, hardened by decade after decade of disaster—appeared by his side. She reached over the prone form to where his black satchel lay, tucked it under his reaching arm. Less chance now that it would be thieved. Less chance it would be forgotten whenever his murky morning dawned.

The neighbourhood around Metro 1905 Goda was shabby even by Moscow standards. Squares were completely overgrown and disintegrating, as if their lawns and benches and fountains had been accidentally left off the district's maintenance and trimming schedule for a decade or two. Fronted by massive wrought-iron gates and a few score flower sellers, the vast cemetery was, in contrast, both genuinely beautiful and tenderly tended. Under thick, towering trees, coins of sunlight scattered on the avenues of graves. Crowds strolled the paths. Inside the endless ranks of gated and fenced enclosures, families worked on their loved ones' plots with rakes or pots of paint. Many stones listed profession first: "Painter: Dmitry Shevschenko, 1903-64."

Even in a graveyard also holding the beloved poet Yesinin and his lover Galina Benislavskaya (who shot herself on his grave), and containing the mass burial plot for the fifteen hundred killed during the crush at the ill-fated coronation party that opened Nicholas II's ill-fated reign,

206

Vyssotsky has the position of honour just to the right of the main entrance. A group of twenty or thirty pressed up to the low fence. Inside there were hundreds of fresh, brilliant bouquets. A few candles, flames jerking in the breeze, had been lit at the base of the dramatic life-sized bronze: Vyssotsky is chained to a pillar; a guitar rising from the pillar behind him morphs into a horse's head facing away from the singer. As I watched, one of the candles went out, snatched by the wind.

Deeper in the graveyard's hundreds of acres we came across more recent history, the events of the week before our own arrival in Moscow: the superb but harrowing memorial to the three young men killed defending the White House in August 1991. The site was arresting, without losing sight of its twin functions of rendering homage to the dead while recalling the horror of their deaths. Two completely different styles and effects were juxtaposed. To the left, three modest, realistic busts of the dead were mounted on slender five-foot-high granite steles. Their faces were thus rendered historical, via allusion to classical statuary, while retaining a domestic intimacy through the realism of the sculpture and the fact that their faces, disembodied, were set at the same height as in real life. These busts, with their everyday expressions, faced, about fifteen feet away, something else altogether: constructed of rusting iron, a large, tortured figure, limbs contorted, barely human, face half torn away, gaping in horror, crucified on a tank trap.

Ilya Krychevski (28), Vladimir Usov (33), and Dmitri Komer (25), died in a rogue tank flourish two years earlier, a few days before our own arrival in Russia, while I sat alone and bleary-eyed in the External Affairs Operations Centre in Ottawa, with dawn approaching, waiting for news of the great Red Army assault against Yeltsin that never came. This made my kinship with them admittedly remote, but my eyes were blurring and blinking nonetheless, and I was wondering how I could have forgotten to bring flowers.

7

OCTOBER AGAIN

In Moscow, being paranoid doesn't mean
doom is not on the way.
                                David Remnick

At the burial of an epoch
No psalm is heard at the tomb.
. . . .
Some day it will surface again
Like a corpse in a spring river.
                                Anna Akhmatova, "In 1940"

The events of October 1993, symbolised for most by the stark image of the charred White House smouldering in the Russian night like a giant tombstone, composed a hall of mirrors in which the country's leaders found themselves face to face with their alter egos, their old roles switched. The heroic underdog of 1991 had become the brooding President in the Kremlin towers with tanks at his command, a spectre to illustrate the proverb that nothing is more dangerous than your dreams come true. His reformist allies had become xenophobic conservatives in unholy alliance with as nasty a rabble of Nazis and Stalinists as the *zeitgeist* had on hand: bravado-spouting rhetoricians, they had been reduced to cowering in their own prison waiting for the army they supposedly worshipped to blow their house down. Gorbatchev chuckled sadly on the sidelines, diminishing whatever stature he had left with inane and insensitive comments. The ghosts were in full blood and the living had disappeared, out of camera range.

It was to prove the end of an era, though an era which had lasted only two years. Not the end of reform, since that word had been accumulating unwieldy baggage ever since Gorbatchev first mouthed it; not the end of innocence, as the true euphoria had lasted only a month or two in autumn 1991. The progeny of Stalin's ghosts were mercifully inept at innocence. But it was the end of the illusion that large-scale bloodshed could be avoided. The weeks and months that followed would have a harsher, more dangerous edge, with the genie out of the bottle. It was the beginning of Yeltsin's tragedy. Though he was not most at fault, much of the blood was on his hands. And of course it never, quite, washes off.

In late September, two years after the coup-plot against Gorbatchev had so ignominiously collapsed, Yeltsin engineered another, less military putsch, though in this case one sincerely designed to defend reform and democracy against a parliament that had become increasingly reactionary and erratic, increasingly contemptuous of Yeltsin's very real electoral mandate, increasingly vicious. Many will find that characterisation simplistic, since the maneuver—the dissolution of parliament—also happened to shift almost all power to himself. (It bore not a few resemblances to Alberto Fujimori's "auto-putsch" in Peru the year before, but was not accompanied by widespread restrictions on press freedom.) But I will stick to it: Yeltsin's motives were as close to pure as political motives can be. He had profound democratic instincts, was reluctant to use force, and hesitated at length when the shedding of blood loomed. Which is not to say, with hindsight, that it was a move with long-term positive consequences. It wasn't. But there was no hindsight available at the time.

There had only been glimmers of warning. When Foreign Minister Kozyrev hastily convened a meeting of G-7 ambassadors in the early evening of 21 September, the embassy knew something was afoot, but not precisely what. In a memoir, Yeltsin would assert that he had made the decision in early September, but told not even his own closest aides. He calculated, rightly, that he sat on a powder keg. The government was aware weapons were stockpiled inside the White House, so Yeltsin planned to make the announcement on a Sunday when the parliament was empty, and follow it with an immediate deployment of the crack Derzhinsky Division to take control of the building. Leaks of Yeltsin's draft decree, which had by now been seen by the inner circle, caused a disastrous two-day delay and made possible the White House occupation by the speaker (and brains) of the opposition, Ruslan Khasbulatov, and the parliament's quickly named "president," former vice-president Alexander Rutskoi, an Afghan war veteran with a superb moustache but little, many suspected, between the ears.

We sat at home all evening and checked the TV regularly, but there were no interruptions of the wildly popular Mexican soap operas on the main channel. The skies above the Kremlin were clear, but a convoy of two dozen army trucks was lined up outside the Interior Ministry building across the street from us, bumper to bumper like one long segmented animal. On the other hand, there had been three times that many assembled for city-wide anti-mafia raids the week before. There was nothing to do but wait for morning.

The next day the legislators were preparing impeachment proceedings and calling on the armed forces to defend them. Since his basic condition of "no casualties" could not be met in any attempt to forcibly dislodge them, Yeltsin opted to let them sit and fume, confident their irrelevance would gradually become clear as elections to replace them approached. Certainly for now the army was studiously ignoring their pleas. Defence Minister Gratchev and Yeltsin went for a pointedly symbolic walkabout together on Pushkin Square, chatting up the lines outside McDonald's.

Yeltsin may have dismissed Rutskoi's donning of the presidential mantle as "unserious, laughably amateurish" (one couldn't help being reminded of competing medieval enclaves of Cardinals naming competing popes who immediately excommunicated each other), but the potential for chaos was real. Russia had two presidents, two defence ministers, two interior ministers, and two governments with two seats of power staring at each other up and down Novy Arbat. With the presidents of the Commonwealth of Independent States due to meet in Moscow another day hence, everybody was wondering if Rutskoi would try to show up to chair the get-together. The parliament had already begun to show its true stripes by naming as defence minister Vladislav Aachalov, a supporter of the clearly totalitarian-minded bunch who had briefly ousted Gorbatchev in 1991. The Constitutional Court, increasingly anti-Yeltsin for months, had dutifully declared the presidential decree dissolving parliament to be unconstitutional. But given that the only partially democratically elected legislature had amended the constitution a few hundred times in the past year, constitutionality seemed a mug's game. Yeltsin's manoeuvre may have smelled of autocracy, but perspective was required: a clearly democratically elected president was dissolving an asinine, erratic, semi-democratic parliament and calling immediate new elections. This was not Tiananmen.

In the great Russian tradition of horrible weather in times of national crisis—this was the country that had greeted both Napoleon and Hitler with the most ferocious winters on record—the next two days poured cold rain, and it barely reached ten degrees. For two weeks, nothing happened. The almost entirely male Parliament met to pass innumerable resolutions in increasingly unshaven sessions— Khasbulatov in particular looked more and more like a coal miner—while waxing and waning crowds milled angrily outside, waving a scattering of fists and Kalishnakovs, and were addressed by a motley crew of anti-Semites, fascists, Stalinists and the odd monarchist united by the yearning to trash Yeltsin and welcome the old republics back into the union fold like the stray sheep they deemed them to be. The Kremlin let them yell, cordoned the area off, and tried to look as busy as possible arranging new elections. As police lines were bolstered and the crowds got nastier, the school where Teresa taught had to close, located as it was on U.S. embassy grounds almost next door to the White House.

Stasis favoured Yeltsin, who seemed fully in control. And the parliament had to be concerned at the spectre of sitting holed up in the White House while the rest of the country held elections to replace them. There was talk the resolve of some parliamentarians was weakening under a government promise to let them keep their Moscow apartments—the closest thing to a gold standard in the Russian economy—if they were willing to come out now with their tails between their legs.

But the nastiest elements in Russia's splintered opposition had other plans, almost certainly with Khasbulatov and Rutskoi's tacit consent, almost certainly not under their complete control. The days of uneasy calm were numbered.

*

Television coverage of crises distorts them most profoundly by radically narrowing the aperture. One might go so far as to suggest it represents the endgame—as the millennium closes—of Renaissance painting's rediscovery of foreground and background and the laws of parallel lines which appear to meet: the camera trolleys back to vantage points providing a clear view of the climactic event free of intruding undergrowth, behind the scenes activities, or murky events in the wings; it stands up a reporter in front whose cardinal law is to never admit she doesn't know what is going on or what is going to happen next; it frames this with the TV box and hangs it in living rooms around the world, less an electronic hearth than an icon or Holy Family tableau since its claim is to show us what is true. We know it is true, because it is "live." It has permanent twenty-twenty rear-view vision; it always assures us that what has just happened was both inevitable and easily predicted. It is back-seat driving *par excellence*; the correspondents are a mini-conclave of Olympian gods.

But inside the unfolding event, and no place more than at its centre, is a dense woods. You can't see what is going on. There are no clear pathways, and it is uncertain which way you should be facing. No obvious routes lead to the conclusion. Whichever way you turn, the crucial vista might be the one behind your head. You are foolish, blind, scared. Little information is available, and what there is might be wrong. But you are, at least, a human being in the real world. That is one thing, by definition, the camera can't show. Families and careers and marriages and deaths are also in these dense woods, if less condensed, less easily defined than the great public crises, and also go forward—or sideways—one step at a time.

On October 2nd the lines of political force in Moscow came suddenly to their node, when no one was looking. On a (finally) sunny and almost warm Sunday, deadly violence broke out around the city, but there were no trailers or promos to let you know when and where, and no grandstand seats were provided. We later learned, and saw, that a parade of opposition marchers with blood in mind had started out past Gorky Park, within view of our apartment; that they had broken through lines of largely un-

215

armed police, and had beaten several to death and maimed others; that pitched battles with truncheons and rocks and, increasingly, with gunfire, had been fought on the Ring Road just past the end of the Arbat.

We were out strolling, only a few blocks away, on Moscow's lovely old Boulevard Ring, a gracious parkway of eighteenth- and nineteenth-century buildings and trees and benches and paths, and had stopped in at the dusty but charming Museum of Oriental Art before walking half-way up an Arbat crowded with families enjoying the sun-shine and queuing for ice cream. Yet, that close—another five minutes of walking, at one point, would have brought us to a maelstrom of smashed windows, bleeding militia-men and rampaging protesters—we had no inkling that anything was up.

Back at the apartment, as afternoon turned into early evening, information trickled in, and with it the first claus-trophobia, the sense of branches in front of your face, sweat in your eyes, of being unable to *see, dammit.* One friend called to marvel at the level of destruction they had seen at the junction of the Arbat and the Ring Road, the Sadovoye Kaltso. They had come back from an outing and stumbled upon the scene, quickly retreating to find another route home. *Where?* we sputtered, astounded. The television was reporting police lines broken again near the White House. CNN was contradicting itself by the minute, with serene confidence.

Dusk was coming down, the air over the Kremlin was quiet. But the monumental palaces within were dimly lit. Why? No beehive of activity? Where was Yeltsin? An-other Canadian living in the north of the city had seen convoys of armoured vehicles heading toward the Ostankino tower, where the main Russian television networks were housed. Convoys on which side? He wasn't sure: they didn't make any announcements, and no one was about to ask.

When Katya, our babysitter, called, I heard fear in her voice for the first time. A radio report said the opposition had taken the mayor's office, but the TV was reporting that the mayor had changed sides, adding that this was unconfirmed. Some troops had joined the opposition. No, we were assured the rag-tag forces of the opposition had instead seized a few army trucks and armoured personnel carriers.

We sat, watched the screen. An APC with a Soviet flag flying. Out the window the Ring Road was quiet, traffic light. Snippets of confused data. Rutskoi and Khasbulatov had appeared outside the White House to address a mob that by now had tasted blood and was rampaging in various sectors of the city in armed attacks on key government centres. It was clearly an attempt to take power. General Albert Makashov, whose views were to the right of Attila the Hun and the left of Stalin simultaneously, was one of a number of leaders who seemed to be more or less free-lancing with impromptu battalions. A few swastikas were seen in the crowd, a vision so astonishing and nauseating to Russians that even many bitterly opposed to Yeltsin would later cite their appearance as the last straw, convincing them the President had to prevail. Late in the afternoon Rutskoi "ordered" an attack on the Ostankino complex—but it was never clear whether the politicians in the White House were orchestrating events or merely reacting to them.

After dark we began to get the first film footage of the siege at Ostankino. Panicky cameras tossed and tilted streets and buildings as they swung wildly across night-lit scenes of sprinting troops and ducking journalists. No one seemed to be sure what was going on, even who was attacking. It was clear from what we had seen that this was deadly serious, that people were being killed, that Ostankino might well fall, thereby putting the opposition forces in control of the country's central broadcasting facilities. In the finger pointing afterwards, it was often forgotten that the Yeltsin government had patiently ignored the opposition's increasingly openly armed defiance, and that it was the opposition that began the shooting and the killing. And would have shot and killed many more given more firepower.

At 7:30 we sat numbed, grim, eyes fixed on the screen. Channel One had cut away from the regular programs it had been stubbornly—or ominously—allowing to unreel. Now we watched a single, sweating news reader, Victor Vinegradov, with tie askew and top button undone, wearing no jacket. His voice was one of controlled calm, but he was speaking too quickly, running his sentences together, darting from paragraph to paragraph. We strained to keep up. He didn't know how much longer he would remain on the air. The attackers were in the building. Gradually he began to lose control; his cheeks glistened with tears of fear, or rage, or both. At 7:39, with the reader in midphrase, the broadcast abruptly ended. A test pattern flashed onto the screen.

It was time to get the kids ready for bed, a domestic chore which, it occurred to me, never seemed to be mentioned in the dramatic accounts of historical crises. They were more than a little frustrated with mom and dad's fixation on television news. But it was difficult to haul ourselves away from the set. The test pattern persisted; our hearts sank; we felt real alarm. Surely this could only mean Ostankino had fallen? Surely Ostankino could not fall unless the army was splitting, or had joined the parliament's forces, or was staying in its barracks ignoring Yeltsin's orders? Where *was* Yeltsin? Was he in the Kremlin? Was Gratchev, the Minister of Defence, with him?

Flipping to CNN, we got another deluge of rumours, unconfirmed reports, endless repeats of the same stand-ups meant to highlight the reporter's intrepid-on-the-spotness. But the forest remained all around us, in front of our eyes. We couldn't see.

All of Russia's principal radio and television stations were to remain off the air for several hours. From the window I counted armoured personnel carriers and army trucks rumbling by on the Ring Road—to do what?—and called in my figures to one of the Canadian military attachés. His wife took the message: he was out there, somewhere, trying to keep track of events. I hadn't noticed all the useful details she needed about the vehicles: logos, precise type, size, regiment.

No one that night gave a coherent account of the events at Ostankino. For the media it was somewhat the equivalent of the fire department trying to handle a blaze in their own building. Later we were to learn how bloody it

219

had really been, that it had never fallen completely into the control of the rebels, but that it had been a very near thing. Fighting had flared throughout the night; troops loyal to Yeltsin did not quell the attackers until near dawn, and even then sniper fire continued through much of the next day. Crowds supporting the parliament had begun arriving in late afternoon following Rutskoi's dramatic—and murderous—orders at the White House. Makashov arrived soon after, screaming through his megaphone that, "This is the free territory of the USSR." The storming of the building began about 7:30. The fifty-odd OMON guards crouched behind a pile of chairs in the lobby faced grenades and automatic weapons fire. No army support arrived until five APCs appeared just after 9:00 p.m. Over the next two hours about sixty people were killed, and four hundred injured. Demonstrators—many armed—and journalists hid behind cars in the parking lot. Bodies—the universe of each mind gone—lay scattered in front of the main doors, like a Schwarzenegger film gone real. British cameraman Rory Peck was one of the dead; four other journalists were injured in their thirst for "live" footage. In an attack on the radio building, a truck was driven through the plate-glass facade, with Makashov striding in behind it. Eventually the lower three floors of that building were under his control.

We heard some reports that Yeltsin had just arrived at the Kremlin by helicopter, and we stood gazing out our windows into the night, troubled by how dim the lights were above the onion domes, as if those inside the great battlements were worried about air strikes. Some journalists had heard that this or that regiment was actively cooperating with the parliamentary mobs.

The subconscious kept emerging as blatant cravings: we wanted order. We wanted to know who was in charge. We wanted *somebody* to make the situation clear. The profound fear of chaos, our bodies taught us, was not restricted to some quirk of the authoritarian Russian psyche. As any number of Shakespeare's plays trumpet loud and clear, in most nations and in most eras, the general public's opinion about whichever strongman is running things is a minor point compared to their subsuming conviction that *one* strongman running things is infinitely preferable to the cannibalism of civil war, the disintegration of the state. This disintegration now seemed startlingly easy. The epic monstrousness of our century's quartet of Hitler, Stalin, Mao and Pol Pot has obscured a broader historical truth: whether we like it or not, in virtually all other situations the populace suffers less from nasty leaders than from disorder. It was not for nothing that after the crumbling of the Roman Empire—hardly a beatific enterprise—western society dreamt for a millennium of putting it back together. This is not at all a pleasant truth; the myth of the noble savage is far sweeter; and the suffering that disorder causes is not an excuse for brutal dictatorships. But the importance people in places like Russia place on a clearly defined, even if authoritarian, power structure, and their disgust and fear when it is *not* clear, is not based on stupidity or immaturity, as Western media commentary often likes to imply, and does not mean they wouldn't, sure, like a nice Swiss hands-on democracy with Swedish social programs and American zest, in the best of all possible worlds. Their convictions are based on intelligent self-interest.

This explains, I suppose, the surprisingly strong sense of *relief*—mixed with both dismay for the Russian people and a good deal of personal apprehension (Would my family be split up? Would they be evacuated? Or all of us? None of us?)—the relief felt when initial reports were increasingly confirmed both on TV and then by phone calls from friends in other districts: in the early hours, all along Leningradsy and Leninsky Chausees, in response to Yeltsin's written orders, long columns of tanks began entering the outskirts of Moscow.

*

October 3rd would be our most nerve-wracking day in Moscow, the day when the violence which until then flared only on the periphery of the old Soviet Union—in Tadjikistan, Georgia, Armenia, Azerbaidjan, Moldova—arrived at the centre and touched us, however slightly. I wondered whether White House sieges would come to seem the bookends of our brief passage through Russia's long history.

It was a tense night, getting up every hour or two to turn on the TV and check out the windows, wondering whether the tanks had come right into the city, whether Ostankino was back under government control, whether Yeltsin was fully in command of the government.

Yeltsin, we would later learn, had been spending Sunday the 2nd with his family at their dacha near Zavidova, two hours' drive north-west of the city. Reports of the deteriorating situation in Moscow were phoned to him through the afternoon, until at 6:00 p.m. he signed a decree imposing a state of emergency. He would later express remorse that for "several terrible hours Muscovites did not know whether someone was defending them" without explaining why this silence had occurred. He arrived by helicopter at the Kremlin at 7:15, just as the fire fight was about to break out at Ostankino. A meeting with the heads of the "power ministries," Minister of Defence Gratchev and Interior Minister Yerin, was held immediately. Meanwhile, a frenzied Khasbulatov was reporting to the parliament that Ostankino was already taken and that the Kremlin would be next. Another group of gunmen was entering the ITAR-TASS wire service building to try to bully the staff (unsuccessfully) into informing the world of a change in government in Russia.

Despite Gratchev's repeated reassurances to Yeltsin, the army seemed painfully slow to respond. Whether this was due to lack of organisation or hesitation as to which master to obey is still not entirely clear. Even by 2:30 a.m. Yeltsin was still banging his fist on tables, wondering where the troops were.

By seven we were up and watching TV footage of tank lines crawling down Kutuzovsky Prospekt, a major artery which leads to a bridge spanning the Moskva immediately in front of the White House. It was also a street with the apartments of a number of Canadians. One colleague would later describe the stirring yet quasi-comical vision of his driver unexpectedly showing up to take him to work, his Zhiguli darting boldly around a tank to pull into the building driveway. Long rows of army trucks were barricading the Interior Ministry building across the street from us. Initially, of course, we had to deal with getting the day going: dressing the kids, brushing teeth, fixing breakfast, perking coffee. The school where Teresa taught had already been closed for a few days. Now Caitlin's kindergarten was shut too. But after a quick phone call I learned the embassy had decided to open.

By all accounts the Ring Road in our sector was free of tank traffic, so I decided driving seemed wiser than the metro, which the authorities might close. Coming to the stoplight in front of the Interior Ministry where I make a right turn to the Ring Road on-ramp, I faced a half-dozen nervous-looking pimply youths, officially uniformed, carrying submachine guns. My main concern was that nothing startle them. I hoped their safety catches were on, but doubted it.

The embassy was extremely quiet, more watchful and waiting than tense. About half of the local staff had shown up; those from northern neighbourhoods near Ostankino had wisely opted to stay put. Much of the inner part of the city, where the embassy is located, was shut down, most shops—but far from all—closed. The pedestrian and vehicle traffic was thin, but the streets could not be called deserted. A few people even showed up to apply for visas; they were processed quickly, and by midafternoon we had closed the front door and were assigning embassy vans to take local staff to open metro stations, since there had been snipers reported on the Arbat, only a block away.

At the White House, two kilometres distant, central Moscow was seeing its heaviest military activity since the Bolshevik Revolution seventy-six years earlier. Television focused only on the photogenic tank cannonades that presented the world with the startling image of heavy shells being lobbed directly at the front of the country's parliament building, generating a series of fires that gradually charred the entire upper half of the huge building. But there were gun battles at a number of locations around the city, including an evening assault, even after the surrender of Rutskoi and Khasbulatov, on a pro-Yeltsin newspaper. It was the stream of reports coming in via military attachés that added to the sense that the situation was far from under control even as large crowds watched the shelling of the White House—which began with fusillades from tanks and howitzers at 9:00 a.m.—as if spectating at a one-sided sporting event.

There were anxious moments back home at the apartment. First came the unnerving spectacle of tank columns passing on the Sadovoye Kaltso beneath our windows. Then, at midmorning, two carloads of black berets in full battle gear flung to a halt in the back driveway of our building at the precise moment Teresa and the children were returning from a hurried trip around to the front of the building to buy bread. (There had been unusually long lineups: Muscovites know a hoarding occasion when they see one.) The soldiers burst out of all four doors of each Volga. Teresa's heart stopped. In Moscow, right now, you had no idea who was on what side, and you were by no means confident that the "right" side meant you were much safer. The soldiers, packing submachine guns, seemed to be looking for someone; they sprinted into one of the building entrances near our own. When Teresa called me at work, mentioning that Caitlin had started to cry upon realising her mother was terrified, I was suddenly and irrationally furious, banging on a wall and cursing to my empty office in an attempt to burn off a trapped sensation, loudly haranguing the world's hard men who had no *right*, dammit,

225

to frighten my daughter. The primal human instinct: at the heart of goodness, but also useful in keeping wars going: raid TV towers if you like, blow down the parliament with tank fire for all I care, but don't you *dare* make my daughter cry, not her, not my own. A tragi-comic response, in retrospect. I wasn't laughing then.

The steady static of automatic weapons fire, hour after hour, punctuated by the thud of larger shells against the White House facade, was unexpectedly exhausting. I tried sporadically to work, frequently flitting to the embassy basement where the TV in the club room was tuned to the BBC, or upstairs to the office of the *Chargé d'affaires*, to catch CNN flickering on the portable set in the corner, with a shifting group huddled around it. A ghostly, postmodern phenomena: when tank blasts struck, we could hear the explosion first from TV, then, a second later, the duller *whump* from out the window. The networks were not merely live, they were *quicker* than live. By that evening muscles literally ached from the stress, from the come-down off a twenty-four-hour adrenalin high.

Later footage showed Khasbulatov sitting autistically in a corner as rifle fire and smoke washed around him, while Rutskoi screamed orders over the phone to imaginary Air Force acolytes, demanding they bomb the Kremlin. After snubbing last minute offers to come out peacefully— the strong rhetoric of rows of tanks drawn up facing the building was not sufficiently convincing—and thereby leading to another sixty deaths and hundreds of wounded; after a long afternoon of ascending lunacy, those inside began large-scale surrenders just before 5:00 p.m. After negotiating guarantees they would not be shot, Rutskoi and

Khasbulatov gave themselves up at 5:30 even as elite Alpha Unit troops continued to fight their way upward, floor by floor, through the building's notoriously labyrinthine corridors. Rutskoi and Khasbulatov were taken to Lefortova Prison. As months passed, their trials gradually fell apart, and they were all eventually released unconvicted of any crime, evidence of the inadequacy of Russia's nascent "rule of law," but also sufficient indication that the irritated Yeltsin, who did nothing to block their acquittals, was no tyrant.

By Monday evening, with the smouldering White House still throwing last flames into the night sky, it was time to take stock. Although not all those who had taken up arms against the sea of reform were in custody—sniper fire crackled sporadically in some areas for another two days—the back of the rebellion was clearly broken; Yeltsin was undeniably in charge. He would go on to hold more or less free and more or less fair elections as promised, and would accept the distasteful results: again, so much for the Yeltsin-as-dictator rumblings common in the Western media. But for the president there was a moral cost. The events of October 1993 involved, he would write, "shrugging off and cleansing the remains of the filth, lies and falsity accumulated for seventy-odd years." In other words, the flushing out of Khasbulatov and his crowd was the completion, not the reversal of the defeat of the putsch of August 1991: the two years had concluded rather like a stage strewn with villains where, in the middle of the denouement speeches, one or two revive enough for a last lunge and must be run through with rapiers a second and final time.

There is certainly an element of self-congratulation in this formulation, and of the almost inevitable creeping conviction (one that grew overwhelming in Gorbatchev, also a decent man), that his power needed to be preserved because no one else could do the job. But one difficulty surrounding our era's encounters with such events is that the experience is filtered through a medium—what we call *news*—that knows no gradations between sainthood and cynic. The fact that Yeltsin in the end disposed of the parliament with tanks led to the easy summation that he was no better than the putsch leaders of two years earlier, and no better than the bully-boys who had set out to storm Ostankino after bludgeoning a few policemen to death on the barricades.

But it is too simple to proffer the choice between a) the defeat of the parliament was a triumph and Yeltsin a democratic hero, or b) the tank attack was a tragedy and Yeltsin a bloody-handed villain. The truth was that the event was a tragedy, but Yeltsin was not the villain.

Those who eventually surrendered to the big guns were a rabble cohering around no idea but hatred, no political strategy other than scapegoating, no idea of governance other than coercion. They included a number of ill-defined groups with leaders of varying degrees of obscurity. Makashov, more or less the military commander of the Sunday blood bath, had told an interviewer a few days earlier that he sought a return to Soviet Communism. There is no sense mincing words: that means his political philosophy embraced grand-scale imperialism, totalitarian control of the individual, social engineering including mass relocation of populations, prolific corruption, the Gulag, and bullets in the back of the head for a panoply of perceived sins. Neo-Nazis were also on hand, most prominently represented by the Russian National Unity Movement, which had been established by members of the virulently anti-Semitic group Pamyat: they favoured swastika armbands. The group was to lead the attack on the Mayoral building near the White House by driving commandeered army trucks through the lobby windows.

Yeltsin was, I believe, genuinely loathe to use violence—he would later castigate himself mainly for not understanding earlier that it was the only tool appropriate to the opponent. Local editorials on Tuesday tended not to blame the president for unleashing the tanks: the chilling memory of Sunday night, the sweating newscaster cut off in midsentence, the fleeting possibility of a Khasbulatov indebted to the Makashovs of the world actually running Russia, were still too fresh for doubts on that score. Instead they criticised Interior Ministry troops for lacking both the training and the proper equipment—tear gas, rubber bullets—to disperse the Sunday demonstrators and thus prevent the early, catalytic violence. The killing on Sunday was carried out by those opposed to Yeltsin, and the first blood spurred them to nitroglycerine highs. Yeltsin had left the increasingly well-armed "parliament" and its supports to sit inside their barricades for thirteen days, determined not to be goaded into using the army, an action he sensed would constitute the failure of much that he had worked for. Even on Monday morning, with the tanks arrayed on Kutuzovsky bridge and the headquarters of those who had attempted an armed take-over in their gunsights, he sent in offers to allow a last-minute surrender without firing.

But while it is not clear Yeltsin had any choice but

bombardment by Monday morning—after all, he was far from in complete control: parts of the city were still subject to armed bands and the army was vacillating—the attacks by the rebels and Yeltsin's dramatic and bitter reply, couched in unforgettable images, was a tragedy. A large number of people were killed, certainly over one hundred, each of them a husband or sister or mother or son or lover. In a larger context, the action *renewed, revivified* the military option. Tragically it did so at a time when there had actually developed inside Russia itself a quite forceful pacifism, a deep repugnance against the jackboot after seventy years of internal terror, and of Hungary, of Prague, of Afghanistan, of Vilnius. That revulsion against the use of the military in civilian conflicts—a revulsion so evident in Eastern Europe in 1989—had taken on a wonderful momentum of its own that is already difficult to recall. A deeply rooted conviction that the army had no place in politics had grown up, and this conviction was one of the most valuable, and most unexpected, features of the finale of Soviet Communism. Khasbulatov and Rutskoi, along with their erstwhile allies, were primarily to blame for the violence of October, but that does not change the final sum: it constituted a crucial failure of Yeltsin's presidency. After October, the darkness and menace that already haunted various small rooms and war-torn republics of the post-Soviet sphere moved to the centre. It made it a lot easier to use the army next time. And the next time would lead to the devastation of Grozny, in Chechnya, where a military run amok killed thousands of civilians in a pointless purging of a two-bit nasty dictator; would lead, indeed, to a Yeltsin far too steeped in blood.

Journal Notes

Attending a conference on citizenship issues in Dagomys, on Russia's Black Sea coast, I realize that I am witnessing one of the last hurrahs, at least linguistically, of the old Imperium. A rare occurrence: a good deal of arm-twisting by the organisers (and the lure of warm sunshine in November? Palm trees by the sparkling sea?) has enticed representatives of fourteen of the old republics into the same room, including the Baltic states, who normally refuse to have anything to do with events that seem to imply membership in Russia's "near abroad." (Only the Turkmen were absent, apparently due to a national holiday.) The fair-haired Estonians, the Turkic-featured Uzbeks and Kyrgyz, the broad-faced Kazakhs with their hints of Mongol blood, the fabulously densely bearded Armenians—all sat around the tennis-court sized conference table behind their national flags, and spoke Russian. Corridor chat between Ukrainians and Georgians took place in Russian. The handsomely inimitable Russian Federation representative, Abdulakh Mikitaev, was about as Russian, ethnically, as I was. He had pointed out to me his homeland in a remote valley of the Caucasus from the windows of the Ilyushin as we flew over the ice-cliffs

231

on the way down from Moscow. When charming and in-
timidating the recalcitrant (or sensible, from their point
of view) Latvian or Estonian delegates, he used the lan-
guage of Pushkin. The language's lingua franca role, use-
ful and resented throughout the old Union, is surely on its
last legs outside of the three Slavic countries and western
Kazakhstan. The same meeting, twenty years hence, would
almost certainly see delegates fiddling with headphones
and casting irritated glances at the interpreter booths.

Above the conference hotel the deep green furrows
of tea plantations climb in terraces into the mist. Del-
egates headed late one afternoon to a samovar museum
and fairy-tale wood-carved tea house near the summit,
crowding around tables headed by samovars filled with
superbly aromatic local tea and laid on with sweet breads
and hazelnuts. Waiters ferried trays of cognac and vodka.
Accordion and balalaika and whistles played while the
whole heterogeneous lot sang sentimental Russian folk
songs and applauded folk dances with genuine enthusi-
asm. The Soviet Union had dissolved in an eye-blink in
1991, and its death was richly deserved. But it is not so
easily eradicated from the lives of its former citizens. The
cheap but real sentimentality that was so much a part of
state-sponsored Soviet culture supplemented rather than
contradicted all the lies and brutality, and brought these
peoples together in some portion voluntarily and in some
portion against their will, and did change them, lay down
links, sediment layers of similarity. The shared traditions
will fade, a necessary thing; for some a wonderful thing.
Human beings cannot, however, be unravelled and disen-
tangled overnight—the ethnic mixing of the Union is one

*of its most enduring legacies. The Azerbaidjani delega-
tion contains an ethnic Belarussian, the Armenian team a
Georgian woman born in Azerbaidjan who speaks Russian as her mother tongue.*

*Looking around the table I noticed that in spite of
the racial potpourri the Soviet Union had been, it was
still easy to distinguish the delegates from the observers
(a Canadian, an American, a Swede, a German, a Swiss).
It had never before been so strongly impressed on me that
the Soviet Union had been not only a political contriv-
ance but also a society, however artificially induced, whose
ghost will fade as slowly as those of other empires. Kids
still play cricket in the back streets of Kathmandu. Many
who hated Soviet hypocrisy and brutality had loved its
ideals, and thus on some level loved it in spite of itself.
Though their futures lay elsewhere, the assembled all came,
whether they liked it or not, from the same country.*

*Moscow, once a bargain basement for Texans and Ber-
liners, is rapidly becoming a one-star city with five-
star prices. The rouble, at twelve hundred to the U.S.
dollar, has dropped by only twenty percent since May,
a period during which inflation totalled seven hundred or so percent. A metro ride, still cheap, costs thirty
roubles, two hundred times its fifteen kopeck price when
we arrived. The kopeck coin has disappeared into folk-
lore. The restaurants are rapidly moving out of reach
of all but Western oil men and Russian businessmeni. A
couple can effortlessly spend one hundred dollars U.S. to
eat poorly.*

Late in the month there is an early cold snap, minus ten day after day and the Moskva starting to freeze over. By the Kievskaya Hotel—from which you can watch imported Turkish workmen revamping the black White House and marvel at the rapidity with which you, and everyone else it seems, have forgotten the names Rutskoi and Khasbulatov—there is a tractor trailer sitting on the snow in the parking lot, a bonfire dancing underneath the cab, thawing a frozen gas line.

DECEMBER

Orson Wells once wrote:

> *This hand that touches you once touched the hand of Sarah Bernhardt—can you imagine that? . . . When she was young, Mademoiselle Bernhardt had taken the hand of Madam George, who had been the mistress of Napoleon! . . .* Just three handshakes from Napoleon! *It's not that the world is small, but that history is so short.*

In Russia the same sensation is often with me, that history is brief, much briefer than one had imagined, less theoretical and more personal. Stalin is not (only) a shrouded and distant demiurge like Genghis Khan. My first Russian teacher back in Ottawa had as a boy been chosen from out of a children's choir to present flowers to the dictator in the Royal Box at the Bolshoi—and had shaken his hand. For that matter, he had also known Shostakovitch, perhaps our century's greatest composer. In Russia, The Great Patriotic War against Germany is

234

always close at hand. During our years here history has continuously been confronted, rewritten, disputed—in short been accepted into the present. Crowds demonstrate against the closing of the State Lenin Museum. The parliament and the media debate the fate of his pale, manicured corpse in its ghastly purple viewing chamber under the cobbles of Red Square. At a meeting in the Ministry of Education one day, I found myself in the office once used by his widow, Krupskaya, the old furnishings intact and her formidable gaze lording from a wall portrait. The Blue Guide to Moscow lists twenty-one monasteries, fifty-four major monuments, eighteen palaces, and a hundred and three museums, though no doubt the editors missed a few. We have only made it to nineteen of the museums so far: a lamentable record. I have read my poetry with Bella Akhmadulina, who has made many recordings of her poetry and who is exactly the same age as my mother—but also a personal friend of both Anna Akhmatova and Boris Pasternak. Pasternak as a child often opened the door to Tolstoy when the novelist came to visit the Pasternak home. It is from such a cultural matrix that one can feel the full force of Osip Mandelshtam's rending cry of his own extinction: "And somebody strange is in a hurry to have me forgotten."

It is not simply a question of being present here while history is being made—a phrasing which, in any event, presumes a rather limited idea of history—or of knowing people who have known famous people. The sensation rather is of the presence of the past in the mental orbit of everyday life, living alongside it, and thus in some sense living alongside the future. The Russian inti-

macy with history is as severe for both good and ill as the Canadian estrangement from it. Just because this is a cliché does not mean it isn't true. This estrangement, part of every Canadian's sense of homelessness, is also of course one of our great advantages, a leg up. Situated on the temporal and geopolitical periphery, we have an edge, a perspective, others cannot hope for. But it is an advantage we pay for dearly, forced into a different sort of prison.

JANUARY, 1994

Yesterday, after a week of rain and sloughs of dirty-pablum slush, the temperature dropped, a foot of fresh snow fell, the sun dazzled from a huge sky. We found the sliding hills in Ismailova park and tobogganed along with scores of other families where a great semi-circular bluff plummets into a dell of deep powder. Each twig balanced a white shadow twice its own thickness.

At a concert that evening at the Conservatory—surely our favourite single spot in Moscow—the brilliant Pavel Kogan was conducting the Moscow State Symphony's Fiftieth Anniversary Concert. Two rows in front of us sat those epitomes of denouement, of belatedness, the Gorbatchevs, looking fitter and younger than one expected. Gorbatchev endures now the odd indignity of breathtakingly low political popularity combined with titanic celebrity: even in the hallowed hall of the Conservatory he had to sign autographs while the busts of Mussourgsky and Rimski-Korsakoff and Tchaikovsky looked on. His cheerful, unlined face, after over six years in the toughest job on the planet, bespeaks a consti-

236

tution of unfathomable resilience. At the first pause, while Kogan wiped his brow and gathered the orchestra's energies, Yelena Bonner came in alone from the side entrance, small, wizened, dishevelled, yet brisk with energy. The great human rights activist (and widow of Sakharov) passed directly in front of Gorbatchev on her way to her seat. They did not look at each other. Between them, however much at odds, they contain the force of a hundred of the rest of us.

According to the local papers, the rynoks *of Moscow, where one can buy anything from car parts to sable coats to antique icons to pantyhose, have recently exploited the growing demand for* used light bulbs. *Under the old system, it was considered a grave disadvantage to have a job that provided no opportunity to plunder state supplies, nothing to sell or barter. This is captured in the classic joke about the factory where, to cut down on pilferage, exit gate inspections were instituted. As one worker passed out with a wheelbarrow covered by a sheet, the guards stopped him and ordered the sheet drawn back. Nothing. Night after night they checked—an empty barrow. Weeks later the guard supervisor was hauled into the manager's office to explain the continued loss of factory property. He protested that every worker, without fail, was searched on leaving. That may be, retorted the manger, but we're losing wheelbarrows like crazy.*

Still, burned-out light bulbs? This stumped the paper's columnist, who had until now considered himself adept at divining the uses for the innumerable odd items up for sale. It was one of those mysteries having a solu-

tion which, once known, seems self-evident. Burned-out light bulbs are extremely useful—to replace the functioning *light bulbs you are stealing from work.*

8

DARKER ROOMS

LIVING SPACE:
YEKATERINBURG, WESTERN SIBERIA

As if the depths of Siberia—forest and tundra spanning a third of the earth's circumference—had turned inside out, the broad, winter-crisp boulevards of Yekaterinburg had gone. Snap: a small pocket. I found myself in a very narrow space.

He peered at me, grinning around his cigarette, glancing to the rows of silent uniformed men—unofficial uniforms—lining the walls, crowding us in.

—So why, he expostulated, with hearty fake benevolence, have you been visiting the *Jews*?

*

Yekaterinburg, the size of Vancouver, had two decent restaurants and one good hotel, where I *wasn't* staying. But in early December 1993, the weather was giving me good impressions of western Siberia, the Urals region, just east of the line of hills marking the start of Asia and Siberia, twelve hundred or so kilometres east of Moscow. Brilliant sunshine presented the spaciously laid-out, open-to-the-sky

239

city in its best light; the cold, crisp air, the occasional siftings of snow (without visible clouds) had splendid clarity. The roads, the sidewalks, every twig of every tree was white with hoarfrost; vapour clouds billowed from every car, signalled every breath and word. Tough economic times had not yet dampened a native openness and informality: though thousands of miles of cold and rock and forest lay further to the east, dotted with cities, military sites and massive industrial dinosaurs, Yekaterinburg still had a bit of a frontier edge.

And it was a new city, even if it had been one of the earlier way stations on Russia's eastward march after the crumbling of Mongol-Tartar power, a march which paralleled, chronologically, the movement west of European settlement in North America. It was little older than Denver or Edmonton. Russian settlement began in the area when Old Believers, fleeing the persecutory aftermath of theological schism, arrived at the start of the eighteenth century. A fort and ironworks followed in the 1720s, but there was little population growth until the Trans-Siberia railroad came through in the 1870s. Names make their point here: the city, originally named after a Tsarina, became Sverdlovsk in "honour" of the chief assassin of Nicholas II and his family there in July 1918. It was now Yekaterinburg again, but was still capital of the Urals Region of Sverdlovsk.

Until recently closed to foreigners, in its present form it was an exemplar of Soviet central planning and its emphasis on heavy industry and science—for which it was now paying the price. It had been force-fed on Kremlin *dictat* and fattened into one of the major industrial centres of the old Union, with over two hundred factories—metallurgical and chemical machinery, steel, rubber, mining, diesels, and a sizeable armaments sector. It also housed the Urals branch of the Soviet—now Russian—Academy of Sciences, and boasted forty-three scientific and research establishments, and a dozen universities. This meant it had hundreds of thousands of industrial workers wondering what privatisation meant, not to mention four *thousand* scientists (i.e. holding PhDs), and another six thousand scientific technicians, all of them knowing there would *not* be forty-three research institutes in a decade's time. The city, and the region of almost thirty million it centres, was something of a test case for the issues of unemployment, cheap government credits to industry, privatisation, defence conversion, and the brain drain, all of which were increasingly preoccupying policy makers by late 1993.

Cities like Yekaterinburg were facing for the first time, on a large scale, many of the social realities associated in Russian minds with the West—unemployment, market-shift dislocation, unplanned migration—while still saddled with those endemic in the Soviet system: savaging of the environment, obsolete industry, unwanted consumer production, severely underdeveloped service sectors, shortages of housing. The "Soviet" factory directors I met seemed genuinely appalled at the notion of sending workers off into unemployment to fend for themselves. This in itself was certainly a refreshing change from their Western counterparts, whose current managerial *raison d'être* was slashing staff. Severance from the workplace had particularly serious consequences here in Yekaterinburg and in scores of other industrial behemoths like it from Novosibirsk to

241

the Pacific. State unemployment benefits were risible. Large firms had normally also provided housing, upgraded medical care, access to grey-market goods, even heavily subsidised vacation packages on the Black Sea, often at company-owned facilities—not minor frills if you lived in a polluted Siberian industrial city in a tiny flat. In other words, Yekaterinburg was in many ways a company town with the population of San Francisco. So far unemployment remained statistically negligible. Enterprises whose production was plummeting avoided the stigma of shedding workers through reduced hours, long unpaid or partially paid vacations, rotating layoffs, or simply by paying idle employees and running up unsustainable debt. No one was eager to jump onto the official unemployment rolls, where, after the first year, one's entitlement was seven thousand roubles a month, the current going rate for three kilos of Grade C sausage.

City housing officials dolefully recited their ghastly statistics with the sort of perverse pride Winnipeggers use to talk about January weather. Although there was now a small private housing market, the desperate shortage of apartments led to prices simply out of the question for most people. State-issue flats were available for the patient—and long lived. The queue was sixteen thousand families long. The lucky people now at the top of the list, itching to move in their things any day now, had been waiting for thirty-two years. That isn't a typo (though since places on the list were a tradeable commodity, it is not clear how many actually waited it out). And to get *on* the list, one must have either no housing or fewer than seven square metres per person, a size known to most Canadians only with regard to their second bathroom.

This in a broad-boulevarded town with all the space of Siberia to grow in. I got to know more about the city between official meetings than during them, killing time and seeing the sights with my interpreter, Yuri. Yuri was young, blonde, without regular work, and embroiled in disputes over his free-lance fee with the city Foreign Relations office, which was perfectly prepared to charge the wealthy Canadian government triple the going Moscow rate for a car and driver while paying Yuri peanuts. Yuri's smiling face—he seemed always to manage simultaneous cheerfulness and scepticism, and I came to think of this, rightly or wrongly, as the Urals and Siberian character—and fluent English were most welcome my first morning in the city after a late-night Aeroflot arrival.

He met me outside the Tsentralny ("Central") Hotel. Its centrality was, unfortunately, its sole virtue. Our reception there (I was travelling with two other men, Perry, an embassy colleague, and Carol, a Canadian election observer) had been less than soothing. At first the woman at the desk—a table behind a window the size of a mail slot—assured us she had only one room, which we could share. Perhaps a bribe was expected, but we just got mad. The hotel appeared abandoned that evening except for the prostitutes being matched up with their clients by a traffic-directing hotel staffer in the main lobby. Okay, she did—following a complex final check—have a couple more rooms. The hallway linoleum induced seasickness. My room was huge, and had hot water, so complaints were out of order in spite of a decorating scheme consisting of a massive black vinyl couch, an orange polyester bedspread, a brand new smoked-glass side-table bearing a *mauve* telephone, a green carpet, and shiny gold curtains. The effect was nauseating, so as I unpacked I reminded myself regularly about the hot water.

It was 10:30 and we hadn't eaten. Aeroflot had served a glass of fizzy water. We regrouped in the restaurant. An odd, cube-shaped stage cut into one wall held a four-person electric band trying to play 1970s Western pop. Only two other tables were occupied, and we saw no sign of food. A surly staff member said to order from a *waitress*, not her. None were in sight.

While Perry headed to the kitchen to take matters in hand, a short, plump woman in a large plum sweater tugged drunkenly on Carol's sleeve and pleaded with him to dance. I interpreted. Carol said *nyet* all on his own. Five minutes later she tried again, this time half lying on the table to make the point. But no food. A helpful kitchen cleaner looked dubious at our suggestion there must be some other restaurants nearby still open, but did consent to give us one phone number to try. Closed. We consoled ourselves with the almost universally high quality of Russian breakfasts and went to bed famished. But after dragging ourselves out into the dark morning eight hours later (it remained pitch black until past nine), we found only a *buffyet* offering stale bread, Snickers bars, and a counter selection of dried chicken parts. We went with Snickers. Yuri would eventually, after a morning of light-headed meetings, find me a thoroughly decent restaurant in the old Party hotel, where I ate for so long we were late for the first afternoon appointment.

Over the next two days, during gaps in my schedule, I took advantage of the car and driver to look around. The weather was beautiful, with a brilliant low sun steaming off the frosty city and throwing long shadows across open spaces. Wide avenues took us to the city centre. Traffic was light. Though Yuri assured me an indigenous mafia was already developing and importing dark-windowed Mercedes to prowl the streets, they were so far little in evidence compared to Russian models. The downtown had many of the white-trimmed plaster-over-wood classical buildings in yellows and greens common to Moscow and St. Petersburg: here in the oldest part of Yekaterinburg, many of the structures were from the turn of the century. Much of it was attractive enough, more so than I had envisaged, although a hideous leaden box ten stories square squatted at the very heart of town: the city hall had been built with the labour of German prisoners of war in 1949, and appeared to have been designed by someone trying to capture the spirit of decaying steel mills.

Where the Iset crossed through town and had been dammed to form a broad lake, there was a pleasant promenade with multiple wide flights of shallow steps leading down to the canalised river below the sluice gates and to the flanking museums and art galleries. Railings were of intricate cast iron, a superbly rich colour achieved only in the foundry, never by paint, a cobalt-tinged black, where the tone comes from the depths rather than being laid on the surface. Cast-iron sculptures flavoured the lamp posts and pathways with their dark solidity. These were preparation for the city museum, an excellent one in that it adopted the region's natural attributes as its subject matter. The city's industrial origins had been dominated by iron foundries and workshops. In many places the Soviet glorification of heavy industry can produce museums of stultifying but occasionally hilarious kitsch of the same genre as the odes to tractors churned out by Writers Union lackeys in the thirties while the real poets rotted in silence or Siberia. In Yekaterinburg the subject matter came naturally, and they really had something to brag about. In addition to discombobulating samples of local gemstones upstairs—pure garnets the size of bookends, clusters of feldspars in every imaginable tinge, gigantic rubies, compelling black crystals of manganite—the main gallery was dominated by a light-as-air filigree summer-house, of virtuoso intricacy and grace, *made of iron*, cast for the World Exposition in Paris in 1900. Large enough to house tea for twelve, its delicacy would have been remarkable enough had it been twined together from wicker and wood laths. Made of cast iron it was the most impressive testament to the foundryman's craft I ever expect to see.

As we walked back up the steps to the main street we could see across the man-made lake. Because of the sunshine, a slight mist hung over its ice- and snow-covered surface, an expanse dotted with strollers and ice fishermen. Beyond the mist, ranks upon ranks of white apartment blocks, each thirty stories high, gave an inkling of the blander conformities of Homo Sovieticus.

Yuri took me to lunch the next day at one of his favourite *stolovaya*, the cheap and usually grungy institutional cafeterias that dot all Soviet cities. One travel-writer rightly advises visitors to "think of school meals" when deciding if they want to sample *stolovaya* fare. But Yuri's—

entered through a pitch-dark basement that would fend off all but knowing locals—was spartan and clean, with tasty *pilmeni* (dumplings filled with lightly spiced meat) that seemed to have encountered real butter along the way, and a friendly server on the cafeteria-style line who suggested we wait a minute since a new batch was on its way from the kitchen.

More than once we found fifteen minutes to visit his favourite café. Tucked into the corner of the Cinematographic Institute, it was full of hopeful filmmakers and actors with, Yuri assured me, a hundred schemes in mind to convince Western firms to finance their projects and make them all both rich and famous. I wished them the best, knowing full well that the first wave of Western aid money and co-op ventures was already receding, and that a lot of disillusioned Russians, including a few young directors from the Urals, would be left stranded. But the coffee was good—perked in heated sand—and along with shots of vodka warmed up both us and the rest of the crowd.

Late in the morning of my second day in Yekaterinburg I had meetings arranged with representatives of the region's Jewish community. But we had an open half-hour. Yuri gave instructions to the driver. On a main highway leading to a wide bridge over multiple railway tracks (the city is on the Trans-Siberian, so that foreign entrepreneurs are more apt to be Korean or Chinese than American) giving views to the vast industrial enterprises on the outskirts of the city—scores of smokestacks bruising the sky—we came to the simple wooden orthodox cross set about twenty feet back from the curb. We pulled off and piled out. Painted white, the cross was about twelve feet high, an understated monument erected by a few local monarchists. Small photographs had been taped to the upright. The base was strewn with a dozen frozen roses.

After Emperor Nicholas II's abdication on March 15, 1917, plans were made to send the family to England (they were closely related to the House of Windsor), but due to the objections of the hardline Petrograd Soviet, they were shipped to western Siberia instead. In July 1918, as anti-Bolshevik White armies, tenuously allied with Czech legions who had taken control of the railway, approached the outskirts of Yekaterinburg, the danger of a royal rescue and revival became very real. It was a month in which the Bolshevik Revolution hung in the balance. In addition to the White advances in the east, Socialists had staged a coup attempt in Moscow after assassinating the German ambassador, and there were left-wing uprisings against the Leninists in Yaroslavl and other northern cities. The British were planning an incursion from Arkhangelsk on the Arctic Ocean, and did manage to land an expeditionary force at Murmansk in June. A Socialist Revolutionary government had been established in the south-east, at Samara on the Volga—the socialists had, after all, polled fifty percent more votes than the Bolsheviks in the November 1917 elections. In the south, Armenia, Georgia, and Azerbaidjan had declared independence in April and May, and British forces were sitting in Tiflis (Tblisi).

Under the circumstances, the Bolsheviks returned to their root instincts. They began to systematise the Red Terror. Not that the circumstances fully explain the terror. Perhaps one hundred thousand were shot over the next year. There was always something beyond "necessity" in

Lenin's violence, something exceeding even an amoral *realpolitik*, an aesthetic of excess, like Hollywood with live ammunition. Lenin's policies contained the inexplicable extra, thirsty and vindictive, a glorying in carnage that defies the logic of the very real social and economic forces underlying the revolution itself.

Mass class warfare, with its Nazi-precursor "imagery of public hygiene" ("The towns must be cleansed of this bourgeois putrefaction," wrote *Pravda* in August), began at the symbolic top. On the night of July 16th, the Tsar, Tsarina, and all of their children were taken to the basement of the nondescript house where they were confined, and shot. Yes, it is important to remember that the revolutionary heroes put pistols to the heads of the children and pulled the triggers. The bodies were then burned and thrown down a mine shaft. The man in charge of the operation soon gave his name to the city. He was Jewish, as were many of the leading Bolsheviks, which would not of course prevent the Soviet era, after an initial liberalisation, from eventually becoming rabidly anti-Semitic.

The site remained unmarked until local party boss Yeltsin ordered the house torn down. Now a tiny chapel, octagonal and built of wood in the old style, had been erected a few yards away. A couple of fur-bundled women stood outside hopefully, but it seemed to be locked. As I turned to gaze back at the cross, obviously now a minor pilgrimage centre, I started: in a coincidence of icons, a historical tableau appeared. From this angle, directly behind the cross on a small rise across the street, stood a copy of Moscow's famous "Worker Lad and Peasant Girl" statue, he with a hammer, she with a sickle, striding boldly into the future. Directly behind *them*, neatly aligned, was the tall sky-blue bell tower of the city's old Orthodox cathedral, recently renovated. The Soviet era, it appeared, was bracketed by older, and newer, loyalties. Only a Snickers billboard was missing to complete the vista.

Lenin's ferocity, inherited and perfected by Stalin, was a formidable legacy, laying deep roots of hatred ready to put out new shoots at any time. In the car, hurrying toward a meeting after lingering too long at the assassination site, Yuri was telling me a little about the reawakened Jewish cultural groups in the city. They had sprung up in the late eighties, encouraged by *glasnost*. Yekaterinburg's was a relatively small, highly secularised community, as old as the city itself. About fifteen thousand remained, now benefiting from the end of state persecution, but buffeted by economic crisis and emigration to Israel and America. There had been no synagogue since the 1960s.

Out of the blue, Yuri added,—I went to a few meetings, but I couldn't get interested.

I failed to hide my surprise. Yuri was fair, blue-eyed. He grinned and tapped the bridge of his nose.

—Well, maybe, I said. Barely.

He mentioned the insults he used to get at school, and presented me his face in profile. I shook my head. It was a mystery to me how Russian anti-Semites could identify their targets.

*

Yuri and I rested on a bench in a broad hallway on the fifth floor of the mayoralty building. We were waiting to go into

250

a meeting—I forget now with whom: the labour people, or housing experts; maybe the fellow in charge of resettling ethnic Russians from Kazakhstan. Down the hall, steamrollering, came a swarthy man, oversized—more in motion and energy than in actual physique—and barrel-chested. He swerved immediately on catching sight of me, thrust out his arm as I stood, and beamed while he shook my hand into submission. He was perhaps sixty, with a face bespeaking either decades facing into the wind on the steppe or regular fifths of vodka. He wore moustaches and a classic Soviet suit, that is, dark blue, pin-striped in black, ill-cut, at home on a 1970s left-overs rack in the basement of Eatons. On his lapel he bore a pin designating him as a member of the last (disbanded) Russian parliament.

I explained who I was. He introduced himself in the manner of someone using a megaphone, attempted briefly to speak some long-since dissolved school French, announced his status as a deputy (no longer technically true) in such a way as to suggest he could throw some weight around for me if I were having any problems, and extolled the virtues of Canada. My homeland was like Russia—vast, noble, cold, and not American. My host from the mayor's office, a Mr. Lomovtsev, came up at that moment with a mixture of exasperation and disgust on his face. He and Yuri groaned at each other and rolled their eyes. As soon as the deputy stomped off, an aid scurrying in tow, I was regaled with tales of the ex-parliamentarian's scandalous behaviour: he was a drunk, they said, a Cossack (ironically, as it would turn out, I first thought they said "Kazakh") who had no real Cossack roots but was fiercely chauvinistic anyway, and who was infamous primarily for an endless drunken speech he had given, on television, as the region's representative at a Japanese film festival.

Mr. Lomovtsev headed off again to shepherd my meeting, asking Yuri and me to wait. While we lingered, the Cossack came back. And hijacked me.

Gripping my arm, getting me to my feet again, he declared that fortunately he had a moment free. He and his men (his men?) would be delighted to discuss important issues (issues?) with an important Canadian official. (I was a Second Secretary . . .) I feebly protested that I had a meeting. Who with? he barked. Yuri, trying to keep close to me, gave a name off my schedule. The Cossack snorted. Don't be ridiculous. He'll wait.

He and his lackey strode us down a side corridor and stopped in front of a closed door. In we went. I was looking back over my shoulder as I entered, hoping Yuri got in behind me. He made it, loyal as velcro. The man's Russian was guttural and strongly accented. I had only vague ideas what he was talking about.

The office was dingy, narrow, ill-lit. It seemed completely filled with desks, filing cabinets, miscellaneous chairs, and smoke. Eight or ten men in odd, quasi-military uniforms I had never seen before stood silently along the walls as if waiting for permission to exhale. The Cossack took me to them, stopping sombrely in front of each and introducing them with a solemnity suggesting we were all about to undertake a death-defying mission together. We weren't, were we? One he named as his head of security, a second his director of counterintelligence. The last, a pimply youth, was a "cadet," with the understanding that he was glad simply to be in our presence. All of them—Yuri would explain later—were enlisted in the Cossack Army of the Urals.

He stationed himself behind a scarred desk in need of a good sandblasting, a smelly feudal lord with bad teeth, and proffered cheap Russian cigarettes. We smoked. So. What brought me to Yekaterinburg? I gave my set piece, described a few of my meetings, adding that I was late for one now with Mr.—.

Mr.— could wait. He waved a crabbed hand dismissively.

—So. Why have you been meeting the Jews?

Taken aback, I explained that Canada had a large Jewish community, that many Russian Jews want to visit Canada, that we were interested in questions of migration pressures, human rights, minorities in the new Russia . . .

—*We*, he said (we who? Me and him? Those in the room? Cossacks? Siberian Cossacks? Russians? Soviets?), *we* hate people who abandon their motherland. In a war, it is the Jews who are the first to run away. Don't you agree? It is an historical fact. They don't have the same feelings for the countries they live in as we do.

At this point I was not catching all of Yuri's translation, which was entangled in the booming hammer shots of succeeding Russian sentences. I actually asked him to repeat it all. Yuri did, translating slander against himself a second time.

—They will leave as soon as things get bad. Trust me, *Gospodin* Manicom, you in Canada will learn your lesson. If you have a lot of Jews in Canada, they'll leave as soon as you have some trouble.

Some ridiculous (but precious?) instinct of civility prevented me from simply telling him he was a foul-mouthed idiot. Or maybe it was only surprise. The outer reaches of anti-Semitism were until that moment something I had encountered only second hand. Maybe it was the narrow room, and the shadow of the chief of counter-intelligence behind me. At the time I felt no sensation of fear, but afterwards I wondered if "cowardice" was a word that needed applying.

He was still going on. It wasn't that he didn't like Jews. He had lived in Odessa for many years. Many of his friends were Jews. (Yes, he said that, word for word.) But Jews have no love of their native soil. Kazakhs, Turks, Jews. All the same. But the Jews were more dangerous, much more dangerous.

I tried sarcasm. I wondered, with feigned innocence, whether Cossacks were *native* to western Siberia? Hadn't *they* abandoned their home and native land along the Don to come here? (The Cossacks—the term is Turkic for "no-mad" or "adventurer"—were a semi-ethnic, semi-cultural group, originally Tatars, who had settled the south and south-eastern fringes of the Tsarist empire. They had also spear-headed parts of the Russian advance into Siberia.) He replied proudly that indeed they had, almost a century ago. The point was lost on him.

I had to *say* something. By this time Mr. Lomovtsev of the mayoralty had tracked me down and stuck his head in the door. I pleaded my meeting. I stood up. I said I had to leave. I told him I disagreed with his opinions about the Jewish people. I said it politely. Firmly, okay, but politely. I said it in Russian, but out of habit Yuri repeated it anyway, correcting the grammar. The Cossack couldn't hear him. So Yuri virtually shouted at him: *I disagree with your opinions about the Jewish people!*

He didn't even blink. He stood up, gazed at me with watery eyes. He clasped my hand heartily.

—Fine! We are civilised men, no? We are free to disagree, no? We are free men.

I was in the hallway, breathing hard. The room was closed behind me, though now I was much more aware of that doorway, how easily it opens, aware that the Cossack, the General, the People's Deputy and his men are always there, smoking, refining their uniforms and titles until they are called out for service.

STARVATION IN THE VIENNA CAFÉ: TBLISI, GEORGIA

More than anywhere else in the former Soviet Union, Tblisi will not leave my head. I have added its textures, I suspect, to my melancholy moments. It stays put, well-glued photographs.

*

A thin, lemony sunlight, out of a January sky, lent a bit of warmth to the brick streets of an old quarter of Tblisi. If you wore a dark jacket you could sense heat on your back. Dry brown leaves held to the limbs of the sycamore out of habit. The slopes above the valley were grey in the midst of the brief Georgian winter; shreds of mist near the Kura River gorge where it passed through the city had burned off before noon. I could see the river from here, at the bottom of the street—clean metal.

I had just worked my way down the winding streets descending from the rock in the centre of Tblisi that arrests the eye like the keel of an overturned ship, after a traipse over the crumbling remains of the fifteen-hundred-year-old fortress that clings there, the town's permanent ghost of past glory. Everywhere has a past glory. Tiny Georgia, geographically now on a scale with the Switzerlands and New Brunswicks of the world, had its own imperial past, and was even today reviled as an imperial power by splintering Ossetians and Abkhazians. This was Shavteli, the main street of the old town, a gracious rising curve paved in good grey stone. It was a street of unnatural calm on a quiet autumnal day (although it was January). The sidewalks should have been bustling. Everything held a sensation of displacement. At first I couldn't see why the mood of the city was so strange yet so familiar. Finally I recognized the gentle melancholy of ruins and archaeological digs, the landscape of accomplishment abandoned, whisperings of folly and the scale of time. Yet this was a living city, not Troy or Philippi; this was the home of a million people.

It was not empty, though it was emptying, an hourglass overturned by three civil wars. Thousands of residents had fled, to be sure, to live with relatives in the West or in other parts of the old Union, or into the countryside to grow their own food. But the quiet was as much a factor of the palpable weariness of the population, and the scarcity of gasoline. And hunger, malnutrition.

It had been one of the gardens of the Tsarist and Bolshevik Empires; now a famished and crumbling beauty, a winter sycamore. Three civil wars had bled the city of

256

its legendary vivacity: in the bullet-scarred capital, the struggle between president-poet-dissident cum madman Zviad Gamsakhurdia and the more or less reformist forces allied to former Soviet Foreign Minister Scheverdnadze carried on; bloody ethnic strife in the breakaway region of South Ossetia on the northern border with Russia continued; and slaughter followed secession in the Black Sea paradise of Abkhazia. Tblisi's spirit of élan and leisure had vanished. My secretary in Moscow had assured me Georgians rarely worked. In her memoirs, Nadezdha Mandelshtam describes the respite from the chaos of revolution and war they found while they "lingered in rich and happy-go-lucky Georgia." Only three years before my visit, observant travel writers were still extolling its handsome and friendly people: "The whole republic exudes an atmosphere of colour, fun and *joie de vivre.*"

I stopped and turned and waited, framing it all, setting a mental aperture. On my right, a small flight of stone steps led to a stone balustrade in front of a high white fence, with greystone gateposts bearing pale Stars of David. Made of the same small red bricks that crumbled off so many of the city's buildings, the synagogue was tall and square, and seemed in good repair. But I knew from a visit to the (heavily guarded) Israeli embassy that Georgia's ancient Jewish community was packing up and leaving forever, succumbing not to anti-Semitism—Georgia had known less of this than almost anywhere else in the Judeo-Christian world—but to civil unrest and economic privation. The community was moving en masse, mainly to Israel, accompanied by those Georgians who, lining up daily outside the embassy, were able to hoodwink Israeli consuls with

257

embroidered tales or scrounged documents about Jewish grandmothers.

A woman in a dark blue overcoat and kerchief stood, hands in pockets, at the top of the steps, staring through me. Her gaze as old as Georgia. I am almost certain she was there. If I could find the right negative I could show her to anyone, demonstrate her immobility. Oddly, the door was open behind her, an empty doorway.

Back down the street, the way I had come, I could see across to a broad paved square and down to the tree-lined—sycamore and cypress and linden—promenade along the river. I counted a total of only six cars in this both broad and deep urban panorama, all Zhigulis or Ladas, five parked, one moving. A gaggle of pedestrians loitered at a miniature market along the sidewalk, where a half-dozen tables bore socks or hand-knitted sweaters. I saw no one make purchases. Salaries here were worthless. Bread was rationed. The city's only crowds gathered when government-issue milk or eggs or bread appeared. Meat was gold.

I turned again, faced directly across the street. Late afternoon took colour from the air. The grey paving stones of the street were at the bottom of the picture; then the grey-brown bricks of the sidewalk; then a low cement wall punctuated by wrought-iron lamp posts; then, across the centre of the view, lovely old buildings in ochre and white behind tree trunks stretching up into thin limbs and a scattering of sand-coloured leaves on a white sky as upper border. Three sellers had established a poultry market. A man in a cap and long brown coat had just passed them by and was moving out of the left side. Only these four peopled the scene. There was a becalmed nakedness. Against the low wall, two stocky women in black and brown with their wares: a few dried chickens on a board. Between them, something for the rich, a major sale (the family's last substantial asset?): the seller was an elderly gentleman with a posture of perfect patience. His coat and shoes and trousers and cap were all black. On a clutched leash strutted a huge gobbler, a fat, red-wattled, beady-eyed turkey as high as the man's waist. The Georgian currency was at a hundred and fifty thousand to the dollar. The fellow was worth millions.

*

Business had evaporated. Half the shops were shut; most others had little to offer. Even government officials, not bothering with brave fronts, described industrial output as "nothing"; optimists at the American embassy spoke of production as six—not sixty—percent of capacity. A senior bureaucrat's monthly salary would buy a kilo of onions. Even in a land renowned for its bounty and its brandy, the largest private market downtown offered only a few root vegetables, greens, fish. Vendors outnumbered customers amid the cavernous stalls. I went into a nearby store. It sold a bit of everything. Nylons. Shirts. Soap bars. Auto parts (literally: a fender here, a door there).

At a display case near the front I stood helplessly watching an elderly woman. Arrayed for sale were a few cheap plastic combs, the style without handles that teenaged boys wore in their jeans pockets when I was in high school. A little ticket beside them gave the price. The woman could not seem to move her feet. She stayed where she was.

She picked up a white comb, she turned it over, she set it down. She picked up the same comb, she turned it over, she set it down. Her hand hovered. I waited. She picked up the same comb, she turned it over, she set it down.

* * *

The architecture is as rich as the people are poor. It is unexpected, difficult to place: not Italianate, not Asian, not Germanic, not Classical nor Renaissance nor Gothic nor Baroque. Seen from the ruined fortress of Shuris Tsikhe, the sloping red roofs are a sea of shambles. Near the main boulevards—Rustaveli, named after an epic poet, and Melikishvili—remnants of a Turkish wall have been exuberantly crowned by wooden houses with grand, multicoloured balconies in peacock blue and tan and green that would not have been out of place, save their colour, on Ontario farm houses. Their conjoining with the stone ramparts is fun-loving, unconcerned with proprieties.

In back alleyways whole thirds of houses have fallen free of their foundations; great splits filigree the brickwork; laths stand exposed as if a museum display designer had had his way; boarded-up churches have wide seams down their centres and sod flowering on their roofs. Angled from view in a courtyard, the ancient scarred door of a chapel is bolted; a huge-fendered 1970s Ford sits on blocks. The seven-hundred-year-old church on the cliff-banks of the Kura is built of massive brownstone slabs, eaten and scrubbed by weather. Its windows, narrow-slitted as if to give cover for archers, are bordered in intricate abstract designs that hint both at Celtic and Islamic calligraphy, and of course at the dense curvings of the Georgian alphabet.

*

The local hotels are full of refugees from Abkhazia, as are the sanitoria within which the Party once cultivated its privileges. Rooms are available only at the five-star Metechi Palace, a gleaming dozen-story modernity on a hill that looks as if it arrived yesterday from outer space. An Austrian firm put it up in 1990, eyeing a *perestroika*-loosened Georgia as the next great holiday destination for bored and sun-starved Mitteleuropa. It is three-quarters empty, but somehow—Alpine stubbornness—keeping up appearances. Fronds flourish in a soaring atrium, glass-walled elevators slide upward like an old Jetsons cartoon, a pianist by the waterfall tinkles Chopin to the detritus of diplomats, aid organisation reps, optimists, and the hardiest of scavenger investors gathered at chic little tables with Scotch or cappuccinos. Desperate for repeat business, the management gives me a room big enough for a small wedding reception and lays on champagne in an ice bucket with sweets and flowers. The TV has the NBC Nightly News off some satellite perched over Africa, affording me play-by-play coverage of an L.A. earthquake.

But the Cowboys and Indians days are not over. My time here is tranquil by local standards; a burst of machine-gun fire a few blocks away during one meeting (those present flinched but did not duck), a distant rifle crack or two during the night hours. Armoured personnel carriers are few in the streets, though army checkpoints still guard all approaches to the city centre. But weaponry is rampant. The Metechi Palace deals with the situation as best it can without sacrificing its European *hotelier* sense of decorum. A walk-through metal detector has been installed at the main entrance. Just beyond, an elegantly scripted little sign on an aluminum stand reads *Guests are kindly requested to check their firearms.* New arrivals cause loud beeping, and once through the gauntlet dutifully hand in their weapons at the coat check. Nevertheless, over drinks in the lobby, one local tough advises a colleague to always have protection, and pats a conspicuous bulge in his suit. But, wonders his tablemate, how do you get past the metal detector? No problem, is the reply. I always carry two. One to hand over, one to keep.

*

Georgi Vishikadze had out his refugee charts. The backs of his pale hands were covered with thick black hair; I couldn't stop noticing them, their pallor in the lousy light, the dark hairs heavy as iron filings. There were two types of charts, two methods of organising and displaying human displacement. I had been in the hallways of this government building only minutes earlier, and had seen what that displacement meant close up: cramped legs, damp, sitting on your last belongings, a crying baby screaming along the quivering cord of your stress, waiting and waiting. One method was geographical, spatial. Here is a map of Georgia. Each coloured dot is one thousand refugees. Here are some in that town. Two dots. Over here six. Look at that.

The deputy head of the Housing Division of the Committee for Refugee Affairs laid down his colour-coded map and picked up another sheet bearing dry lists of numbers. His wrists nestled in the cuffs of the thick grey sweater, as roughly and warmly textured as that of an Aran fisherman, that he wore beneath his black wool suitcoat. It was a pleasant enough day in Tblisi, but it *was* January: ten or twelve degrees Celsius. Inside this government building there was no heating, and the night chill lingered. It felt like the inside of a fridge. It was hard to pay attention to these numbers—this hotel in Kutaisi held two hundred and fifty refugees, that one a thousand. I kept noticing the thickness of the sweater, the heavy lines of its ribbing, the coarseness of the knitted yarn.

I had tracked down the Ministry's building with the help of my interpreter, loaned by the Georgian government. But in the decrepit shell of the lobby—walls unpainted or peeling, no staff at the coat check, no one at all really, lights burnt out—even he was daunted, and we wandered a number of corridors before fetching up in the ice-box office with its battered furniture. Had it been a refugee holding centre I would have acknowledged its grimness with a sinking stomach. But this was the government headquarters, home of senior officialdom—yet it was as dank and oppressive as a nineteenth century prison. Given the principle that such institutions almost unfailingly reserve the best for themselves, the cheerlessness of the fate of the non-elite—never mind the refugees—was difficult to visualise. The hallways were lined with displaced families waiting to visit one arm or other of the bureaucracy, to install themselves on one list or other that might save their

263

lives, that might feed their children. They sat numbly on chairs in the unlit vistas, nursing babies on the grimy floor when the chairs were full. They wore heavy coats, heavy stockings, heavy boots.

The statistics were daunting for an impoverished nation of six million. The take-over of the Black Sea coastal region by Abkhazian nationalists—aided by Caucasian mountain peoples and elements of the Russian military—had produced a humanitarian disaster dwarfing the earlier struggle over Ossetia, which had itself produced thousands of refugees. In a rampage of ethnic cleansing as sweeping as anything achieved by the Bosnian Serbs, the Abkhazians, themselves a small minority in what they considered "their" homeland, drove out a chillingly high percentage of the non-Abkhaz population, effectively depopulating many areas. Something like two hundred and fifty thousand people had been displaced, mainly ethnic Georgians but also Armenians, Greeks, Jews and Russians. Of these, one hundred thousand had exited in a panicked flight following the fall of the regional capital of Sukhumi six months earlier. Up to ninety percent of the Georgian population fled across the Inguri River frontier, tens of thousands over snow-filled mountain passes, leading to many deaths. These were the people now housed in hotels and sanitoria throughout the country. Every town held a few hundred, every city at least a few thousand. Given what I was seeing in the building where I was sitting, I was not optimistic about conditions in these holding centres. When asked, Georgian officials glumly asserted only that "we can give them something to eat." Georgi Vishikadze then gave me another number. In Tblisi itself, the capital of the garden of the old Empire,

264

twenty to thirty residents—refugees?—*residents*, die of starvation every day.

He stared listlessly at his columns of figures, waiting for my interpreter to finish passing his summary from Georgian into French. I thanked him for his time. He shrugged, didn't bother to rise. As I stood, I noticed the red coil of a tiny heater, no larger than a child's lunch pail, squatting on the floor behind his chair, the only colour in the room. I didn't blame him for not showing me out, though I felt a sort of impersonal disgust. The cold corridors were brimming with human flotsam. He had to work here every day; it was his job; he had to survive enough to have a life, tickle his children when he got home, kick a soccer ball about when they wanted to play. And even the mere lists of misery were as much reality, hour in, hour out, as could be borne. A little heater, a thick sweater, pale hands.

*

From this angle you cannot see much of the street; you have no panorama, you focus on what is in front of you, passing through this lens. Not much to look at; washed out. On this side of the street the degenerating sidewalk seems in places to be concrete, at times beaten dirt. A bit of litter, and a single barren tree; not an impressive tree; a badly pruned trunk knobbed with the scars of hacked limbs, spindly branches holding up a thin freckling of dried leaves. A man passes in front of it, foregrounded. His hands are deep in the pockets of a calf-length overcoat in a dark colour, rounding his shoulders. The back of his balding head gleams against the dull background, but its angle suggests

265

a downward cast, eyes fixed on the ground, no vistas. Just to the right of the tree, there is an ironic counterpoint in danger of arousing sarcasm: a pedestrian crossing light on a thin pole. You can't see the light from here—doubtful if it works—because it faces the street, in which from extreme left to extreme right of your view there is not a single vehicle and not a single crossing pedestrian. Why would a pedestrian cross the road, in Tblisi?

The man in the deep-pocketed coat shows little interest, moves on. The opposite street corner bears a bulky two-story building ending, toward the back left of your picture, at an alleyway down which another figure disappears from view. Beyond this, though you barely notice, there is another two-story building, in faded cream paint. A slashing split runs down one side; near the roof the split spreads, becomes a foot wide. It only appears to be intact: it is a pile of fragments not yet fallen.

Back to that corner building nearer by. It is fronted with brown concrete on its lower floor, and above with paint that was once perhaps blue or once perhaps grey but has now become neither. Neither this nor that, neither here nor there. Life gets away. Large sections of the painted plaster have fallen; the upper floor bears the appearance of stripping and priming for a new paint job—but all in reverse, all toward decay. A bit of colour—a red signboard—cuts diagonally across the face nearest the pedestrian crossing, with a shut door set in the hypotenuse. A café, or a bar, but closed tight.

But to the left of the unimpressive tree there is something else entirely: a knot of people, a dark cluster, all the dark coats in one grey-black mass, though with white or

266

pale blue hats or kerchiefs of the women dabbing colour, individuating heads. You can't see, quite, from here, why a score of them herd into a crammed semi-circle under a bit of awning. A small black-lettered sign over their heads is in the round-shouldered Georgian script—Greek to you. But the stir of energy, the elbow of hurry, are evident even in a freeze frame. And from a little further along your side of the street as you now continue forward, changing the view, you can see the flour-dusty loaves coming up over the heads of those in front out of a little unseen window in the wall, as the lucky lift free and slide ration-card discs of Georgian bread into plastic bags and begin to move away. In the upper left above the splitting building, sketch in a corner of blue sky.

*

The Ministry of Foreign Affairs of Georgia was putting on a small dinner. I was pleased: a chance to chat in an informal setting after too many you-on-your-side-of-the-table-me-on-mine meetings, with nothing more personal than business cards traversing the gap. My colleague Graeme and I were led through a winding series of corridors. Night had fallen outside, and the ministry building interiors were just about as dark. Half the rooms seemed unused, inhabited only by ghosts of Soviet desk-officers cementing fraternal socialist ties. The hallways were dank, undecorated, unlit—the whole place needed to engage the services of a plasterer and painter. From one point of view this might have been an encouraging sign: even a key ministry headquarters was in rough shape, meaning the government of

267

this ground-to-a-halt state wasn't lavishing its dwindling resources on posh digs for the diplomats. This didn't strike me as likely. I rather suspected a grimmer scenario: there wasn't even enough wealth lying about Georgia for successful corruption.

Leonid Chartishvili and Valeri Zedginidze, midlevel members of the consular and protocol divisions, gamely pursued a path through a doorway which seemed eventually to lead to basement storerooms, turned left off the first landing into another gamey, gloomy stairwell, up a few flights, through an abandoned chill antechamber with chairs standing on their heads on tables, and into an even chillier but softly lit cafeteria, hung with purple tapestries. Here our guides conversed rapidly with one of the staff—the first evidence of humanity in this wing of the building— and passed on into a haven, a long private dining room where space heaters lent a glow to a table big enough for twelve with places set for four around one end, and bearing enough food—and enough bottles of Georgian wine and brandy—to satisfy eight more guests.

We ate and drank, of course, as valiantly as possible, and I felt we were in a small boat, warm and dry, afloat in the cold sea of the huge building; or that we were the last light in the tower. But as the soup gave way to the spicy mutton I was most interested in what I noticed happening to the geography inside my head as Leonid—a young deputy-director with mournful eyes and a habit of frank pessimism—talked bitterly of what was going on in Abkhazia, along Georgia's once-coveted Black Sea coast.

I had earlier in the day been handed a copy of the local human rights commission report on the carnage in

268

Abkhazia, page after page filled with names of murdered families, mutilated grandmothers, mothers and daughters raped then burned in public squares. This was the Georgian version, to be sure, castigating an enemy that had just chased a humiliated Georgian president and his army out of Sukhumi. On the other hand, the flight of virtually all ethnic Georgians from the region, and the rocketing of *two* passenger airliners, spoke sufficiently clearly of the rebels' clarity of purpose and disregard for the lives of inconvenient civilians. For Leonid all this had struck close to home. He told me about his aunts and uncles in Abkhazia, his mother's siblings. Three of them were dead. One had died in the exodus. An uncle had disappeared in the disintegration and chaos of the fall of Sukhumi, details unknown. His aunt, however, had been executed. In a village north of Sukhumi, she had decided to stay after the Abkhaz takeover. A few weeks later, residents were asked to register with the new authorities. The next night, soldiers went door to door, killing Georgians, now knowing exactly where to find them.

Horrible, and, from Bosnia to Croatia to Afghanistan to Rwanda, a 1990s commonplace—in this respect identical to all preceding decades—of the hyped-up tribalism we call nationalism, at root similar in maturity to nine-year-olds claiming *My daddy is better than your daddy.* But there was something else in Leonid's story, in his amazement that the Abkhaz—a cultureless minority, as he considered them, beneficiaries in his view of first Soviet then Georgian attempts to develop their homeland—should not only have the bloodthirsty stupidity, and the thanklessness, but the *ability* to turn on their now majority neighbours and hurl them back across the river. Of course the Russians had helped, it was assumed (and some had, while others were assisting in the sea-evacuations of the refugees), as had the mountain Caucasians to the north. But still . . .

Here, in the small wedge of land between the Caspian and Black Seas, between Europe and Asia, the whine of unappreciated imperialism droned beneath the genuine human grief for Leonid's massacred relatives and compatriots. Here, in *colonised* Georgia, in recent centuries a football for the Turkish and Russian empires, in recent decades Sovietized and culturally, linguistically, and politically dominated by the mainly Russian elite of the Communist party. But to the Abkhaz, and, I assumed, to the Ossetians, Tblisi was a hated Rome, a despised London, casting its giant shadow over the freedom of small nations, over their will to govern their own affairs.

We were sipping Georgian brandy, essence of sun and grape and summer sea-breezes, coveted—and now hard to find—throughout the old Imperium. The heaters whirred, knives clinked on tableware. The windows gave back the night.

It is easy to forget, but the former Soviet Union teaches you over and over again: imperialism may be an active evil, an aggressive imposition of the national self on the autonomy of others, a roughshod run of the powerful's values over those of the (for the moment) less *puissant. But to be colonised accords no positive virtue.* It only means you have been colonised, not that you are thereby free of the imperial urge. The colonised have no moral force, because they are no more or less virtuous than the colonisers—only weaker. An impolitic truth, to be sure. Long after the great fifteen-hundred-year arc of Saxon expansion passed from early landings on the coast of fifth-century Celtic Britain to the gates of Kabul and the out-back of Australia, Scotsmen—earlier victims of the English Imperium—proved ferociously able administrators of the Raj. Armenia, crushed under the Ottomans, once held sway over weaker neighbours all the way to the coast of the Mediterranean, a "Golden" (i.e. domineering) age now only visible in the anomalous Armenian "quarter" of Jerusalem's Old City. Long before the Iroquois were rendered despoiled and culture-shocked "aboriginals" on a European polity's reservations, they did their best to exterminate the Hurons, a "lesser" people speaking the same language, whose hunting grounds and lock on the fur trade looked appetising. A Huron remnant—today we call them refugees—wandered what is now the American midwest for a few decades, then vanished. A few minutes observing wealthy Delhi or Bombay *paterfamilias* interact with Nepalese or Bangladeshi hotel clerks shows that the jewel in the crown has learned its own imperial swagger. The safest thing you can say about a colonised people is that their turn will come, and that they will grab it when it does. By 1993, the Lenin-and-Stalin-drawn map of the Soviet world was exhibit one.

*

From the bread line, I kept walking, all the way back. Despair is the great devourer of energy. I had found the entire day enervating, drained to a depth I had never reached

271

before. *Here* was the culture I knew nothing of, the culture of war and hopelessness and hunger and unrelenting loss, the culture where the arc of a visible future, which sustains us even when we are unaware of it, has been destroyed; the culture of the blank wall, of the life like a crumbling balcony, the citizens ghost-characters in an unfinished novel no one was left to imagine. I was trying to struggle out of this new species of exhaustion. For the first time I thought of weariness in terms of claustrophobia. As evening fell I arrived at the gleaming Metechi Palace, floodlit on its hill.

In the lobby there was light everywhere. A pianist caressed the keys; no doubt a member of the Tblisi Symphony shilling for dollars or deutschemarks. The fountain added its own notes. I sighed a five-star lobby sigh. Wanting to organise my semi-legible scribbled notes from the day's meetings before I forgot too much to decipher them, I made my way to the bar off a quiet back corner of the lobby. Another elegant sign on an aluminum stand greeted me, and I noted for the first time that I was entering the Vienna Café.

It was tranquil within, half the tables filled, crystal and silver and calm conversations. The carpet was plush, the armchairs that drew up to carved and polished wooden tables were deep and receptive. Hidden speakers delivered a Mozart string quartet; for an odd instant I wanted the composer, seated in silence while his quill scratched notes onto staves in Vienna or Salzburg (the Alps quiet behind him, but the cold thrum of the Salzach's water cutting under like a cello), to be able to stand at the window here, gazing over dimmed Tblisi, and listen to his own music in such an unexpected place. A waiter brought a classically scripted menu on heavy stock with a braided cord

272

and tassel. They had everything the heart desired, lovingly described in Georgian and Russian and German and English. Impossibly, I was hungry. It seemed imperative to eat something, the more special that something the better. An amulet of immunisation, I suppose. I ordered coffee, cognac, and Black Forest cake.

I got out my notebook and began to extract prose from my jottings. The coffee and cake arrived. Many layers high, the hefty cube of icing and cake was topped by filigreed chocolate and maraschino cherries. I sipped my coffee as an amber vessel of cognac appeared. For a moment I simply admired its colour, then inhaled its fumes and sipped. Fork poised, I dug vertically into the soft cake, and with the chocolate still lingering against the cognac-trace in my mouth, wrote, "Govt bread rations normally available. Office from state cttee for Refugee Affairs stated twenty to thirty city residents die of starvation each day."

METROPOLITAN DARK:
YEREVAN, ARMENIA

In that vicinity the eyes need more salt. You pick out forms and colours but it's all unleavened bread. Such is Armenia.

Osip Mandelshtam, "Journey to Armenia"

I'm still the same, my heart has not grown fainter,
Lover of light, sworn enemy of gloom,
I lie and fight with phantoms in my room.

Gevorg Emin, *Songs of Armenia*

Dust and ochre, and the solitary white mass of ancient Ararat meditating over Yerevan.

But at night a medieval darkness and chill in the Armenian capital, a metropolis of one million people. Lenin, the gremlins of Soviet central planning, and the pathogen of nationalism had combined to turn out the lights for three million Armenians.

In 1921, the mountainous region of Nagorno-Karabakh, populated primarily by Armenians but with an Azerbaidjanian minority, was assigned to the newly formed Soviet Azerbaidjanian Republic by Narkomata, Lenin's Commissariat for Nationalities. Although officially worshipful of the many "nations" within the comradely Union, Lenin's policy, long before Stalin perfected it with artificial famine and mass deportations, had been to divide and fragmentize whenever practicable. Early in the *glasnost* era, Armenian resentment over what seemed to them the partitioning of a homeland already amputated by Turkish imperialism and genocide quickly boiled to the surface. In 1988 a Karabakh Committee was able to bring a half-million people into the streets of Yerevan and push a resolution demanding the "return" of the region through the Armenian Supreme Soviet. Anti-Armenian rioting erupted in Azerbaidjan in response, and eventually led to Moscow imposing direct rule in Nagorno-Karabakh, a compromise that made all parties furious. A few years later, with the Union structures dissipating like smoke in a breeze, Armenia and Azerbaidjan were at war, even if, officially, there were only Armenian "volunteers" fighting in the vicious battles outside Stepanakert, the capital of the enclave.

Karabakh had been functionally independent for over a year by spring 1994, and "Armenian" forces now also occupied a corridor linking it with Armenia along with a "security zone" inside Azerbaidjan proper. There were plenty of refugees on both sides. Given the shakiness of government control on the ground, a particularly nettlesome problem for the Red Cross was that of privately held prisoners of war, kept under often very poor conditions by families bartering through back channels for the release of loved ones held on the other side. The taste for dying to regain a bunch of dry mountains full of obstreperous Armenians who fought with the tenacity of 1948 Israelis was fading fast. Baku was having trouble getting men to the front. The odds of getting Karabakh back were lengthening.

But if Armenia could not be defeated on the battlefield, it could be made miserable. Armenia obtained much of its fossil fuel needs in the form of natural gas from Caspian fields, via pipelines across Azerbaidjan. This tap was turned off. The principal alternative—given the hostility of Turkey on its western border—was Turkmenistan gas via Georgia, but Georgia was disintegrating, and this supply arrived only in fits and starts, interrupted by Georgian nonpayment of transit fees and periodic bombings of the pipeline (probably by Azeri agents). In one of those curses of historical bad timing which Armenians feel the gods arrange to strengthen the national fibre, the main nuclear power plant, providing thirty percent of the country's electrical needs, had been shut down due to understandable ecological concerns following the catastrophic 1988 earthquake. The overall result was energy generation meeting about one-sixth of the country's needs. There was virtually no heating or hot water in a country whose winters—always severe given the dryness and elevation (Yerevan sits at over nine hundred metres)—were unusually harsh in 1992 and 1993, with lows touching minus twenty. In the capital there was about one hour of electricity per day.

A colleague and I stepped out of the hotel and walked into a gulf of darkness. Our hotel, where most embassies and UN agencies were housed, was provided with electricity much of the time (and with the aid of an electric prod resembling an oversized hair curler one could even heat bath water, though only by risking electrocution). Debbie had been in Yerevan before and knew the way: it wasn't far to the apartment of our local staff members Artashes and Narva. It was the chilly but still pleasant ending of a balmy March day. The city had felt reawakened in the hazy sunlight and the sidewalks were busy, the people upbeat. We had found a café putting out a few tables to take advantage of the warmth. When a group of black-suit-coated men at the next table learned we were visitors, they insisted on buying vodka to upgrade the meal. That evening we had decided to walk. As we passed from the hotel's pooling light we entered a strange realm.

The human mind is still somewhat accustomed to nature's dark, the ink of a nighttime forest, the blindness of the country yard beyond the porch lights, loud with crickets. But now we moved across city intersections, past a twenty-story apartment block, into commercial streets lined with shopfronts, across a six-lane street, then up a hill and into a residential quarter filled, we knew, with the grand old ochre-stone buildings—many of volcanic tuffa—six or seven stories high; we moved in utter night. So dark that

276

we stepped cautiously, feeling for curb edges, squinting for broken sidewalks. The city's shapes were black on black. The sensation was of desolation, of life walled up, shut in, muted; of the era before gas lighting when sunset meant only darkness and the small pods of candlelight that pointed out, rather than extinguishing, the great power of night. We were in the middle of a city of a million people and could barely see our feet. Having found our way to the correct street, we were approaching our destination when I saw at the last instant an open manhole, and stopped short, startled heart pounding at a near miss.

Our seeing improved. Night is never absolute. There was some thin cloud cover and no moon as yet, but stars showed dimly here and there. Gradually we felt the sky give off, if not exactly light, some sense of space and contour. Artashes had reminded Debbie: "X" many doorways from the corner. Stopping in front of the entrance, searching her memory, she decided this was the one. We went in.

Now it was dark. Dead teenagers lay scattered across the barren land on the frontier of Nagorno-Karabakh. Continuum. A pitch dark hallway, darker than the dark outside the way truly black cloth will reveal the impurity of blue-black set beside it. Artashes was waiting for us, and had been watching to see if we would detect the correct entrance. I could hear the grin in his voice, but there was also the formidable Armenian stoicism, and a bitter pride, all too aware of the foolishness of such pride and how it traps a culture. He went first, telling us how many steps there were to the first landing. I laid my hand on the newel post, then touched the bannister. A game of blind man's bluff on a grand scale, on a war-vast scale. I was hooded, trussed. My foot found the step. One. Two. Three. The ascent had no shape, no sense of space. We were invalids. In the territories of true darkness we had previously known, there were no five-floor walkups.

At the landing Artashes' feet stopped and his voice came back to us. Landing here. Fifteen steps to the next. Up we went. Off each landing, we knew, were apartment doors, but they remained invisible and thus the sense of depopulation was sharpened. For unclear reasons the brooding sense of unease, of hidden lives, that settled over me came to remind me of Joseph Conrad novels, not only *Heart of Darkness,* where the darkness gives a sense more of moral blindness than helpless isolation, but *Lord Jim, Nostromo, Nigger of the Narcissus.* Again—how many times?—Artashes' disembodied words came down out of the silence, and again we found the pausing place, the upward twist of the bannister turning to the right, the recommencing of counting. Ten flights eventually, two per floor. Then we stopped. Artashes and Debbie were suddenly beside me. There was no sound but our breathing. I heard Artashes turn the key and the door swung.

We had come back from a great distance, back to light, and stepped into a faintly lit—but so beautifully un-dark—entryway. There was a single bulb burning for the apartment's four rooms, I would shortly learn, a bulb saving sanity through the winter nights, a gift earned by hard labour, stubbornness and luck and ingenuity. But now, here, it simply gave a welcome dim warmth as we took off our shoes, following Artashes' example, and greeted his family.

*

278

In the first three terrible winters of their independence it was the darkness that Armenians came to dread the most. Their minds cried out for colour, shape, illumination. In central Yerevan, unlike most cities of the old Soviet Union, you could be unblindfolded and know instantly you were in Armenia. The city is not so much beautiful as it is *spirited*. Its buildings combine stolidity with the ornateness and rich tones of native stone in a way appropriate to a people so adept at blending fatalism and *joie de vivre*, long-sufferingness and passion. Built of basalt and marble, onyx and volcanic tuffa in a gallery of styles, they create a unique cityscape based on varieties of ochre and an indigenous stiff late-classical early-medieval building line.

One of the main streets, still called Lenin Boulevard on the map I had, slowly rises until it gives a panorama of the early spring city behind you as you climb. At its crown stands a modest yet dramatic building of grey stone, dominated by a central arched porch with blue stained glass rising to three quarters of the structure's height. Along a balustrade six Armenian sages, carved in the same grey stone, survey the scenery. Below them, beside a plinth inscribed with each of the Armenian letters, his eyes closed and his two hands held up in the old style of prayer, sits Mesrop Mashtots, creator of the alphabet. One of the oldest of languages, Armenian can be traced to the seventh century B.C. Its unique script of thirty-eight letters is attributed to Bishop Mashtots and dates to the end of the fourth century A.D.

Inside the austere building behind him, the Matenadaran Library holds an infinite amount of light. Armenia stakes a claim as the oldest Christian nation, converted early in the fourth century, at a time when Constantine was still offending the locals by not partaking of Rome's pagan rituals. The Matenadaran contains two hundred thousand ancient documents and incunabula, including over twelve thousand scrolls and manuscripts in Armenian script, scores of them from before the year 1000. In one of the most remarkable single rooms in the world, a high-ceilinged circular space on the second floor lit by the great window above the entrance, display case after display case holds the jewelled pages of the great Armenian illuminators, from huge volumes in which every page must have occupied a month's labour, to tiny gem-works for a monk's pocket.

There you can see the gospel miniatures of Tzerus, a fifteenth-century monk, cheerful but not resplendent in his favourite tones of dark olive, sombre red and golden yellow, little worlds where Adam and the Virgin and God the Father all have wide open, mischievous eyes busily taking a delighted look at things. When his Christ laves the apostles' feet he takes a good firm grip and grins while he's about it. They are populist pictures, startlingly lively and fresh under Matenadaran glass after six hundred years, reminiscent in tone of the English medieval Corpus Christi dramas in which Noah is apt to get in a smart remark before rounding up the animals.

In another case are the darker dramas of Arag, a century older and from eastern Armenia; he was a painter-scientist more in touch with the broader Byzantine world, favouring a rich yellow-brown field and more solemn faces, familiar to anyone viewing Russian or Greek icons of the same era. In his "Removal of Christ from the Cross," black and gold radiate from the border; the Virgin kisses a torn and twisted Saviour even while his feet remain nailed in place.

And so many others, glowing in the glass-and-wood cases. The near-pastel levity and bestiary imaginings of Toros Taronatsi from the early 1300s. Sargis Pitsak's fabulous purples and ochres in almost-Arabic twinings—his unparalleled birds, letters and angels burnt into the parchment, still hot to the gaze. And most compelling of all to my colour-sated eyes in that room full of enormous yet tiny windows into the heavens and the mind—stained glass in reverse, the artistic fire cast outward through the panes of colour—was the work of Grigor. From the mid-1200s, his miniatures resound with dark tones and dark eyes and strange tilted buildings. He is the master colourist of them all, generating blues I could link only to Chagall and the upper reaches of Chartres' triforium on a sunlit day, mixing reds neither scarlet nor vermilion but touched with both, worlds of fervid nightscapes.

A millennium later, the colours flourish. Nitpickers will point out that colour is the breaking up of white; but after my own journey to Armenia I would never again think of it as anything but an inroad against darkness.

*

Now it was spring in Yerevan, late March, and if the city's remaining trees—much of its once famous greenery had been scavenged for fuel—were not yet quite in leaf, the scent was in the air, the sun was warming the rich ochre tones, and kids were kicking soccer balls under the white

281

flapping sheets on courtyard clotheslines. The nights were still bracingly cold, but the buildings held some heat.

Artashes was a serious man, of medium height, with black hair cut short and a dense, closely-cropped beard. He wore a long, heavy sweater of dark grey-blue, the sort of sweater prized in a city without heating. Energetic and sombre at once. When Osip and Nadezdha Mandelshtam visited Armenia in the early thirties, the poet, with typical frank clarity, noted that Armenians were defined by a "rude tenderness." There was something of that in Artashes' stripped-down manner, an abrupt friendliness without coddling or frills. Naira, his wife, was at the door to greet us, petite with a pale face and coal black eyes of great beauty and sadness, framed by thick hair, jet, to her shoulders. Two children also: a son, nine or ten years old, and Astrid, at six, the age of my own daughter, as dark-eyed as her mother. The entrance hall was in deep shadow, but beyond it a large room was spilling light toward us through an open door.

Artashes gave me a tour. It was a tour of their survival, the salvaging of his family, a visit to their ingenuity, persistence, and luck.

The apartment was large, enormous by Moscow standards: probably seventy or eighty square metres, with this pleasant open hall, a large sitting room, separate kitchen, bath, and one spacious bedroom. Six people lived here. I was soon to meet Artashes' elderly parents, arms crossed on the living-room couch and thoroughly bundled in heavy socks, layers of vests and sweaters, his father wearing a beret suited to the cafés of Paris.

The vestibule revealed a surprise: the walls, papered in dark floral patterns were bare. Most apartments of "Soviet" intellectuals were dense with paintings, sketches, prints, antique plates, photos. Artashes saw me looking.

—The paintings are all wrapped and stored in closets. We heat with wood. (Not tonight, so far I as could tell: it was chilly inside.) The soot would ruin them.

He lit a candle; we proceeded into darker rooms.

The kitchen held an electric stove. Artashes showed it off. Puzzling. Though I knew gas was also in short supply, I was certain electricity was almost non-existent. He had arranged some sort of swap; I've forgotten the details. I didn't want to pry, so saved my questions (they would be answered soon enough). In the bathroom he demonstrated their solution to constantly interrupted city water supplies and an utter limpness of water pressure: above the tub, suspended in a wooden frame, hung a plastic tank the size of a coffin. He must have bartered for it from some industrial plant or other; it certainly wasn't a standard household item. Time for a demonstration. The tank was linked by plastic tubing to the showerhead. When Artashes opened the spigot the great weight of overhead water did its job: the Emins had a pummeling shower stall with water pressure worthy of a fine hotel.

But the living room sobered me. Convivial, less chilly, lit, cosy, it nevertheless told of too much suffering. Here was where the family lived. Excursions out of this room required candles and an extra sweater. Two large couches along one wall could be turned into beds. The walls were papered in yellow-brown. Lighter rectangles demarcated where paintings had hung, faint windows to memory. A table to one side was for meals and, right now, the children's homework. Glass-doored corner bookcases. An overstuffed armchair. And in the centre of the room a wood stove, squatting on a square of tin, with a venting pipe doing an elbow at six feet and heading across a dozen feet of open air to exit through a hole sawed above the door to the balcony. On the wall above the couches a single florescent tube had been mounted. It was illuminated. A few feet to the right of the stove, a television. It was on. How?

Artashes showed me his pride. Back in the entrance hall, tucked in a corner and running under a table, stood an array of six huge liquid batteries, sleekly black, like bombs. Wires skipped between them, then disappeared into the darkness.

This had been salvation this winter, had rendered it merely an ongoing aggravation. Artashes' work required him to travel to Moscow at intervals. On each trip over the past year he had managed to purchase and lug back one of these batteries. (Our own flight down, on a crammed Soviet-built Tupolo with no flight attendants, broken seats, and a dangling ceiling panel, had been lengthily delayed once everyone was seated while the captain and co-pilot loaded flats of eggs into the hold.) Now, with six batteries, the horrors of the previous winters had been chased away, chased outside the circle of the fire. These batteries could build up enough charge, even on only one hour of electricity from the city grid a day—which, most days, they got— to power one light bulb and either the TV or the kitchen stove through the evening hours.

The wood stove lording awkward and raw over the room's centre had not been lit this evening. An extra sweater and thick knitted slippers would suffice. After all, wood here was precious.

To complete his tour Artashes led me to the balcony. He gestured at his victory with the air some men in other dimensions of the universe use for a new Saab or the view from their patrician dock as the sun touches the water. Fifteen feet long and perhaps six wide, the balcony had been enclosed with tacked plastic sheeting. It was full, from end to end and floor to ceiling, with stacked firewood. To have this on hand as spring came, rather than desperately scrounging week by week as the thermometer and sun both sank and snow dusted in the little trenches across city streets here electricity thieves laid their lines, was in Yerevan something roughly akin to having retirement looked after at age forty: unusual security, peace of mind for loved ones.

And crucial, because, as Artashes explained while we sat around the same table where the children laboured on their homework by the one glowing tube, he would not be here next winter. Naira was unable to contain a shudder, a turning inward of her dark eyes. She and Artashes were laying out plates and saucers, serving rich herbal tea and exquisite homemade baklava. Artashes had won a Fulbright Fellowship and would be going to the United States for at least a year to do graduate studies at Georgetown or Harvard.

A doorway out, but also a ticket back. The Fulbright came with generous allowances: penny-pinching in America would mean a few thousand American dollars to bring home, a relative fortune in the collapsing-currency world. He and Naira were not *all* practicality: with wood in the bank to keep elderly parents and children warm, with the battery array to provide a light, a stove, a TV, they could in good conscience at least talk about the possibility of Naira visiting for a month during the Christmas break, just when the days in Yerevan were darkest, the assault on the psyche toughest. They might rent a car, they speculated, or with better luck borrow one; they would drive through Virginia and Tennessee and Louisiana, see New Orleans, meet America on its own terms, on the highway.

We talked in our funnel of light. The children finished their homework and moved on to drawing pictures for me to take back as presents for *my* children, who had never thought twice about a light bulb in their lives. Naira often silent; Artashes' mother smiling, watching television, knitting, murmuring at the children; his father, with whom I had chatted superficially—mainly in Russian as he was uncomfortable in English and I knew no Armenian—turned the pages of a collection of prints, looking up every few seconds at the TV. We talked about the war. Armenia would win; Azerbaidjan had no real interest and would eventually realize it; of course the government here was helping the Karabakh forces but not, it seemed, with regular army forces. There were some stories of "volunteers" conscripted at gunpoint. It wasn't clear if they were true.

One of the family's main concerns was education. The schools had just reopened with the warmer weather, and would stay open through the summer, after having been closed for five months to preserve fuel. International aid organisations were providing gas heaters to some of them. Many students were morose and languorous from too many hours in the dark and from poor nutrition. Naira was concerned the children's progress was suffering. She and Artashes were not the sort of parents to be satisfied that at least their children were keeping up with their local peers. A poor education was a poor education. Artashes broached one possible plan—Naira wincing again—to somehow finance sending their son to an academy run by Armenian monks in Venice, where he could get a *real* education. He was particularly irritated by what he considered low-quality language training: his son was learning "only" Armenian, English, and half-hearted Russian. The daughter was fine for now; she was younger, and seemed to be suffering less from the psychological batterings of the winters. Maybe the situation in Armenia would improve in time for her.

This winter, Artashes explained laconically, had been less horrific, both for the family and for the city as a whole. People were better prepared. Many arranged to leave for "warm" regions (i.e., with energy supplies) in Ukraine, Russia, or wherever relatives or friends could take them in. In the bowled-over post-Soviet world, people headed *north* to escape freezing to death. One aid organisation, the Armenian Assembly of America, had told me that unused ration coupons suggested twenty percent of the population had fled this winter. Those who remained tried to organise fuel supplies in advance as best they could, insulate their apartments, scrounge for wood stoves and then for wood, lay in food supplies from rural relatives. There had been fewer casualties this year. During the nightmares of the two preceding winters the weak and the unresourceful had already died—the elderly, the sick, the foolish, the unlucky. Even a thousand miles to the north in Moscow we had heard the horror stories of retired professors feeding the pages of their libraries into their stoves to stave off the terrible cold.

287

Except for the grim topic of conversation, and the fact that family members disappeared into the dark every time they went to the bathroom or to the kitchen for tea, it was a cosy and unremarkable domestic scene in the apartment of Artashes and Naira Emin. The terrors, here, were at bay. I caught glimpses of them, though, in the practised routine of the children when the big event of the evening occurred. There, in the middle of our tea, without warning, the city electrical grid kicked in. The apartment, every room, was dazzled with light. Leaping up immediately, the boy sprinted into the hall and unplugged the TV extension cord from the array of batteries and plugged them into the wall socket to begin charging. Simultaneously, Astrid hooked the TV into another wall socket so as not to interrupt the program her grandmother was watching, and unplugged the florescent tube to relieve any drain on the charging batteries—it was now unneeded since every lamp was ablaze. Everyone's spirits visibly lifted. I realized how dim the room had been. This douse of electrical benison meant not only the temporary splendour of good light but, if it lasted (it did—for over half an hour), topped-up batteries to get them through *tomorrow* evening.

Shortly after the lights went off again and the children ran their routines in reverse, we rose to leave, with a busy day planned for tomorrow. We shook hands with everyone, and I tucked away a batch of cheerful drawings wishing hello to my children from the southern Caucasus. As we stood at the door making final farewells and preparing to navigate the inkwell of the stairs, I noticed on the wall, in the pale rectangle of light cast from the living room, a faded poster. It was a publicity announcement for a po-

288

etry reading in a major London hall in—as I remember it—the midseventies.

My eye had been caught by the names of those who would be reading English versions to accompany the recitation in the original languages by Russian and Armenian poets: Vanessa Redgrave and Richard Harris. In addition to a few of the heavyweights of contemporary Russian verse—Yevtushenko for one—there was a name I did not at first recognise, but which I realized, from the company it was keeping, that I *should* know: Gevorg Emin. After a moment of stupidity my synapses made the connection. This poster was hanging at the doorway of Artashes and Naira Emin. I looked back to the living room, where he still sat on the couch, deep in the colour plates of his book, one of Armenia's leading poets of this century as I would learn, turning over the leaves, imagining what the colours of these paintings would be like if only he had a little more light.

Along the city streets on the way back to the hotel, with nothing to look at save the faint edge of the sidewalk that the sliver of risen moon showed, I was thinking back to something Naira had said about their first winter without light. We had stood talking at the door, parting delayed while Artashes dug out copies of two of his father's books in translation—one of which, his paean for his country, *Seven Songs About Armenia*, lies on my desk as I write this. These were a superb trade for the copy of my own most recent book the Emins had out of politeness insisted I send down from Moscow. Decades earlier he had described himself in verse—a bitter prophecy in the end—as "lover of light, sworn enemy of gloom." In spite of how terrible the cold had been, Naira had murmured, a chill that could never be excavated from your bones, it was the darkness she dreaded. With quiet certainty she said that if she knew she must face another winter like that one, she would either leave Armenia or go mad. Evening after evening the family had sat, gathering in one room for the warmth of whatever flammable objects had been quarried, scrounged, bartered that day, in the dark. They could not read. They could not write. They could not knit or sew. They could not watch TV. They could not see each other's faces. If someone cried silently, no one knew they were sad. Sometimes, she said, she began to feel that no one else was there, that they had all died, or that she had died without realising it and become a ghost who could no longer touch the real world. Rarely, they would buy a candle: they were hard to find, and cost what a desperate market would bear. All they had were each other's voices; but they found themselves talking less and less. They waited, their sense of time itself gradually fading, in silence, in darkness.

Even this was not the worst, she told me. The worst was that the darkness got into them. They spoke few words. They cared little. It became enormously difficult to make any sort of effort, whether to get food, to plan the next day, to clean themselves under the icy taps. The worst, the worst of all, was that sometimes, just for a few minutes, the lights came on. The apartment burned in their eyes, a terrible vision, glowing with the force of a hundred chandeliers, light blazing painfully against their clenched lids. They resented the light. The light meant an unbearable revival of obligation, of responsibility, an effort to rouse yourself, to do something, to activate your mind and your emotions, to think about lines of verse or where you could buy soap or thread to darn a sock. They hated when the lights came on, attacking their torpor, reminding them they were not yet dead.

Journal Notes

MARCH 1994

It now costs 1792 roubles to buy one U.S. dollar. In much of the former Soviet Union, though, amidst tengs and soms and carbonovets and drams, the Russian currency is considered admirably stable and convertible compared with the local pocket chaff.

I met a man today who was on his way from Tomsk, in Siberia, to Saskatchewan. Fiftyish, quiet, solid, his hands as worn as old baseball gloves. He worked as a machinist. He was going to see his father, who had kissed him goodbye on his way to the front in 1941, when Leningrad was in the first year of its siege and Kiev and Odessa had fallen. When he was two years old. He had not seen his father since. Like many soldiers, this one had disappeared in the chaos. The family had waited, given up. Perhaps, captured by the Germans and having heard what Stalin had in store for "traitors," he had been afraid to go back. Maybe the chance to go west was simply too alluring, or he thought his family was dead, or he allowed himself to think this because he didn't want to go back, his emotional attachment a weave worn too thin by years of separation and carnage. Perhaps the war had little to do with it; perhaps the grand forces of history barely touched him. Perhaps he simply didn't love his wife. A less poetic tale, but just as likely. Not all victims are saints; lost love cannot be willed back; those swept into war are noble or disloyal in the same proportions as humanity in general.

Then, in the '80s thaw, contact had somehow been reestablished. I never learned the details. An aunt spoke to a cousin who worked for a man who had heard that his brother's first wife . . . That sort of skein, no doubt, some sequence of improbable, Dickensian chance. Elderly now, with a Canadian family, the Russian war veteran sends an invitation to a middle-aged Tomsk machinist, attaching a long and agonized letter in Russian, a language now partly forgotten. Or a short, inarticulate note, empty of emotion? So one ends up with a ham-fisted metalworker whose previous travel adventure was one two-week outing to the Black Sea in '86, seated in an embassy waiting room with his shapka in his lap, on his way to the Canadian prairie, where, offspring of a ghost, he will recognise only the flatness and the cruel cold. When he recovers his suitcase off the airport carousel and turns to face the crowd he will, with great difficulty (using a mailed photograph) pick out a stranger leaning on the arm of his half-sister.

After a few weeks, full of emotion and facing emotional chasms that can never be crossed, he goes back to Tomsk. After a few years his father dies.

MAY

May Day was bright and balmy and part and parcel of the recent stretch of (relative) political stability. The post-coup blues seem to be the tune still, everyone too bushed to attend to the apocalypse. The Communists were out on our neighbourhood square of course, their flags the colour of dried blood as snappy as ever in the wind. But the numbers were modest. As I walked in the milling crowd they didn't seem very worked up, more like the Canadian Auto Workers at a Labour Day picnic than the remnants of the great and terrible machine. An American on the podium yelling "Long live Communism" in English got the biggest rise, but nothing like a mighty roar.

The next day was Easter Monday on the Orthodox calendar. At 9:30 p.m. it was almost dark when the church bells began, a single first note that was then echoed and reechoed from all directions, some close, some haunting from afar, a beautiful weaving of rhythms. The tolling picking up pace. Who would have thought one of my memories of Moscow would be the sunset full of church bells, sombre yet joyous, set against the dusk?

We're pretty excited about gasoline these days. The saga of keeping our car's tank filled over the past three years has been the story in miniature of the transmogrifying Russian economy. When we first arrived petrol was in plentiful supply, and, with the requisite Soviet-style bureaucratic hoop jumping, could be more or less always counted on. It was simple. If you had a foreign-built car

294

like we did, and needed gas with more than trace amounts of octane, you just had to write the embassy a cheque on your Canadian account to obtain U.S. cash—a week later—from the embassy accountant, visit one of the two or three places in the city that sold roubles for U.S. dollars, and take your roubles back to the embassy administration, which was authorised by the Soviet government to issue diplomatic gas coupons, with which, at specially selected state gas pumps a mere ten-minute drive from the embassy, you could put reasonably adequate gas in your tank after no more than a six- or seven-car lineup. Not quite like popping into the Petro-Can self-serve for a fill-up on your way home from work—plus a loaf of bread and a cup of coffee on your credit card, in and out in five minutes—but with a week or so of planning, careful record keeping, and patience, the system functioned.

Then Moscow abolished diplomatic coupons and ran out of gas. It also ran out of roubles, so in late 1991 and early 1992 you played on your lunch hours the double game of scouring likely spots for rouble purchases and then, roubles in hand after only five or six wasted tries, beginning regular stops at functioning gas stations in your region of the city on the off-chance they might have some. After a while you used the car only to shop for gas.

But then foreign investment began to arrive. This meant an Italian corporation built a real honest-to-god gas station with coffee shop, a dozen self-serve pumps, car wash and garage, on a piece of barren land three-quarters of the way to Sheremetyeva airport. Most of the pumps had lineups stretching a hundred cars back down the road, but the two "high" octane pumps for non-local products—at triple the price—had no lineups and always had gas. Well, almost always. They did have a quirky system requiring you to buy coupons for x-number of litres of x-octane at the cash register inside, then shove the coupons through an outside window and shout through a thick pane of glass to get the woman inside to turn on your pump. But that was nothing. It was a half-hour drive each way from our apartment, a nice way to blow a Sunday afternoon. And of course the drive back took the top off your tankfull. I thought it was great.

Now, this spring, progress by leaps and bounds. We have discovered a wonderful spot, underneath a bridge across from Gorky Park mere minutes from our door, where an entrepreneur with a gas tanker truck parks regularly to dispense perfectly acceptable wares. You just turn off the Ring Road on the way home from work, execute a couple of tricky U-turns in front of the New Tretyakov Art Gallery, find your way down a dark alley-like lane, and back your car up to the truck. He has a high-octane truck and a low-octane truck. He takes your money, pumps you full in no time, and even says please and thank you. Before you know it he'll be putting in rest rooms. Gasoline as a challenge is disappearing from my mental horizon. I can do whatever I please with a Sunday afternoon. Life just doesn't get any better than this.

The political stability, or at least the absence of visible collapse, of jitterbugging along the rail edge above the chasm and not yet falling off, is, however, accompanied by a continuous crumbling of the civic veneer in day-to-day life. If last year's bull in life's china shop was inflation and all it said about economic value going puff like smoke, this year's is crime. We have been personally smacked by it three times, but as we are safe and sound and un-impoverished we don't feel particularly hard done by, just a lot more wary, our privacy well fingered, and freed of any "it won't happen to us" instincts left over from happy childhoods. Our Jetta was broken into in broad daylight around the corner from the embassy by semi-pros jacking at the radio: they couldn't get it out but did enough damage to render it mute. Once Teresa had her wallet spirited from her backpack on the metro home from work: a few hundred bucks in U.S. dollars and roubles, and the aggravation of reassembling all the bits of plastic and paper the banks and governments like us to have so they will give us their benisons. And once we had the pleasure of a gentleman in our bedroom at 4:00 a.m., a cat burglar who five minutes later would attempt to disorganise my face with the leg of a dining-room chair before exiting out our ninth-floor kitchen window. His presence—the moment of accepting it—was the cusp of a nightmare one couldn't wake out of.

But we feel lucky enough. The current fear about town is from a spate of attacks by fake (maybe) policemen, complete with uniforms and machine guns, who knock on doors, gain admittance, and beat up the inhabitants before cleansing the apartment of valuables. A colleague who had two appear at his door last week was smart enough not to take off the chain, and found to his surprise that a fierce, universally-understood English

297

"FUCK OFF!!" sent them traipsing back down the stair-well. And on the weekend, serving as embassy duty officer, I spent a Sunday afternoon tracking down a hospitalised Canadian lawyer. He wasn't easy to find in a massive downtown hospital complex with fifteen buildings and no reception desks. But a summary of his reported wounds got me into the right sector, where regularly repeating Canadski? *to floor nurses enabled me to home in. He was in a ward, barren and charmless but more or less clean, his head, chest, arms and legs heavily bandaged. He had been operated on late the night before— bone settings and repairing of massive lacerations. The previous evening he had opened his door to a driver at his law firm, an employee he had had to fire—but, he thought, the parting had been reasonably amicable, so let him in. Mischance had drawn the fellow's attention to an ornamental but sharp sabre mounted on the apartment wall, which he used to beat up the lawyer. After which he chained him to the toilet, turned on the gas, and left. A neighbour had saved the day, and one life, by breaking down the door. The lawyer was pleased to see me, already in a surprisingly chipper mood. After the surgery he had woken up. Alive. Delighted under the tape and gauze.*

The quickening of spring, the accelerating days, the lingering light are welcome in few places more than in Moscow; but for us the flowering and opening is twisted with sadness and a sense of ending inappropriate to the season, like a love affair ending rather than beginning in the lovers' month of May. Though any love affair with this place is a turbulent one, shadowed by recurrent loathing, buffeted by stress and disgust. The thought of leaving actually makes me physically nervous, for reasons I can't pin down. It is a sensation of dismay, of things going wrong, off track. It is no doubt in tiny measure what binds Russians themselves to their difficult land, what made the anticipated great migration to the West—so feared in Western Europe in 1990 and 1991—never happen. (Canada's immigration program in Moscow, covering two hundred million people during tumultuous social and economic and political times, remains very small, five or six hundred families a year.) Moscow isn't the sort of place you pop in on, on the way to or from somewhere else. So it's a real goodbye, though we'll be back, sometime, somehow. My Russian teacher never stopped giggling at the English phrase "pop in." We won't be popping in anytime soon.

There's a Russian word, tosca, with no precise English equivalent. One writer defined it as "ineffable longing for something lost or far away." I have more tosca now. It is Russia's gift and curse. I thought of the word a lot as May came to an end with the arrival of Aleksandr Solzhenitsyn, stepping on Russian soil for the first time since he had been bundled onto an Aeroflot flight along with seven KGB agents and a doctor, stripped of his citizenship, and led down the steps onto the tarmac in Frankfurt twenty years earlier. Sad photos of him taking a last look at his Vermont home appeared in the press, followed by unexpected glimpses of him beaming (had we ever seen him smile?) on the ground in Vladivostok. He is now in a country he will love and loathe, with plenty of tosca *for many different things, a country he will not be able to change any more than his writings—indirectly but powerfully, a deep undercurrent altering the landscape— already have. He will be—like Gorbatchev—a titan now in the wrong era. But then he had reminded us all, in the pages of* A Day in the Life of Ivan Denisovich, *that the forces of history are incarnate only in individuals. So that's okay. An old man—troublesome, irascible, brilliant, arrogant, brave and unflagging—is finding his way home.*

JUNE

St. Petersburg, a brief last visit, long final strolls. White midnight on the Neva, the hovering of the Winter Palace. The ethereal light drawn out hour after hour like the held note of a violin.

9

A DAY IN THE COUNTRY

Let me cut the hill and its campfires into layers.
There'll be no time to grow forests. . . .

Let me take this mirror country lying on its back
and button a long coat over it and keep it warm.

Osip Mandelshtam

It wasn't exactly a day in the *country*. But I am not about
to change the title. Let me try to explain.

On the longest day of the year, a sunny Moscow
Sunday to begin our final week in Russia, we were invited
for a picnic—that was the word—by Katya and her family. When Teresa had taken a teaching job during our second year in Moscow, we had lucked onto Katya—a friend
of a friend's maid knew her mother; something like that—
an unemployed twenty-year-old kindergarten teacher
whom we hired to look after John—aged three, later four.
She was shy in the beginning, but warm, reliable, intelligent, stimulating for John—apt to head off to a day at the
zoological museum on intricate bus routes, so that when

we came home from work our three-year-old would be explaining about the hinge on a snake's jaw—and a joy to know. Most importantly, she loved John. More, I am afraid, than he can ever know or understand. And if she learned more English from him than he did Russian from her (though he mastered all the key words to try to get his way), we were simply delighted that he was so obviously delighted. In the end, her grief at parting from him was one of the hardest things I have ever had to look at.

Katya lived with her mother just beyond Moscow's outer Ring Road, a brawling and dangerous ill-repaired rally course orbiting the city about fifteen kilometres from the Kremlin. We piled into the car in late morning and drove out Kutuzovsky Prospekt, past the rewhitened White House, going fast on the wide, straight boulevard in the light Sunday traffic. The main route west out of the city, "Kootz" as we all called it had served too often as the artery of Russia's terrible encounters with conquering lunatics out of Europe. A few kilometres past the classic wedding cake kitsch of the Ukraine Hotel—facing the White House across a bend in the Moskva, it is Stalinist monumentalism at its "best"—we zipped under the snorting bronze horses astride the grandiose Corinthian columns of an archway commemorating the victory over Napoleon. Here, on a modest slope, the French Emperor had waited for the city to surrender. Instead, of course, General Kutuzovsky abandoned the burning city to permit the French to lose the war by winning the battle—all with winter rapidly coming on and the inadequately provisioned *Grande Armée* some two thousand kilometres from home. Gradually opening on the left on Poklonnaya Hill was a great green space, hundreds of acres in the middle of the city, cleared to build a complex of monuments and museums—still unfinished—to honour the even vaster struggle against Hitler. It was out Kutuzovsky Prospekt that the bulk of the Red Army marched during the unexpected counterattack that drove back the German troops from the outskirts of the capital.

Kilometre after kilometre: straight and open to sun, electric buses balking and tilting their way up to thin day-off-work crowds at the stops; Zhigulis and Ladas wheezing and tut-tut-tutting past, wheels visibly wobbly; long marching rows of apartment blocks and peeling state store shop fronts; the trees filled out above a scattering of sunlit aluminum kiosks where now, in Moscow, a mother out with her toddler could pick up a Mars bar or a bun, and a heart-long-ago-torn-away drunk could lay his hands on everything from peppermint schnapps to Budweiser, King of Beers. Kootz was, in these outer reaches, officially Prospekt Marshala Grechko and then eventually Mozhoyskova Chausee as it sloped gently downward toward the outer ring; it would become the M1, en route to Smolensk and the western frontiers. The kids were bouncing about in the back seat wondering if we were there yet. It is a good question, one worth answering "yes" to, however far you've gone.

Just inside the outer ring we turned off onto a side street which, with startling rapidity, snaked into woodland and dipped under the freeway and outside the city limits. A dead ringer for an Ontario country road headed through big boss dacha territory—you never actually saw the dachas of anyone *really* important, but plenty of cops lingered at all the turnoffs—past streams and un-cattled pasture and stands of birch and poplar and oak and Russia's shaggy, silver-tinged version of maple. Left again onto a smaller macadam road. Down the hill a portly man in tiny shorts had his shirt off to scrub his car, which he had parked with its front wheels in a brook. His dough-pale flab was no less blissful for its pallor and extra pounds. Then onto a sort of double laneway with an overgrown grass median leading past a bus stop and a not-quite-cleanly put together concrete bunker which housed, the sign said, the local cultural centre, medical clinic, and pharmacy. This appeared to include a library and small theatre for the inhabitants of the local apartment fortresses and was, like many things in the former Soviet Union, a good idea badly executed. The sidewalk out front was frost-heaved and cracked, and the Bus Stop sign had its message erased by rust.

Now we could see the community these amenities served: a half-dozen high-rise blocks hunkered in a Stonehenge-circle around us, crappily built—sections visibly off-kilter—and poorly finished. Balconies were streaked with rust, or broken off, or growing shrubs out of their crumbly cement. Driveways were choked with undergrowth and deeply rutted. The central courtyard-playground we skirted as we searched for Katya's building was a sad menagerie of weary, empty swing frames and rust-speckled climbers rising from weeds and (where there was gravel) a low-explosive minefield of tin cans and broken bottles. Perfect for tots. But many people were out nevertheless, strolling, resting on the half-broken benches, or fixing their cars, curious but trying not to stare at the oddity of our bright red Jetta with diplomatic plates toiling into a run-of-the-mill (but deemed a cut above the average, a good break for those who had landed a spot) outer Moscow apartment cluster.

Katya met us as we unloaded ourselves from the car, with her niece Nadia in tow, a four-year-old china-skinned beauty with blonde pigtails and big dark eyes. John danced a jig around Katya and tried to avoid being swept into a hug. His *nanya*'s eyes were glistening.

Upstairs we stepped together from the dingy hall-way—painted dark green and decorated with filthy ceramic tile—into the apartment. The spotless hardwood floor had been laid with a thin, finely braided mat in red and white, as clean as a table runner. There Katya's mother Elena, a widow to alcoholism of about fifty, greeted us warmly, kissing the children and exclaiming excessively over the simple salad and bottle of French red we had contributed. She is a woman of cheerful weariness, as if life were a perpetual Thursday afternoon, but one to be made the best of. The apartment was Soviet Standard: two medium-sized rooms plus a kitchen alcove. It was now relatively spacious, as only Katya and Elena lived there; but for many years it had served a family of four. Decoration was spartan. The family had no extra money, and Soviet consumer culture offered little beyond bland kitsch with which to brighten an apartment. The walls and couches and bookshelves, the icon in one corner, the dining-room table, were all scrubbed and dustless, as clean as a stereotypical Dutch kitchen in the midst of Russian muck.

We also now met Katya's sister-in-law Olga, slender and fine-boned like her daughter, but of the darker Russian type in complexion, with brunette hair. Neither she nor Elena spoke any English: Katya's had been improving rapidly, but through the day our Russian had to generally serve. Olga's husband Anton had gone ahead, we were told vaguely, to get things ready. But what did you need to get ready for a simple picnic?

Wicker baskets and cloth bags were already stuffed and waiting in the entranceway. They were good weight in our hands as we rode down in the narrow brown cage of the urinous elevator and walked out into the unreasonably beautiful June sunshine. The children jigged around the adults as if around Maypoles, then darted off, then circled back to hold a hand. We passed other families, one child each, making the most of things on the scruffy lawns or in the prehistoric playgrounds; we passed a greenhouse complex (where Elena worked) backing onto the grounds of the apartment blocks; and then entered the countryside that surrounded all such outer urban pods of Moscow. We first traversed a not-very-thoroughly cultivated field that would yield something like half its potential crop of corn (it appeared that, after the ploughing, one haphazard run with rude cultivators had been deemed sufficient; the earth remained in hard clods as big as baseballs; knee-high corn stalks were scattered, rather than arrayed in neat rows, across the expanse of farmland under a line of high tension wire); we passed across the field and broached, with delicious suddenness, as if dropping into cool water, the shade and green air of mature deciduous forest.

The woods brimmed with silence. The city was shut off, like a fridge rumbling to a halt in a nighttime kitchen. However, along the submarine paths, picking up our feet over a calligraphic intricacy of tree-roots, brushed and whispered by dense vegetation, I realized we were not in

306

nature—or, rather, that the nature we were in was shared with human nature. The path was well travelled, the interlaced roots made more prominent by the wearing away of soil. Larger roots on the way were as polished as old door jambs. From time to time the forest opened out into small clearings or larger meadows of sun-silked grass where we could see logs pulled together around the bare patch of a regular camp-fire site, or where we could see a solitary fifty-year-old man, his shirt off to put sun on his pale stomach, reposed in his own world of grassy sea with a book and a bottle of juice or vodka, a Russian Antaeus getting his strength back. We went on and on, our bundles getting heavy. The route was intricate, and lengthy: clearly it was not a matter of ploughing into the woods and grabbing the first good spot. Some sort of etiquette was involved, and some sort of concern for the perfection of the day, a remaining faith.

For a time we skirted the edge of the woods along a less frequented path—only a vague parting of the grass, as if a comb had been run through it—densely canopied by a brake of lilac bushes now past flower. The backs of nearby warehouses reminded us where we were before the path turned back into the forest. Then we came to a wide but enclosed meadow—perhaps five acres—where the thigh-deep grass was stippled with hundreds of yellow flowers and threaded with scores of delicate white teardrops and occasional bluebells. The sky was bluer because of the flowers. Ahead of us, where a few trees stood out a bit from the forest wall to create a space below them that was both sheltered and open, both wood and meadow, Anton stood hailing us, hard to see at first in the shade of the old maple above him. The children broke away and dashed on ahead through the surf of grass.

As we approached, Anton was squatting again, intent on his work, but he stood and turned to greet us as we arrived and set down our baskets, lending the brief solemnity Russians prefer in greeting before smiling warmly.

It is indeed a perfect spot; bringing us here is an intimate gift. Two trees give us shade. We are near the woods but not in them; the expanse of meadow surrounds us, opening our eyes and lungs a little wider, but the trees give the space contour and confinement. A weathered trunk fallen years ago, silver grey and scrolled by wind, defines the area further and provides seating for four or five a dozen feet from where Anton is preparing a fire. Under the trees the grass is sparser for us to spread blankets and unpack the hampers.

Anton, a slender young man, appears to be about thirty and by the rule of Russian males (a diminishing species) is thus probably twenty-five. His daughter has her arms wrapped around his leg. He is very cleanly shaven; his short sandy-brown hair is neatly trimmed. Dressed in freshly washed Levis and white T-shirt, he carries a hatchet in his right hand. He addresses us in Russian, which that day I am loving even in its unrelenting complexity, asking us how we are, how are the children, asking if we are pleased with the blue sky, which is surely especially for us, for the picnic.

This isn't barbecuing over a gas range with dual temperature controls on the back deck. This is a lot of work. Anton has been foraging. He has assembled some larger branches of dead wood, trimmed to provide both kindling from the trimmings and heavier fuel from the shorn limb. A portion of these have been laid out in the bare-dirt centre with kindling tucked beneath. At the four corners of an imaginary square containing this wood he has made spits. Taking the Y's of four branch forks about as thick as broom handles, he has stripped them clean and sawn neatly across the tops just above the fork. Then with the head of his axe he has driven the base of the Y's into the hard packed earth, leaving the crotches about a foot above the ground. These branches are green and, where he has cropped them, white. He crouches back to his work, gathering shavings to feather beneath the kindling. Satisfied at last, he snaps the head off a kitchen match with his thumb and sets it against the curling white edges. With the twigs beginning to crackle, and slow wraiths of smoke twisting upward, he shoos us away from the baskets. He needs coals, embers. The fire will be ready for cooking in twenty minutes. We should take the children and go for a walk, show David and Teresa the path—he gestures across the meadow—and the flower-clearing. By the time we get back we will be able to put on the meat.

We leave Anton tending his fire, where he is obviously content to be. Children again in hand, we strike out into the wade of grass, heading directly across, to where a seam in the woods opens on the far side of the clearing. John and Nadia are already picking fistfuls of the yellow and white flowers sprinkled around us, but this lovely space is only preparation for what lies beyond.

Approaching the gap, we see it widen into a broad boulevard between the trees, a prospect of lush, waist-deep grasses interlaced by a panoply of flowers flourishing in the dappling of sunlight, a rich river of white and yellow blooms swaying against each other so that we must plough through them, our legs awash in colour-laden stems. We are ravished. The children leap through the flowers like dryads. We pass through to where the woods open again into a still larger clearing. The wild flowers fill it completely, a span of brightness that makes us stop and stare.

We gradually work our way back, this time cutting through a dense glen, through dark wood-shade, fists clutching bouquets. Elena falls behind, to search amongst the tree roots for medicinal plants. When we emerge back into "our" meadow, the children again sprint ahead to greet Anton, who is just rising again from his crouch by the fire, stretching his legs. Drawing near, we see that the fire is still burning fiercely but is now doing so over a bed of charred logs. Anton feeds it no more fresh wood, so that the flames gradually settle back into the jewelled wood as Katya and Elena open the largest hamper. Inside is a huge covered dish.

The amount of meat is staggering. And humbling. A month's salary? The cubes of beef have lain soaking all day in oil and spices. Elena unwraps a dozen metal skewers from a tea towel—each is a good eighteen inches long—and begins to spear the meat onto them, assembling the *shashlik.* Each skewer would serve, in an average Canadian restaurant, as an entree for two people. Here, we are six adults, with three children. There are at least a dozen skewers now heavy with beef. This will be a roasting suitable for feast time in a Greek epic. Anton takes two empty skewers and lays them into his wooden Y's, then places the *shashlik* crosswise, tight against each other, roofing the fire in raw meat. Which begins immediately to scorch and roast and drip and sizzle, and baste in clouds of wood smoke.

Katya and Olga spread a large plastic tablecloth, checked red and white, between the fallen tree trunk and the embers Anton is now stirring. Elena is playing with the children; some contest involving tossing leaves at a twig stuck in the ground. Tess and I help empty the baskets, increasingly abashed as we compare our poor contribution to the feast awaiting us. Cultural miscue: we had thought "picnic" implied an informal snacking. In addition to the meat, there is plentiful *zakuski*: fresh cucumbers and tomatoes, sweet black Russian bread, cheese, mushrooms, a salad, grapes, bottles of lemonade, juice, vermouth, vodka.

Two passers-by—the first other people we have seen in half an hour—stop and ask directions to Peredelkino, where Pasternak is buried, which turns out to be surprisingly close, a further two-kilometre hike through the woods. We open the wine, saving the vodka for toasts, sip and chat and watch Anton fuss over the meat—salting, peppering, ladling the oil and spices over it—and rake the fire. When he pronounces it ready, he takes a razor-sharp knife with a ten-inch blade and hews kabobs free and slides them off onto plates pre-loaded with the bounty of the hampers.

Our appetites are as sharp as the knife. But first the vodka has to be opened, carefully dispensed. We raise our glasses. Cheers! *Santé! Nash'zdorovye!* and silence descends save the wind and the birds and the occasional chink of cups and cutlery.

*

I stopped, exhausted, at the kitchen window of our flat.

Behind me the apartment was stripped. The walls were bare, the closets empty—not a toy, not a book, not a CD, not a single pair of shoes. All the colour was gone. Even the movers' crates were gone. I looked out toward the Kremlin domes, but it was a densely overcast day, with mist in the air, so that they could barely be made out, just a hint, if you knew where to look. I knew where to look.

After that only a bit of waiting was left, waiting in the car along the Sadovoye Kaltso, past the great curving gates of Gorky Park, over the Moskva with a last glimpse of the Kremlin cathedrals from the bridge, out Leningradsy Chausee to Sheremetyeva; waiting in the dingy departure lounges and then on a Lufthansa jet already carrying us up over the giant, inhuman metropolis that was slowly turning below us and then sinking beneath the surface of clouds above which my reflection floated, just past the plane's wing tip. I felt like I was awaking, or going to sleep; I wanted more than one world, more than one poor life; I longed to keep all of my realms.

*

The food is wonderful, so we keep at it a long time, and don't particularly know what hour it is. After a while, having finished salad and cheese, we take to leaning on the ground to talk languorously as the sun begins to draw out the shadows, and concentrate only on the remaining *shashlik*, succulent and smoky, and the vodka—down to essentials. Stuffed and content, the children have wandered back to their games, Elena and Olga with them, while Teresa and I eat and drink and talk with Katya and Anton.

Anton is a chemist; he has a job somewhere in an institute. He goes there from time to time. But like Katya he is profoundly disgusted both by the constriction and paralysis of the last Brezhnevian decades of Communism, and by the chaotic money-grubbing, social disintegration, and survival-of-the-nastiest milieu that have so far served as examples of "democracy" and "capitalism" in the new Russia. He is glad new possibilities have opened up; he reserves the right to be appalled by those which have been realized so far. As far as I can tell he and Olga are back-to-the-landers in a non-ideological sort of way. Anton has left the family apartment. He and his young family spend most of their time at a dacha—little more than a rough cabin from all accounts—an hour into the Russian hinterland of collective farm and birch forest beyond Moscow. There they work the earth, live simply, need little cash, breathe relatively clean air, try to clear their thoughts and raise their daughter.

It is a cliché of course, but, lying in the dimming beauty of late afternoon, fire-roasted *shashlik* on our plates and fire-essenced vodka in our tumblers, since it is Russia, we end up talking about history with this kindergarten teacher turned nanny for foreigners and her chemist brother, and talking about philosophy, and Tolstoy, and the Russian poets who are always looking over your shoulder and writing about today, and about capitalism and socialism and the state of the Russian soul. There is time to talk, and the ghosts seem far enough away to give us leave to roam freely through our own impressions and emotions.

At one point Elena and Olga begin to pack up the dishes, and then, insisting we stay to finish eating, announce

313

they will head back now, and take the children with them. They mention something about tea. Fifteen or twenty minutes later, full to satiety and in a sunny vodka calm, we ravel our paths back through the forest, where the flowers are darker tones now in the long angles of sun.

When we arrive at the apartment, Teresa and I thinking we have completed one of the most delicious and splendid days of our lives, we find Elena bustling about a fully laid table. A white cloth has been brought out. Plain china is at each place, with silverware. The samovar—a simple one, meant for daily use—stands nearest the wall with the small kettle perched on top. Agog, we gradually accept that more food is planned. Olga is ferrying fresh *bliny* (thin, sweet Russian pancakes) from the stove. Small dishes are filled with jam and *smetana* (sour cream) and caviar. Ice cream and cakes await. Katya puts a cassette of Tchaikovsky in the compact stereo we bought her as a going-away present. Elena is pulling aromatic cups of steaming tea from the samovar as we gather together one last time around the table.

High in the air somewhere over eastern Russia, near the borders of Belarus and Poland, I look back. Anton and Olga and little Nadia have left. It is now the evening hours in that apartment, the long hours of Russian summer sunset, and in some way we are still there. But as Elena and Katya move tiredly about their two rooms, clearing the meal away, they notice that we are beginning to fade, like the slowly draining light, that we are less than solid, ghosts, hard to see now, mere spirits of a brief communion.

NOTEJ

Page 15. "A giant ship." Osip Mandelshtam, poem 101, as translated by Clarence Brown and W. S. Merwin (Penguin, 1986).

Page 18. "The Putative Head Gennady Yaneyev." David Remnick, *Lenin's Tomb* (Vintage Books, 1994), pp. 454 ff.

Page 38. "Homo Sovieticus." Ryszard Kapuscinski, *Imperium* (Knopf, 1994), p. 275.

Page 44. "On that date." Andrei Sakharov, *Memoirs* (Vintage Books, 1990), p. 615.

Page 61. "At twilight the swifts." Boris Pasternak, *Selected Poems*, translated by Jon Stallworthy and Peter France (Penguin, 1984), p. 55.

Page 64. "Do not be ashamed." Maria Razumousky, *Marina Tsvetaeva: Mythe et réalité*, translated by Alexandra Pietnioff-Boutin (Les éditions noir sur blanc, 1988), p. 162. My English version is adapted from Pietnioff-Boutin's French translation version of the original.

Page 64. "To aspire to purity is natural." Boris Pasternak, *Selected Letters and Writings* (Progress Publishers, Moscow, 1990), p. 90.

Page 64. "What had happened in the world." Pasternak, *Selected Letters*, p. 147.

315

Page 65. "The return of historical memory." Remnick, p. 4.

Page 73. "In 1992, even amidst . . . " The anecdote is recounted in the *Moscow Times* (Oct. 1992).

Page 75. "He carried poison with him." According to Guy de Mallac, *Boris Pasternak: His Life and Art* (University of Oklahoma Press, 1981), p. 220. The source cited is Andrei Siniavskii.

Page 77. "According to one biographer." de Mallac, p. 267.

Page 77. "The grieving non-literary crowd." Andrei Voznesensky, *An Arrow in the Wall: Selected Poetry and Prose* (Henry Holt, 1988), p. 285.

Page 80. "Raise it again, man." Seamus Heaney, *Field Work* (Farrar, Straus and Giroux, 1979), p. 27.

Page 80. "And it seemed to him." Boris Pasternak, *Doctor Zhivago*, translated by Max Hayward and Manya Harari (Fontana, 1983), pp. 184-85.

Page 90. "I remember being alone with Chechanovski." Nadezdha Mandelshtam, *Hope Abandoned*, translated by Max Hayward (Collins Harvell, 1989), pp. 416-17.

Page 94. "It wasn't until the 1850s." For this and a number of other historical details I am indebted to Ahmed Rashid's valuable book, *The Resurgence of Central Asia: Islam or Nationalism?* (Oxford UP: Karachi, 1994), especially pp. 107-35.

Page 95. "By 1870 the Kazakhs had lost." Rashid, p. 111.

Page 117. "In his memoirs Sakharov gives." *Memoirs,* p. 531.

Page 122. "He doesn't know what to do." John Updike, *Rabbit, Run* (Alfred A. Knopf, 1981), pp. 308-09.

Page 122. "Sakhalin seems to be the end of the world." Quoted in Remnick, p. 250.

Page 134. "In Kyrgystan the newspaper industry." Rashid, p. 71.

Page 134. "In June, 1992 two factions." The Moscow Times, 29 May 1992.

Page 135. "Yevtushenko scurried." Remnick, p. 284.

Page 136. "While the czar's ministers." Remnick, p. 249.

Page 136. "In 1992 it had already been governed." The Moscow Times, 23 June 1993.

Page 146. "On the Russian folk calendar." Polina Rozhnova, *A Russian Folk Calendar* (Moscow: Novosti, 1992), p. 73.

Page 150. "She only made it to Moscow once." Tatyana Tolstaya, *Sleepwalker in a Fog,* trans. by Jamey Gambrell (Virago, 1992), p. 61.

Page 171. "Into the heart of a perfectly-iced wedding cake." Martin Walker, *The Harper Independent Traveller: Soviet Union* (Harper and Row, 1990), p. 229.

Page 173. "The movement for independence." I am indebted to David Remnick's account in chapters 15 and 25 of *Lenin's Tomb.*

Page 196. "Joyce's *Ulysses.*" *The Moscow Times,* 15 June 1993.

Page 222. "He [Yeltsin] would later express remorse." *The Moscow Times,* excerpts from Yeltsin's memoirs *The View from the Kremlin,* 14 May 1994.

Page 227. "Shrugging off and cleansing." *The Moscow Times,* 14 May 1994.

Page 235. "And somebody strange is in a hurry." Osip Mandelshtam, *Fifty Poems,* trans. by Bernard Meares (New York: Persea Books, 1977), p. 73.

Page 240. "In July 1918." I have drawn details from the account by Geoffrey Hosking (*A History of the Soviet Union,* Fontana, 1990, pp. 73 ff.).

Page 249. "Imagery of public hygiene." Hosking, p. 70.

Page 257. "Lingered in rich and happy-go-lucky Georgia." Nadezdha Mandelshtam, *Hope Abandoned,* trans. by Max Hayward (Collins Harvell, 1989), p. 64.

Page 273. "In that vicinity." Osip Mandelshtam, *The Noise of Time: The Prose of Osip Mandelshtam,* trans. with critical essays by Clarence Brown (San Francisco: North Point Press, 1986), p. 205.

Page 273. "I'm still the same." Gevorg Emin, *Songs of Armenia: Selected Poems,* trans. into Russian by Yevgeny Yevtushenko, into English by Dorian Rottenberg (Moscow: Progress Publishers, 1979). p. 53.

Page 274. "In 1921." See Hosking, pp. 474 ff.

Page 301. "Let me cut the hill." Mandelshtam, *Selected Poems*, p. 109.